Phillip I

C000182376

To be a Saint

By

Phillip M. Drake

For Charlotte, Martyn and Patrick

.

Acknowledgements

Thanks to my parents and children for supporting me during the writing and editing phases. A big thank you to Damien Rogers and Mark Cottell for accompanying me to Saints games both home and away over the years, as well as those fellow Saints fans I have met along the way.

About the Author

Phillip Drake was born in Southampton in 1973, three days after a 2-0 Saints home win against Birmingham City at The Dell. He is a writer and a self-confessed footballaholic who spends far too much time fretting over Southampton Football Club and its transfer policy than is healthy. When not obsessing over football, Phillip likes to spend time with his children, his friends and family, and writing horror fiction.

Phillip can be contacted via Twitter - @pdrakeofficial or his website: www.phillipdrake.online

Other Works

Non-Fiction

The Spooky South – The Haunted Locations of Hampshire and the Isle of Wight

Fiction
Dark Window and Other Stories
The Arrival
Tales with a Twist

Introduction

It's 2 May 1976, an overcast Sunday in Southampton, and a young couple takes their three-year-old son to join an excitable crowd lining a street near to his grandparent's house. The crowd is in an expectant mood, everyone is smiling and in good spirits, decked in yellow, blue, red and white, all of them blissfully unaware of the long hot summer to come.

The couple with the child make their way through the throng to the front, the child bemused by this gathering of strangers, strangers who have come together in salutation, but the boy has no idea what is going on, or why everyone is celebrating.

Suddenly, the hum of the crowd morphs into unbridled cheering, clapping, and singing. A beige coloured open-top bus makes its way slowly along the road, men in suits wave to the gathered masses below, the cheers increase.

The boy's parents point to the men on the bus and encourage him to clap his hands; the men are holding a large piece of silverware, the sun peeks out from behind the low grey cloud and shines down on this tableau of triumph.

The boy still doesn't appreciate what is going on, the bus passes and soon disappears into the distance, some older children chase after it, the crowd begins to melt away, the boy becomes fractious, wants to go and play, he still doesn't understand what all the fuss is about, but he will one day.

That three-year-old boy was me, the young couple my parents, the men on the open-top bus the triumphant Southampton team who the day before had won the FA Cup for the first (and at the time of writing) only time in the club's history. This was my first experience of watching a Southampton football team, and I don't remember a thing about it, all I know is what I've been told by my parents about the day. It still annoys me that I was there in body but not in consciousness. If I had been just a few years older maybe I would have some memory of the day, instead, I have to content myself with the false memories that my brain has cobbled together from what my parents and relatives have told me about the day the Saints team paraded the cup through the city. It would be five more years before I got the chance to watch a Southampton team actually play football.

Although I liked football, snooker was my favourite sport in the early years of the 1980s. I remember watching the great players of the time, Ray Reardon, Steve Davis, Jimmy White, Cliff Thorburn and of course the ever-controversial Alex 'Hurricane' Higgins, and wanting to emulate them.

I recall pestering my parents to buy me a snooker table for my bedroom and ending up with a table so big it barely fit in the room, and manoeuvring the cue was extremely difficult, especially when the cue ball was on one of the cushions.

I wanted to be a professional snooker player, but I was terrible at the game, and even to this day, (although I haven't played in years) my highest break was in the mid-thirties.

Inevitably, football was the main obsession in the schoolyard, and the lure of football was too strong to resist, so when an uncle asked me if I would like to go to The Dell to see Saints and Tottenham's reserve sides battle it out on a bitterly cold January afternoon, I said yes.

I don't remember much about the game itself, although, I do recall that my uncle was hoping to see the club's relatively new Yugoslavian goalkeeper Ivan Katalinic play between the sticks. He was to be disappointed, however, as Ivan's absence signalled a recall to the first team, and taking his place in the reserves was our other moustachioed custodian, Peter Wells.

Despite being a native of Yugoslavia, Katalinic sported a moustache, which was black and bushy, and it drooped down either side of his mouth to his chin, giving him the appearance of a Mexican bandit. Ivan was one of those goalkeepers that could be brilliant one week, and awful the next. Unfortunately, for Southampton fans, it was mostly the latter, although there were one or two good performances during his time on the south coast. Nonetheless, it did not stop some of the more critical and witty Saints supporters from nicknaming him, "Ivan catastrophic."

Although much of the details about the match passed me by, most of my memories are about the way the old stadium felt, sounded, and smelled. Only the west stand was open for reserves games, as this was back in the days when reserve team games took place on a Saturday afternoon, at the main stadium. This was the early 80s, and there was none of this modern fad of playing reserve team games at the state-of-the-art training facilities, although this probably accounted for the state of the pitches back then, which were often mud baths by mid-winter. No, whilst the first team were visiting such exotic locations as Norwich, London or Manchester for an away game, the second string players would be trying to stake a claim for a first team starting place by putting on a good display in front of a few hundred hardy souls.

Having made my first appearance at The Dell aged eight, I had to wait another six years before I managed to get to see the first team in action. Hooliganism was rife in the early to mid-80s and serious public disorder was commonplace somewhere in the UK every week, and so I had to wait until I was a bit older before my parents would let me attend a live match.

Never Gonna Give You Up

Saints 2 Manchester Utd 2   Division 1   15 August 1987

During the summer of 1987 the Football League fixture computer kindly sent Manchester United south for the first game of the season, and with the match being an all-ticket affair, I managed to convince both my parents (who would be paying) and my grandfather (who would be queuing for the tickets) that I desperately needed to go to this match. Thankfully, my grandfather managed to procure a pair of standing terrace tickets for under the West Stand for the princely sum of £3.50 each. So now, everything was set for my first team debut!

The first game of any season is always a hard one to call, there is no previous form to call on other than a few friendlies, and the new signings are still trying to bed into a new way of playing. The opening day of the season really is a day where the form book goes out of the window.

As far as Saints were concerned, their build-up to the opening game of the 1987/88 season had been a turbulent one, with boss Chris Nicholl dismantling what was left of Lawrie McMenemy's ageing squad, a squad Chris inherited when he replaced McMenemy in the summer of 1985.

Chris struggled to match the swashbuckling style of his predecessor with the football served up often being dour with a defence that often leaked goals. Where McMenemy's sides regularly qualified for European competition, Chris's sides more often than not flirted with the relegation zone.

The main catalyst for Chris's overhaul of the squad had occurred the previous season when several stories hit the press of player unrest. Rumours surfaced regarding clashes between the manager and some

4

of his players, some of which had actually erupted into physical violence.

The most noteworthy incident came when Nicholl had a full-on fist fight with our fiery left-back Mark Dennis, who wasn't a man to be trifled with, and his hard tackling reputation earned him the nickname "Psycho", years before that particular moniker was given to Stuart Pearce. By the time Mark hung up his boots, he had racked up an incredible twelve sending-offs, which is even more incredible when you consider that referees were a lot more lenient back then than they are now.

This particular altercation resulted in Mark being sensationally sacked by the club (sacking a player is still something which is still virtually unheard of in football) before he was reprieved thanks to the intervention of the Professional Footballers Association.

Even though the club gave Mark a second chance, his continuing disciplinary problems forced the club to terminate his contract before the end of the season, before resurfacing at QPR.

Following Dennis out of the door in the summer were crowd favourites David Armstrong, Nick Holmes and most noticeably England goalkeeper Peter Shilton. Shilts joined Derby County, and following him to the Baseball Ground a few weeks into the new season would be England teammate Mark Wright. In fact, Wright would be gone before August was out, and a defence that struggled to keep the opposition at bay before their departures now looked decidedly lightweight. Kevin Moore, who was gaining a reputation as one of the best young central defenders in the lower divisions, came in as Wright's replacement from Oldham Athletic for £150,000.

The larger than life character of journeyman John Burridge would fill Peter Shilton's goalkeeping jersey in competition with youngster Tim Flowers, and both men would struggle to make the number one jersey their own during the season.

Another arrival was a familiar face, midfielder Graham Baker returned to the club five years after leaving for Manchester City, and all three new signings would appear on the front cover of the programme for this match against Manchester United.

Everyone remembers the first time they went to see their team play, and the thing I remember most about the morning before the match was the mixture of emotions I felt. Excitement fused with impatience as I watched the clock slowly make its way to the 3 pm kick-off time.

I don't recall what I wore to the match (probably a t-shirt and jeans) but I can tell you what I didn't wear, a replica shirt. Nobody seemed to be wearing one. Even as recently as the late 80s replica kits seemed to be the preserve of young children, the sort of thing you would receive from your grandmother as a Christmas present. When did this modern fixation of wearing your team's shirt start? I know I owned one as a child (bought for me as a Christmas present by my grandmother) but after that, I didn't buy one myself until the 1995/96 season when I was old enough to know better, yet everyone was doing it so it seemed okay. Since then I have bought a fair few, mainly Saints but also some England and AC Milan ones, and I still have most of them tucked away in a cupboard somewhere.

You have to remember that back then in these pre-Premier League days, most clubs didn't really bother with much merchandising. Only the big clubs such as Liverpool, Manchester United, and Arsenal bothered with anything more than the ubiquitous scarf and rosette. The Saints shop at The Dell was tiny, smaller than a Portakabin and only sold a meagre selection of souvenirs.

This was also a time when clubs didn't change their shirt design every season. It's almost hard to believe now that a club would often keep the same shirt design for four or five years on the trot, and as for the away kit, that could be the same simple and plain design for even

6

longer. Nowadays, it is the norm for clubs to have three kits, and another design for playing in European competitions. Football clubs don't have shops anymore, they have superstores where you can buy anything from baby clothes to a fridge magnet all with the club crest emblazoned on it.

Football shirts are big business and clubs seem to change shirt designs every year (or actually during the match if you are Manchester United, but more on that later), and a new signing can almost recoup their transfer fee overnight such can be the demand for replica shirts with that player's name and number emblazoned upon it.

Do I still buy them even though I'm middle aged? Of course, I do, but I often ask myself why. What compels middle-aged men with decreasing hairlines and increasing waistlines to want to wear such things? Let's be honest here, these garments are not very becoming to anyone who is even slightly overweight, and they can be no worse sight on a hot sunny day at a football ground (or the beach) than seeing a lot of balding, sweaty men in tight-fitting football shirts. Yet, many fans will tell you that it somehow gives them a connection to the club, as if wearing an overpriced piece of multi coloured polyester compares with a Christian wearing a cross (other religions are available), but for both, it's a matter of faith.

Back to my first taste of live football, and we arrived at The Dell about forty-five minutes before kick-off, and being my first match I wanted a programme as a souvenir. I soon spotted a programme seller, his little kiosk rising up out of the noisy throng of bodies like a buoy in a rough sea. I paid the humble price of 80p for my match day programme back then, whereas when I purchase its modern day equivalent, it sets me back £4.

My grandfather had wisely chosen tickets under the west stand rather than on the Milton Road terrace, as he deemed it safer for a first-timer like me. The Milton Road terracing was home to our more animated followers and he told me that standing along the side would mean that we had good views of both sets of goals.

The thing that stands out about the day was the varying sensations, everything from that strange clanking noise that the turnstiles make when you push through them, to the sight of the brass band playing pre-match.

However, it wasn't just the sights and sounds that have stuck in my mind, the sickly aroma of cigarette smoke, oranges and Bovril, twinned with the unmistakable scent of freshly cut grass, was a blend of smells that assaulted the nostrils. I remember being overawed by the whole occasion. The size of the crowd (at just over 21,000 it was the biggest gathering I had been to at that time), the noise, the fact that I could swear without anyone taking any notice (although having my grandfather stood next to me meant that I didn't) made me worry that the whole game would pass me by.

I needn't have concerned myself, the match itself was a cracker, with the Saints equalising twice with both goals coming from Danny Wallace in reply to a brace from Manchester United's Norman Whiteside.

Our first was an amazing goal that still has a place in my top ten all-time favourite Saints goals even to this day. Wallace received the ball just inside our half, ran through the middle of the United midfield, skipping past several tackles, before launching a screamer from the edge of the penalty area into the roof of the net. The crowd erupted in celebration, surged forward, and not having had the foresight to stand behind a crush barrier, we found ourselves propelled forward down the steps; it was like being hit by a wave whilst in the sea and at first, it was an unsettling experience. This is the joys of standing on a football terrace that kids these days don't get to experience in their all-seater stadiums, which is a shame because back then, coming out of the ground after a match feeling as though you have just spent 90 minutes in a huge tumble dryer was a rite of passage for a young supporter.

Our second goal was more of a scruffy affair, as Danny's looped cross took a slight deflection off a United defender to wrong-foot the goalkeeper, and at full-time the 2-2 score seemed like a fair result. The whole experience is one that I will never forget and despite not getting the victory I wanted, I went home happy and I was already looking forward to my next match.

The One and Only

Saints1 Sheffield Wed. 1   Division One   5 September 1987

After the United game, I must have read and re-read the programme from cover to cover countless times over the next few weeks as I tried to relive every moment from the match. Kickabouts on the park with my friends resulted in me trying to recreate Danny Wallace's dribble and shot (usually unsuccessfully) and I bored my friends with constant retellings of my day.

In addition to the excitement generated by my first taste of First Division action, something else that gave this season more of an edge would be the resumption of derby matches against Portsmouth, who had been promoted from Division Two the previous season.

This would be the first time the two rivals would face each other in the league since the 1975/76 season when a 1-0 win at Fratton Park at the tail end of that campaign helped relegate Pompey to the Third Division. In fact, this would be the first meeting between the two clubs in the top division, and the good news was that fans of both teams wouldn't have to wait long for the first match, as the fixture computer had kindly pencilled in a trip to Fratton Park on the second Saturday of the season.

Following the Manchester United game, we had won 1-0 at Norwich City in midweek, with Kevin Moore getting his first goal for the club. So with four points from two games, it wasn't a shabby start, and most Saints fans felt that we had a good chance of coming back from Fratton Park with all three points.

The build-up to the game at Fratton Park was considerable, as it usually is when the two teams meet, with the local press needing no invitation to crank up the tension, but this game, in particular, had added significance.

What gave this particular South Coast derby match added spice was the fact that Portsmouth's manager was ex-Saints legend Alan Ball. Alan had guided them from Third Division obscurity to the First Division in only a handful of seasons. Now he was about to face off against the club he had captained under Lawrie McMenemy in two spells covering the late Seventies and early Eighties.

The Portsmouth fans also wanted revenge for Southampton's last visit to Fratton Park, a 1-0 win in the FA Cup in 1984. A game that is enshrined in Southampton fans folklore thanks to an injury-time winner from Steve Moran. Ironically, the extra injury-time came about when a coin thrown from a Portsmouth supporter struck Saints left-back Mark Dennis on the head with so much force that he required treatment.

Their fans inferiority complex was at its peak during that cup match, and it created a hostile atmosphere with not just coins thrown. One of the more sickening sights of the afternoon was the barrage of bananas being thrown in the direction of our young black winger Danny Wallace, which is a sight that has no place at a football ground or indeed anywhere in society.

The rabid atmospheres that these games engender are certainly not for the faint-hearted, nor are they the place to make your debut, but this is what happened to our latest signing, Derek Statham. Derek had

10

joined us from West Bromwich Albion as a direct replacement for Mark Dennis and he found himself thrust straight into the team. A Baptism of Fire indeed.

As it transpired, neither team covered themselves in glory defensively. After Pompey took the lead, Colin Clarke grabbed a brace to give us the lead, a lead we kept until 16 minutes from time. Another 2-2 draw and the south coast bragging rights remained shared.

I didn't attend this match and had to satisfy myself with watching the highlights on TV the next day, but it wasn't long before I got my next taste of live football.

This match against Wednesday was largely unmemorable (on the pitch at least) but a couple of things do stick out in my mind.

Firstly, I took my place on the Milton Road terrace for the first time, and despite telling myself all week that I would try to garner a quiet spot near the front and to the side, I ended up behind the goal halfway up. After all, it seemed quite sparsely populated when I arrived, which seemed unusual, but 5 minutes or so before kick-off the reason for this became all too apparent. I had placed myself slap bang in the middle of our more committed and vocal followers who had just arrived freshly inebriated from the local pubs. I tried my best to join in with the songs they sang, but not being able to decipher all the words exactly, my attempts drew knowing glances and smirks that told me that it was perhaps best to shut my mouth and just concentrate on watching the match. It felt like I was intruding on a private members club.

The second thing I remember about this game was the first glimpse of a young player called Matthew Le Tissier. This wasn't Matt's first game for the club, far from it; he had made quite an impact already. His two goals helped knock Manchester United out of the League Cup the season before, and he had scored a wonderful hat-trick on a snowy and cloyingly muddy Dell pitch against Leicester City that same season. Yet for some reason manager Chris Nicholl decided to use the Guernsey-born midfielder sparingly at first, limiting his appearances to mostly coming off the bench. In this particular game, he came off the bench to great effect, helping to set up the late equaliser that cancelled out Lee Chapman's first half opener for the Owls. In fact, Matt would only make ten league starts this season (with nine substitute appearances) and would not score in any of them. Matt mentions this in his excellent autobiography 'Taking Le Tiss', Chris Nicholl's excuse being that he did not want to rush the young player too soon, much to Matt's annoyance and the fans bemusement.

Shear Genius

Saints 4 Arsenal 2   Division One   9 April 1988

Mind you it wasn't just Matthew Le Tissier who had trouble finding the net this season. The whole team found the going difficult in front of goal, with the total league tally for the season down from 69 during 1986/87 to a meagre 49 for this. In truth, this season had become one hard slog of ultimate disappointment, with very few highs but an abundance of lows.

The most depressing game of the season being a 2-0 defeat at home to Portsmouth in January, which completed an unwelcome double, as Second Division Bournemouth had beaten us over two legs in the League Cup back in September.

We didn't fare much better in the FA Cup either, as our cup run ended on Luton Town's horrid artificial pitch in the Fourth Round.

There were one or two highlights though, such as a 2-0 win at Manchester United a week after the home defeat to Portsmouth, and this thrashing of Arsenal at The Dell, where I caught my first glimpse of a striker who would go on to become one of England's greatest ever centre-forwards – Alan Shearer.

This wasn't a great Arsenal team, in fact, they were going through a bit of a slump by their standards and they were still a couple of years away from being realistic title challengers. Even so, you never expect an easy match against the North Londoners, but they found themselves torn apart on this day and their tormentor in chief was a seventeen-year-old boy from Newcastle.

I wasn't expecting much from this match, and to be honest I was expecting a cheerless low scoring game with us maybe sneaking a 1-0 win. Games against the Gunners were rarely entertaining back then as their manager George Graham had a reputation for producing hard working but dour teams, meaning goals were often in short supply.

I couldn't have been more wrong, as the game exploded into life early on, as the young Shearer headed in Graham Baker's excellent cross to give us the lead with barely five minutes on the watch. Unfortunately, the hapless Kevin Bond put through his own net to level the scores six minutes later thus cancelling out the young striker's opener.

Unperturbed by this setback, the Saints players found an extra gear and on a heavy rain-sodden pitch it wasn't long until they carved out another chance, and it was the indomitable Shearer who bagged his second of the match. It was the kind of goal for which he would become famous, going in where the boots are flying, stooping low in a crowded penalty area to head home. It was a brave finish through a forest of legs, and you don't see many teenage strikers willing to put themselves on the line like that nowadays.

With Arsenal still reeling from the onslaught, and with Shearer's work ethic and spirit seemingly enthusing the entire team, defender Mark Blake (getting a rare outing in the first team) showed a touch of skill to outwit two Arsenal defenders before slotting home to send us in 3-1 up at half-time.

All the same, this was the Alan Shearer show, and it took just four minutes of the second-half for the young striker to complete a memorable hat-trick when his thunderous shot rebounded off the underside of the crossbar, and he was the quickest to react to score from close range.

Arsenal finished off the scoring on a memorable afternoon with a goal 8 minutes from time, but this was Shearer's day. The 4-2 scoreline in no way flattered us, and in bagging himself a hat-trick at the tender age of 17 years and 240 days, Alan had become the youngest ever player to score 3 goals in a game in the top division, beating Jimmy Greaves 30-year-old record. It was a pleasure to be there to witness this historic moment, and the consensus among the fans was that we were watching a future England international in the making, but would he still be a Southampton player when that happened?

Results May Vary

Saints 1 Sheffield Wed. 2 Division One   22 October 1988

If last season had been one big disappointment then this one would turn out to be the ultimate rollercoaster ride, with the season divided into three parts, with a successful beginning and conclusion sandwiching an almighty slump in the middle. It was a winless run that was so bad, that the majority of Saints followers could see nothing other than an end to our eleven-season stay in the top flight.

Yet the season had started so promisingly, with an opening day 4-0 demolition of West Ham at The Dell, although the Saints fans there that day would have no idea that they were witnessing the last opening day home win by a Saints side for something like 23 years!

Two more wins followed that whipping of West Ham, first at QPR then at home to Luton Town, wins that positioned us at the top of the embryonic league table, as well as giving us three wins at the start of the season for the first time in 31 years.

We took our 100 percent record to Highbury to face Arsenal, and what an extraordinary game it turned out to be. With the Saints players now full of confidence after their great start to the new campaign, they stormed into a two-goal lead inside 25 minutes, thanks to goals by Matthew Le Tissier and Rodney Wallace. What happened next was an incident that totally changed the course of the game, and would have knock-on effects for both clubs seasons.

During the second-half, our midfielder Glenn Cockerill had to receive lengthy treatment to an injury to the face that required him to be replaced, and he was whisked to the hospital where x-rays confirmed a double fracture of the jaw. No one had really seen the incident that led to this mystery injury, although the answer would come soon enough.

The match itself had seen Saints doggedly defend their two-goal lead against heavy Arsenal pressure before Arsenal received a rather dubious penalty that they converted with eight minutes left. Saints still refused to buckle though, and with Arsenal throwing the proverbial kitchen sink at them they held firm as the match entered stoppage-time. Thanks to the lengthy stoppage to allow Glenn Cockerill to receive treatment, injury-time seemed to last forever, and with Saints fans desperately whistling to the ref to remind him to blow for full-time, Saints' resolve finally cracked, when Alan Smith nicked a heartbreaking equaliser for Arsenal.

That may have been the end of the match, but it was just the start of the post-match recriminations, as it soon transpired that Arsenal midfielder Paul Davies, who had thrown a left uppercut that Henry Cooper would have been proud of, had broken Glenn Cockerill's jaw. Missed by the referee and two linesmen at the time, the punch hadn't escaped the attentions of one of the television cameras filming the match. The Football League officials used this TV evidence to find Paul Davis guilty of violent conduct, and they saw fit to ban him for nine games and fined him £3,000. Arsenal incensed by this action actually banned television cameras from Highbury for a while, in some small-minded act of petty retaliation, but in my opinion, the length of the ban was totally justified for what was clearly an horrendous off the ball incident.

Whether it was that incident or the throwing away of the two goal lead, or a bit of both but the team seemed to have been negatively affected, as a mini-slump of four games without a win followed, of which this game against Wednesday was the last.

I went to this game with a couple of school friends, Richard and Andy for whom it was their first proper football match. They had heard me describe the matches I had been to previously and after some persuasive chat from me, they eventually came along. Sadly, the game itself was dire, and despite taking the lead via a Derek Statham penalty, we never looked likely to win the match as Wednesday's robust midfield took control, and in fact, the lead lasted a mere four minutes before Wednesday equalised. One goal midway through the second half was enough to give Wednesday all three points in front of a sparse crowd that numbered under 13,000. The only other reason this game warrants a mention is that a little piece of history took place on the pitch. First-team stalwarts Danny Wallace and Rodney Wallace were joined by their third brother, full-back Ray (Rodney's twin). It was the first time three brothers had started on the same team in the league since the 1920's, but this was of scant consolation as we trooped out of The Dell at the final whistle, my first taste of defeat in a match I had attended. As for Richard and Andy, to my knowledge, they never went to another match again, well not during the time I knew them.

The Safety Switch

Saints 2 Manchester Utd 1   Division One   6 May 1989

That mini-slump ended when a fully recovered Glenn Cockerill smashed in two long-range daisy cutters at Tottenham to give us a surprise 2-1 win, as the Saints continued their Jekyll and Hyde early season form. A run of three wins out of four that took us into the top three and Chris Nicholl won the manager of the month award for November.

Many people in football believe the myth that the manager of the month award brings ill fortune for the recipient and his club, and for us that myth soon turned into fact, as two draws at the end of November (including an impressive 2-2 result at Manchester United) contributed to a startling run of poor form.

Saints would play seventeen games in the league and not win a single one! The roll-call of misery included failing to beat Manchester United away (drew2-2), Millwall at home (drew 2-2), Wimbledon away (lost 2-1), Forest at home (drew 1-1), Newcastle away (drew 3-3 after being 3-1 up), Coventry at home (drew 2-2), QPR at home (lost 4-1), Luton away (lost 6-1), Middlesbrough at home (lost 3-1), Liverpool away (lost 2-0), Derby away (lost 3-1), Everton at home (drew 1-1), Sheffield Wednesday away (drew 1-1), Spurs at home (lost 2-0), Charlton away (drew 2-2), Arsenal at home (lost 3-1), and Coventry City (away lost 2-1). That gave us just eight points from a possible fifty-one, a shocking return from a team that had promised so much earlier in the season. In addition to which, we also crashed out of all three cup competitions at home, with Luton seeing us off in the League Cup, Second Division Crystal Palace in the Simod Cup, and Derby County in the FA Cup. To make matters worse, the defeats to Luton and Derby were home replays. To capitulate to both teams at home after doing the hard part away was thoroughly depressing, and throw those cup games in with the league form, and you get a run of twenty-two games without victory in all competitions, a truly horrendous sequence of results.

On a personal note, I had stopped going to matches as the pressure of studying for my GCSE exams had taken up too much of my time and mental energy, and the last thing I needed was to watch a team that didn't seem to know how to break that miserable run of form.

By the end of March, relegation looked a nailed on certainty, a depressing scenario after the club was as high as third place in November, and Chris Nicholl, was rapidly taking on the appearance of a man wondering how long he would have left to turn things around.

His constant tinkering with the starting line-up in a bid to find a winning formula only served to make us worse, but he must have had the continued backing of the board as they allowed him to sign centre-back Neil Ruddock in March, a player who would have a significant impact on the remainder of our season.

From somewhere the players had managed to show some fight, and the winless run ended on April fool's day when Neil Ruddock's 89th-minute pressure penalty saw off fellow relegation candidates Newcastle United at The Dell. It was a massively important victory, especially with the next three games away from home. The 4-point return we garnered from those games was the minimum we needed to keep our necks above water. Despite goalless home draws against Norwich and Wimbledon, the 3 points we secured at fellow strugglers Aston Villa was a huge boost to our survival chances, and with other results going our way, those points helped us to climb to 13th in the table, 5 points clear of the relegation places.

Now we knew what was required, we only needed three more points from the last two matches to guarantee survival, and first up was our final home game of the season against Manchester United.

With so much riding on the outcome, I put my GCSE studies and revision to one side and took my place on the Milton Road terrace amongst the serried ranks of nervous and expectant Saints fans on a warm and sunny spring afternoon.

The rock hard, desiccated Dell pitch did nothing to add to the entertainment value of this match, as players from both sides struggled to keep control of the ball. Nevertheless, this wasn't a match that needed to entertain, this was a match where we required the three points that would guarantee our top-flight status.

It may have been the hard and uneven pitch that contributed to us taking the lead fifteen minutes before half-time, when an uncharacteristic mistake by United and England skipper Bryan Robson, let Matthew Le Tissier in to intercept his short back pass. After trying to work an angle for a shot, Matt eventually played the ball back out to the edge of the penalty area. Waiting to strike was Glenn Cockerill who unleashed one of his trademark long-range efforts past United keeper Jim Leighton and into the net.

The joy of taking the lead was almost short-lived as a few minutes later a long ball down our right bounced awkwardly (that pitch again), and defender Russell Osman's high back pass nearly looped over the advancing John Burridge, but somehow he managed to claw it down from almost behind his head.

We survived to half-time, and although this wasn't a great United team, their new manager Alex Ferguson was still trying make his mark on the club, I knew they still had enough good players to spoil the party in the second-half.

That potential party-pooper turned out to be Russell Beardsmore, who slammed home the equaliser from 16 yards out just 10 minutes into the second period, and just seconds after Leighton had prevented Ruddock from putting us two up.

Now the game was on a knife-edge, and Leighton was in action again, this time at a full stretch to deny Paul Rideout from 25-yards. In fact, the United keeper seemed to be keeping the scores level, as moments later he denied Le Tissier from 6-yards out, with Rodney Wallace's follow-up shot from the rebound being cleared off the line by Steve Bruce. Would we ever score? My nerves were jangling now, as we poured forward in search of a winner whilst trying not to leave ourselves exposed at the back.

It was end-to-end stuff, and our collective hearts skipped a beat when United's Lee Sharpe thundered a twenty yarder off the crossbar with six minutes to go. Then with time running out, a surging run through the midfield by Glenn Cockerill set up top scorer Rodney Wallace to place a sweet shot into the bottom corner from 12-yards with but 30 seconds of normal time left.

Yet again, our celebrations almost proved to be premature, when in injury-time Bryan McClair found himself all alone in the penalty area, but Burridge smothered his weak shot.

When the final whistle sounded the relief around the ground was palpable and some of the players weren't quite quick enough to make it off the pitch as hordes of Saints fans ran on to congratulate a team on surviving what looked like certain relegation back in March.

In truth, the season had been an awful one, with only 10 league wins all season, three of which came in the first three games, as well as early exits in all the cup competitions.

Mercifully, inspired by the new signings, we had managed to finish a respectable 13th and 6 points clear of the drop zone. On paper that looks comfortable, but relegation had been a realistic possibility for a large portion of the season, and in order to avoid a repeat the following season, most fans were in agreement that things needed to improve, and quick.

The Kids Are Alright

Saints 4 Liverpool 1   Division One   21 October 1989

Improve they did, although you wouldn't know it from our opening day loss to Millwall at The Dell, a loss that heralded the start of a long run of unsuccessful opening day home games that would span three decades.

After all the transfer activity just before the previous season's transfer deadline, there would be no more signings during the summer and in fact, not many departures either, with the only notable departure being Derek Statham who joined Stoke City.

Certainly, we didn't really need to sign anyone during the close season as this would be the breakthrough year for the likes of Matthew Le Tissier, and Alan Shearer, whilst Rodney Wallace, would continue to improve.

Despite that opening day loss to Millwall and our now customary thumping at Everton, we had made a solid start to the season and suddenly we couldn't stop scoring. The build up to this game saw us draw 4-4 at Norwich and win 4-1 at QPR, but this Liverpool side would be a different proposition altogether.

Liverpool sauntered into town unbeaten in their first eight games, and they were looking to stretch their lead at the top of the table, although, our recent good form meant that we found ourselves handily placed in sixth, just 3 points behind our visitors.

Saints tore into Liverpool from the first whistle, and it was one of the old guard, striker Paul Rideout, who created the first serious

21

chance when he was unlucky to see his 35-yard thunderbolt of a shot cannon back off the underside of the crossbar. The shot was hit with such venom that it left the Liverpool keeper Bruce Grobbelaar grasping at air, and it wouldn't be the last time this particular afternoon that Grobbelaar would be left floundering.

Despite being denied by the crossbar, Rideout would get his reward a few minutes later when he nipped in ahead of a defender to head home at the near post from Jason Dodd's neat right-wing cross. Dodd was making his first team debut at right-back, yet despite having to contend with the likes of John Barnes and Peter Beardsley, he didn't look overawed, and he also found time to get forward and deliver some excellent crosses into the Liverpool penalty area.

With a fervent and noisy crowd behind them, the Saints players carved out chance after glorious chance. Alan Shearer was next to try his luck when he latched onto a Le Tissier through ball only to see his shot saved by Grobbelaar's legs, then some last ditch Liverpool defending denied both Rideout and Le Tissier.

It was certainly hats off to manager Nicholl for gambling on using a cavalier 4-2-4 formation. The pace of Rodney Wallace on the left and the trickery of Le Tissier on the right supplied the ammunition for Rideout and Shearer, both of whom were more than a handful for the Liverpool centre-backs.

The second goal came on 39 minutes when Le Tissier dribbled past a couple of half-hearted Liverpool challenges before threading the ball through to Rodney Wallace. Wallace controlled the ball smartly, almost teasing the Liverpool defenders around him, before firing a low fast shot past the bewildered Grobbelaar.

Let me assure you, that the default setting of your average Southampton fan is pessimism with a hint of melancholy, something that afflicts Southampton fans from a young age. And sure enough, the consensus among the fans on the Milton Road terrace during halftime was that Liverpool would come out for the second half a different team, and probably go on to win, after all, they couldn't play that lacklustre in the second 45 minutes surely? To their credit, they did come out fired up, more than likely with a few choice words from manager Kenny Dalglish ringing in their ears, and they made more of a game of it for a while. Saints weathered the storm and after regaining a foothold in the match, Rod Wallace scored his second of the game on 56 minutes to extend the lead to 3-0.

It was a goal of exquisite quality. Le Tissier received the ball on the right wing, flicked it over David Burrows before going around him and running down the wing. He then delivered a long deep cross that Rod ran onto to smash home first time on the half-volley through Grobbelaar's legs. It was an amazing goal of skill, flair, speed and accuracy, and one of the best goals we would score that season.

With half an hour left, Liverpool gave their travelling fans a glimmer of hope when a clumsy foul in the penalty area by Jimmy Case on David Burrows gave Liverpool a cheap penalty, which Beardsley converted. This caused some of our more pedantic fans to fear that a Liverpool comeback was on the cards, but their fears were groundless as Le Tissier capped a fine afternoon on a personal level, as well as for the team. This time Rod Wallace turned provider with Le Tissier rising to head home the fourth, and chants of "easy, easy" rang around The Dell.

Looking back it is easy to forget just how big a result this was for us at the time and just how much of a shockwave this sent around the football world. Liverpool, still at their peak, would go on to win the title this season by a 9-point margin, yet we tore them apart in a game that most people thought they would win easily. The result was the talk of the city for weeks if not months afterwards, and now people in the press were starting to take notice of the club, and more importantly the youth policy, with some people calling for Le Tissier, Wallace and Shearer to be given full international honours.

One Man Show

Saints 2 Oldham 2   League Cup 5th Round   24 January 1990

Night matches at The Dell always had a special aura about them. Even if the attendance was below capacity the atmosphere always seemed better than a Saturday afternoon kick-off, and this night would be no exception.

Our form had slumped a little after the thrashing of Liverpool, but we were still banging in the goals. It was just unfortunate that we were letting plenty in too. However, we had reached the dizzy heights of 4th place over the Christmas period, and the 3-1 spanking of Spurs at White Hart Lane in the third round of the FA Cup was a rare treat at a ground where we never seem to do well.

Not only were we doing well in both the league and FA Cup, but we had also progressed to the quarter-finals of the League Cup, where we would face an Oldham Athletic side that was riding high in Division Two.

We were fortunate enough to be playing at home, so I made my way to The Dell in anticipation of a straightforward victory, and with a genuine feeling that we had the chance to go all the way to the final of the competition this year. Due to working late, I had arrived at The Dell five minutes before the kick-off, only to find the gates locked and thousands of disgruntled fans milling around outside wondering what to do next.

Being locked out of a match is not something that younger supporters will ever get to experience, as most football matches in the modern era are now all-ticket affairs, but even as recently as the mid-

24

90s it was possible to just roll up to the turnstile, hand over some money and gain access to the ground. If the match was important and you turned up just before kick-off, chances were that you would get near to the front of the queue only to see the entrance to the turnstiles slammed shut in your face.

Annoyed and despondent, I trudged away from a fervent and expectant Dell, a biting wind on my cheeks feeling like a slap in the face as I made my way back home. By the time I arrived home the second-half was about to start with the Saints a goal to the good and I settled down to listen to the second half on the radio, confident that a place in the semi-finals was as good as ours for the taking.

I hate listening to Saints games on the radio. When I'm watching a game, either in person or on the television, I can see the threat to our goal from the opposition, but when I'm listening to the radio, every shot by the opposition is heading for the top corner of our net, in my mind's eye at least. It is not until the commentator says that the shot has been saved or gone wide can I breathe a sigh of relief, and with a semi-final berth at stake, listening to the second-half of this match was a nerve-wracking experience.

It was a tight and tense half of football with Saints not playing particularly well, and Oldham always carrying a threat going forwards. Actually, the two teams seemed evenly matched, and it came as no real surprise when Oldham equalised through their top scorer Andy Ritchie with just nine minutes of normal time remaining.

Rocked back on our heels by their equaliser, Oldham came pouring forward, and they wasted a couple of decent chances to take the lead before a defensive lapse gifted us a penalty with four minutes to go. Le Tissier scored the resultant kick with the minimum of fuss, and it looked as though we had managed to secure that vital place in the semi-finals.

All we had to do was to hold out for four minutes plus whatever referee Roger Milford added on for stoppages, surely that would be no more than a couple of minutes? Not with Roger Milford refereeing the match, it wouldn't.

The indicator of a competent referee is that he passes through the game unobserved. The sign of a bad referee is that he sees himself as a "personality," which can result in an array of behavioural problems. For example, after making a brainless decision he will jog swiftly backwards while smirking inanely at the players, and the champion backwards-running smirking buffoon in the early 90s was Roger Milford. Roger liked nothing more than to come across as being "pals" with star players, as though treating them light-heartedly and grinning childishly at them would mean that he was somehow their mate.

Long before the days of modern celebrity refs such as Mike Dean and Mark Clattenburg, our Roger always seemed to run out onto the pitch looking as if he was thinking, "Hey everyone, I'm running out alongside these famous players!" His arrogance must have assumed that everyone in the crowd was saying, "Wow, there's Roger Milford, he must be such great mates with these football legends that he shares a laugh and a joke with them!" Whilst in reality what everyone was actually saying was, "oh no, we've got that pillock Roger Milford in charge again today."

Roger's appearance didn't help him either, as he always sported a mullet perm hairstyle and ridiculously short shorts. He looked like a middle-aged man trying to cut it on the dance floor with sniggering teenagers, whilst at the same time thinking he looked cool and trendy.

Southampton fans have a particular reason to hate Roger Milford, and it happened during the last few minutes of this match.

With 90 minutes on the clock, the match entered stoppage time. One minute passed, then two, and the noise of the Saints fans whistling for the final whistle forced me to lower the volume on my radio. Two minutes became three, which became four, then five.

As the match entered the sixth minute of stoppage-time, Andy Ritchie stole in to score a heartbreaking equaliser, a goal that inevitably would be the last kick of the match. Roger finally blew his whistle as soon as we restarted the match, and now we had to face a replay on Oldham's plastic pitch, and our record on those pitches was abysmal, to say the least.

I don't know what emotion I felt the most, anger or disappointment, but I remember feeling absolutely gutted. We were literally a few seconds away from going through to the two-legged semi-finals, and now an almost inevitable defeat in the replay beckoned.

Boos rang out as Roger Milford left the pitch, and the closer he got to the player's tunnel area, the more vitriolic it became, and in my opinion was entirely justified. When queried about the amount of stoppage-time he had added on, he said it was for blatant time wasting by the Southampton players when we were 2-1 up with four minutes to go, yet Oldham was doing their fair share of time wasting when the scores were 1-1 midway through the half.

Saints duly lost 2-0 in the replay, thus meekly surrendering our chance to get to a major cup final for the first time since 1979. It was a bitter disappointment but was always inevitable once Oldham equalised in the original tie at The Dell.

Our FA Cup run ended in the fifth round at Liverpool, as they gained revenge for that 4-1 humbling back in October when beating us 2-0, so now we had nothing else to play for other than league position.

Unfortunately, our league form had also trailed off, probably as a direct result of those dispiriting cup defeats, but one game played around that time will live long in the memory for the way in which Matthew Le Tissier destroyed Norwich City almost single handily.

27

Norwich came into this game on the back a slump of their own, and they were looking to use this match as a chance to bounce back from recent disappointments. We started the brighter but only had a couple of speculative Le Tissier efforts to show for all of our possession. Then, after eighteen minutes and totally against the run of play, Norwich hit us on the counter-attack with a sucker punch, and we went into the break 1-0 down.

The Canaries held their lead until ten minutes into the second half when Matthew Le Tissier suddenly took the game by the scruff of the neck. Firstly, he fired in the equaliser, and then five minutes later he scored a phenomenal individual goal. Receiving the ball just inside the Norwich half Le Tissier fooled two Norwich midfielders (one being ex-saint, and now TV pundit Andy Townsend) into seemingly tackling each other as he whipped the ball away from under their noses, before hitting a sublime low shot in off the base of the post from the edge of the penalty area.

Le Tissier's silky skills seemed to be rubbing off on the rest of the team as well, as centre-back Kevin Moore met a poor Norwich defensive clearance on the volley, which flew into the net to make it 3-1.

Le Tissier's third and our fourth was the most sublime of the night, as he slipped past a defender before unleashing a beautiful almost lazy lob over the advancing Norwich keeper Gunn from 30-yards that went in via the far post.

It had been an incredible individual performance and one that he would reproduce countless times over the rest of his career.

That result helped to heal some of the wounds from our two cup exits, and the team pushed on to finish a respectable sixth place in the league, their highest finish since Chris Nicholl had taken over the managerial reigns from Lawrie McMenemy five years previously.

Nevertheless, the wounds from that League Cup exit at Oldham still hurt, and it would take most of the summer for them to heal.

You're Fired!

Saints 1 Liverpool 0   Division One   1 April 1991

If the sixth place finish and cavalier style attacking football from the previous year had Saints fans hoping for even better things this season, then they were going to be sorely disappointed. I don't know whether our tactics had been found out or that we were slightly more cautious going forward, but where we had scored more than we had conceded during the 1989/90 season, this year turned out to be the complete opposite.

In several matches, we often struggled to create enough scoring chances, whilst at the other end, we were shipping goals with alarming regularity, conceding three or more goals in a game on thirteen occasions out of a season of thirty-eight matches, keeping just six clean sheets.

It came as no surprise that manager Chris Nicholl had kept faith with the squad that had taken the First Division by storm in the previous campaign. Yet, despite still having the likes of Matthew Le Tissier, Rodney Wallace, Alan Shearer and Paul Rideout up front, the forwards were struggling to score enough goals to keep up with the amount we were shipping at the other end.

This led to some high scoring encounters both home and away but we were infuriatingly inconsistent, only managing to win back-to-back league games on two separate occasions through the entire league campaign. That's not to say that there weren't one or two highlights during the season, one being the ending of our plastic pitch hoodoo as we beat Luton Town 4-3 in January, (ironically just in time to see it get

29

torn up at the end of the season, as the FA finally saw sense and banned the bloody things). We also beat Liverpool 1-0 at The Dell in a live TV game, broadcast on ITV's Sunday afternoon show, The Match.

The problem with ITV's coverage of live football was in their chase for ratings and advertisers cash, they concentrated solely on the so-called "big five" teams at the time, namely Manchester United, Liverpool, Arsenal, Tottenham, and Everton. Throw mid-sized clubs such as Manchester City, Chelsea, Villa, Leeds, and Forest into the mix, and you would hardly see any of the other teams in the division. The likes of Southampton, Norwich, Coventry, Derby etc would hardly get a look in, as those in charge of ITV Sport did just not consider them "big box office."

This would be the first time that the Saints would be live on national television since the heydays of the early 1980s. Back then BBC's Match of the Day began showing live football on Friday nights (see kids, it's not a new-fangled Sky Sports innovation), and I watched Saints beat Liverpool 2-0 and Blackburn away in the FA Cup from the comfort of home.

I expect our shock 4-1 thumping of Liverpool the previous season had gone some way to influencing the powers that be at ITV Sport to choose this game for live coverage, although they probably wished they hadn't bothered. If ITV were expecting another mauling of Liverpool, they were to be bitterly disappointed, as we won a rather lifeless game 1-0 thanks to a solitary 4th minute deflected Matthew Le Tissier effort. Realising they had made a mistake; ITV overlooked us for live coverage again before they eventually lost the live rights to Sky in 1992 upon the dawn of the Premier League.

As uninspiring as that victory was, that win put a huge dent in Liverpool's title hopes and helped calm any fears we had of relegation, which had once again become a real possibility. Despite only two relegation places from the First Division (due to its expansion back to twenty-two teams for next season), we had flirted with drop zone once again.

There then came the match that would not only define this season but also act as a marker in the clubs history, with the start of what in future everyone would call "the managerial merry-go-round."

After putting together a run that saw us lose just once in seven games between mid-March and mid-April, we travelled to an already relegated Derby County, for the penultimate game of the season. This was a Derby side that hadn't actually won a game since New Year's Day and had only won four games all season, which meant that they were miles adrift at the bottom of the table. Somehow, we let them come away with a 6-2 victory, and it was such a poor performance that it almost beggared belief. If the board of directors had any doubts as to the future of manager Chris Nicholl, then I think that the result at Derby was probably the final nail in his coffin, and Nicholl became the first Southampton manager to face the sack, although he certainly would not be the last!

There was no doubt that Lawrie McMenemy was always going to be a tough act to follow, and it was true that Nicholl often struggled to impose his ideas and personality on to the players McMenemy had left behind. Regrettably, for Nicholl, by the time of his sacking, he couldn't really use that as an excuse to explain away the frustratingly inconsistent results, as it was now (with the exception of veteran Jimmy Case) entirely his team and his players. The youth team players coming through were good, but they couldn't be expected to win games on their own, and it was often the signings made by Nicholl that let the team down.

After the initial shock when the news broke, I suspect most Saints fans (me included) agreed that Nicholl had had his chance, and although there had been some great football and fantastic results with him at the helm, he had probably taken us as far as he could.

Brand New Start

Saints 2 Tottenham 3   Division One   17 August 1991

Now the search began in earnest for the club's third manager in six years, and I spent most of the summer keeping a watchful eye on the local news for any hint of who the new manager might be.

A few names appeared in the press as likely candidates for the vacant manager's hot seat, but in the end, the job went to Ian Branfoot, a man who had served as reserve team coach under Lawrie McMenemy in the early eighties, and who had turned the job down when McMenemy left for Sunderland in 1985. Branfoot had then gone on to become a manager in his own right at Reading where he had led the Royals to promotion from the Third Division, and where he had secured his place in football history by leading them to 13 consecutive wins from the start of the season (a record that still exists to this day). He would eventually be sacked by Reading as they struggled to adjust to life in the Second Division, and by the time he was offered the Saints managerial post, he was serving as assistant manager to Steve Coppell at Crystal Palace.

For me and for the majority of Saints fans, it was an underwhelming appointment, but most people seemed to agree that he deserved a fair chance to show what he could do. After all, he had taken the Saints reserves side to the championship of the Football Combination (which was a regional league for the reserve teams of southern clubs, the northern teams had their own league) in 1982. Therefore, it seemed that the conveyor belt of youth players the club had been producing would at least get a fair crack of the whip.

Alas, before a ball could be kicked in anger under the new man one such player, Rodney Wallace, had already decided that his future lay elsewhere. His transfer to Leeds was a bitter blow on the eve of the new season, and with rumours of a change in style under the new boss, to one of a more direct manner, some fans wondered whether this had something to do with Wallace jumping ship. Accompanying Rodney to Leeds was his twin brother, fullback Ray, and the combined transfer fee was reported as £1.7 million, leading some of our more witty fans to state that Rodney had cost £1,699,999 and Ray a quid!

With fans less than impressed with the new managerial appointment, it was doubly important for Branfoot to avoid making any rash decisions regarding the playing staff, ones that would alienate the fan base before the season started. Therefore, he went and did the complete opposite when he released veteran captain and all-round crowd favourite Jimmy Case on a free transfer. Whether he did it as some kind of show of strength or because he felt Jimmy was past his best, only he knows, nonetheless, it was a hugely contentious decision. One that had the fans on his back from the start, as despite being 37-years old, Jimmy could still put in a shift, and he was great at breaking up the play when the opposition had the ball. In addition to which, he could still thread a killer defence-splitting pass to our forwards, and his tenacity in midfield gave the side that added bit of extra backbone.

I remember thinking at the time that it was a shocking decision and one that smacked of a man who was desperately trying to stamp his authority on the club, and feelings amongst the supporters was that it was imperative for the new boss to make a flying start to the season in order to keep the fans onside.

The only new player to sign during the summer was a striker that Chris Nicholl had already begun negotiations with before his dismissal. Paul Moody signed from non-league Waterlooville Town, hardly the marquee signing the fans expected after the departure of Rodney Wallace.

I arrived at The Dell on a baking hot summer afternoon and forced my way through a packed Milton Road terrace to see what effect the new boss and his direct style of play would have on the team.

Two minutes in and it seemed as though the effect was going to be a positive one, as Alan Shearer put us ahead with a bullet of a shot into the top corner. It was a great start, but one that we couldn't maintain.

Spurs arrived for this match sporting a new strike partnership in the form of England front man Gary Lineker, and their new signing from Chelsea, Gordon Durie. This new strike pairing was just too much for our defence to handle, with Durie putting himself about, something that had our defenders at sixes and sevens, which in turn gave Lineker lots of space to exploit.

As our players wilted in the summer heat, Lineker equalised five minutes before half-time, before Durie got the debut goal his performance deserved to put Spurs in front on 70 minutes. Lineker put the game beyond us with his second of the game not long after, before our own debutant, centre-back Richard Hall (he had signed during the previous season but had not played for the first team) completed the scoring by heading in. Despite some late pressure, it was an opening day defeat for the new boss, but an entertaining game all the same. Most people felt that with one or two major signings then we would do ok, but we desperately needed a replacement for the departed Jimmy Case, and quick.

Penalty Charge

Manchester U. 2 Saints 2 (2-4 on penalties) FA Cup 4th Round Replay
5 February 1992

That replacement for Jimmy Case arrived in the bulky shape of former Millwall hard man Terry Hurlock from Glasgow Rangers for £400,000 in September. His arrival at the club was probably the least spectacular of any new signing for decades as he arrived for his first day in what I can only describe as a "brickies" van. Turning up in a rust and grime covered van, and wearing a Hawaiian shirt, he looked as though he had arrived to unblock the drains rather than play professional football.

Terry forged his hard man image during his time at Millwall and it preceded him wherever he went, with some justification, as he once set a record for disciplinary points accrued in a single season in Scotland. I remember being more than slightly alarmed at this signing, as Jimmy Case was hard but he also could play a bit, but the signing of Hurlock just sent a signal that we were switching to a more physical type of play.

I saw him make his debut in a 1-0 home defeat to Manchester United where he looked as though his only instruction was to run around and look menacing, and he spent the remainder of the season in and out of the side.

Another new signing brought in by Branfoot came in the shape of striker Iain Dowie, who arrived for £500,000 from West Ham.

Iain had been on our books as a youngster and now found himself back at The Dell as the strike partner to Alan Shearer. If most fans didn't know that we were switching our style of play from a simple passing game to the more direct route, they did with this signing, and although Alan Shearer would benefit greatly from Iain's flick headers, there were some who didn't adapt to the long ball game, most noticeably, Matthew Le Tissier.

Regrettably, for Matt and the fans, Ian Branfoot was a disciple of Charlie Hughes, who at the time was the director of coaching at the Football Association. Charlie concluded from analysing matches that most goals come as a result of three passes or less. The way he saw it was if you get the ball into certain areas of the pitch as often as possible (something he called positions of maximum opportunity) then more often than not this would lead to a goal. It was football at its most basic.

He taught this idea to a whole generation of young up and coming coaches in England, and another great advocate of the Charlie Hughes philosophy was the then current England manager, Graham Taylor. Now there is nothing wrong in getting the ball into the penalty area quickly, but doing it every time makes the match predictable and dour as a spectacle. There is much more to entertaining football than just goals. A 0-0 draw can still be entertaining, just as a 2-2 draw can be uninspiring and dull.

Disappointingly, the FA embraced the Charlie Hughes philosophy and it left us with a generation of players who had little technical ability, and coaches who didn't know how to play any other way. The shortcomings to this style of play became evident when the England national side (under Taylor) failed to qualify for the 1994 World Cup in the USA.

For Saints, the long ball game was becoming something of an issue with the fans and after a couple of heavy 4-0 home defeats (versus Leeds and Arsenal) and an appalling 1-1 draw at home to Notts County in mid-December (in front of a crowd of just 11,054), serious questions were being asked about Ian Branfoot's appointment.

By the turn of the year, we were at the bottom of the table, attendances were plummeting, and we looked like certainties for relegation. We were looking at a long bleak winter ahead.

There was a more than usual need to stay in the top flight for next season, as there were rumblings that the top-flight clubs were contemplating breaking away from the Football League and forming their own super league. The main reason behind this rebellion was, of course, money, and with a new deal in place, the top-flight clubs could keep more of the sponsorship and TV revenue money for themselves, instead of sharing it through all four divisions, which was the current setup. The live TV rights would be crucial for the new league, and now there was a new kid on the block, in the shape of BSkyB.

BSkyB had started showing live FA Cup matches in partnership with the BBC for the past couple of seasons, but now they wanted it all, and they were going to fight ITV all the way to get it. If there was to be a super league, then Sky wanted it all for themselves, as they saw football as being the one way they could boost their stagnating satellite dish sales. But that was all in the future, but would Saints still be in the top-flight to take their place in the new league?

It was in the FA Cup that Saints would find some relief from their dire league form, as in the third round, we drew QPR. They arrived at The Dell on the back of an impressive 4-1 away win over title chasers Manchester United in their previous league match, so despite home field advantage they were not going to be easy opposition. Yet, as is usual with the FA Cup the formbook goes out of the window, and the Saints stormed into a two-goal lead by half-time, thanks to goals from Matthew Le Tissier and defender Steve Wood, and it was a lead we held onto quite comfortably.

The fourth round would throw up a sterner test in the form of Manchester United, again at The Dell, a match that Sky decided to switch to a Monday night for live coverage. The match itself was a tepid 0-0 draw, and there weren't many Saints fans who thought we had a chance of getting a result at Old Trafford in the replay nine days later.

Saints' solitary FA Cup victory over United famously came in the final in 1976, and I settled down to watch the match (again Sky had decided to show it live) with the expectation that we were going to be in for a bit of a mauling. Trips to Old Trafford usually end up with us on the receiving end of a hefty beating, and with our dire form so far this season, another heavy loss would not have been a surprise.

The magic of football, of course, is that it has the tendency to throw up one or two surprises when you least expect them, and this turned out to be one of those nights when the unexpected happened.

Amazingly, with just eight minutes on the clock, a long pass from Micky Adams fell between the United goalkeeper Peter Schmeichel and defender Paul Parker. The pair hesitated with each man assuming that the other would deal with the danger. This indecision allowed Stuart Gray to nip into slot home from the edge of the penalty area. If that had me dancing around my bedroom in celebration, then fourteen minutes later I nearly jumped through the ceiling when a Matthew Le Tissier free-kick caught the United defence napping once more, and Alan Shearer nodded in a second.

Two goals to the good at Old Trafford, this never happens to us, but worryingly we still had three-quarters of the match still to play, and if anyone could throw away a two-goal lead, it was the Saints.

We didn't even make it to half-time without conceding, as Andrei Kanchelskis pulled a goal back, just two minutes before the break, although Shearer almost restored our two goal cushion, his fierce shot was saved well by Schmeichel.

The second-half seemed to be nothing more than one-way traffic, as we desperately clung on to our slender lead, with chances for us to score again becoming increasingly rare.

As the match entered stoppage-time, it looked as though we were going to hold on for a famous victory, but just like the Oldham game two seasons ago, we conceded a sloppy goal with just seconds to spare.

The goal itself was about as comical as they come, as a long ball into the box was headed clear by Neil Ruddock for what should have been a United corner, only for the ball to be headed back across goal by our right-back Jeff Kenna. It appeared as though Kenna had tried to duck out of the way of the ball but had inadvertently sent the ball spinning back into our six-yard box where a grateful Brian McClair was on hand to snatch a heartbreaking equaliser.

Deflated, I slumped back in the chair and contemplated the thirty minutes of extra-time and the certain United victory that was to follow. I knew there was a chance that we wouldn't hold out for the entire match, but to have victory snatched away from us in the dying seconds was a bitter blow.

Extra-time followed the pattern of the second-half, with attack after attack on our goal, but with our players doggedly keeping the United strikers at bay. The only real scare came when a Bryan Robson header looked to have been clawed back from beyond the goal line by Tim Flowers (the TV replays were inconclusive), but we got the benefit of the doubt, and we held firm to take the game to a penalty competition.

This was the first season where there were to be no multiple replays in FA Cup matches. It's hard to imagine now, but before this season teams kept replaying until a winner was found, and it was not unusual for a tie to be settled in a second or even a third replay. This was also the first penalty competition to involve top-flight clubs, as there had been none in the previous round.

Taking the game to the lottery of a penalty shootout was going to be our best chance of securing our passage into the next round, and I fancied our chances, as I knew we had a number of players who were adept at taking spot kicks. My heart was in my mouth as Neil Ruddock stepped up to take the first penalty in front of the Stretford End, but I needn't have worried as he put it away with a coolness that he probably didn't feel.

Neil Webb stepped up to take United's first spot kick and blasted his shot high and wide to give us an early advantage. Micky Adams, Barry Horne, and Alan Shearer then all converted their kicks to give us a 4-2 lead with United still to take their fourth.

Next up for United was a young Ryan Giggs who had to score to keep United in the competition, and I remember the camera focusing on him doing keepie-uppies with the ball as he walked towards the penalty spot, a touch of arrogance that United players always seem to exhibit.

His haughtiness did him no good though, and he hit his shot straight at Tim Flowers to send us through. Tim celebrated by sprinting the length of the Old Trafford pitch towards the ecstatic Saints fans at the other end of the stadium, whilst being chased by his jubilant teammates.

It was an incredible finish to an extraordinary night, and it was the first time I remember actually being both mentally and physically exhausted from watching a football match so nerve wracking was the experience.

Little did I, or the thousands of other Saints fans know, but an even more nerve-shredding experience was waiting around the corner in Round Five.

Salvation

Saints 3 Bolton Wanderers 2 (AET)   FA Cup 5th Round Replay
                                                                           26 February 1992

Despite our abysmal league form, Third Division Bolton should not
have presented us with too many problems when they came out of the
velvet bag in the fifth round draw. All the same, this being Saints, we
never make things easy for ourselves, and so it would prove as the two
ties produced some dramatic and frantic football.

Over four thousand Saints fans (I wasn't one of them as I couldn't
get the time off work to make the trip) made the long trek back to the
North-West on a cold and windy February day to see us blow a two-
goal lead in the original tie. After half-an-hour, everything seemed to
be going according to plan, as two almost identical goals by centre-
back Richard Hall (both headers from Matthew Le Tissier corners)
had put us comfortably 2-0 in front.

The score stayed the same well into the second-half, and it seemed as
though a straightforward victory was on the cards, but that all changed
on 78 minutes when Bolton (backed by an unusually large and
vociferous crowd) pulled one back.

With time running out, Bolton poured forward, and eventually, one
of their attacks bore fruit as they grabbed what was probably a
deserved equaliser, which meant a replay at The Dell ten days later

The replay against Bolton turned out to be one of those games that
older fans still talk about with misty-eyed nostalgia. It should have
been a straightforward home victory against a team two divisions
below us, but no one on the Dell terraces that night had any inkling of
the drama that was about to unfold.

Just over 18,000 fans turned up for the replay, which included 3,000 from Bolton, but although the attendance was below capacity the noise from both sets of fans was deafening.

Standing on the Milton Road terrace the prevailing mood amongst my fellow supporters was that the Saints would probably win but make it more difficult than was necessary. It was a way of thinking that would prove to be very prophetic indeed.

As in the first game at Burnden Park, Saints took a well-deserved lead, and although we had chances to extend our advantage, it came as no real surprise when Bolton equalised midway through the second-half. The game was now a typical cup-tie, with both teams roared on by their fervent followers. It was classic end-to-end football, and both sides had the chance to take the lead, with both goalkeepers called into action on a regular basis.

With 90 minutes almost up and the game heading for extra-time Bolton scored what looked like a certain winner. The Saints defence failed to clear a corner properly and the ball fell to Julian Darby on the edge of the box. His resultant volley flew through the crowded penalty area and into the top corner of the net sending the Bolton fans wild and the Saints fans hurrying towards the exit.

As I was standing towards the front of a packed Milton Road terrace I decided to stay put rather than fight my way out of the ground, and a couple of minutes later I was rewarded when somehow and from somewhere, Saints managed to grab an unlikely equaliser.

To a backdrop of hundreds, if not thousands, of Bolton fans whistling to remind the referee to blow for full-time, Saints piled forward in a desperate bid for salvation. After seeing a couple of long balls launched into the box only to be repelled by the Bolton defence it looked as though it was too little too late. That is until one last long ball wasn't cleared properly by the Bolton centre-backs, and the ball fell kindly for Barry Horne.

42

Barry found himself 35-yards from goal, and with the ref about to put the whistle to his lips, he decided to try his luck with one final attempt on goal.

As the ball left his foot it rose, dipped, and swerved left then right as if he was somehow manipulating the ball via remote control. Despite the Bolton goalkeeper David Felgate being only a yard or two off his goal line, the ball flew past him as he desperately backpedalled in a vain attempt to get a hand on it.

It was an amazing goal out of nothing, causing some fans to spill onto the pitch in celebration, whilst the deafening roar saw a stampede, as those who left early returned to the terraces.

Not content to score such a dramatic late equaliser, Barry Horne launched another long-range effort in extra-time, a low daisy cutter that found its way past the helpless Felgate to give us a 3-2 lead, and one that we held onto this time. Saints fans who were there that night still talk about this match and that Barry Horne goal whenever the subject of late, late goals crops up.

Highlights of the match were shown on BBC's Sportsnight programme that night, and it isn't until you see Barry's shot from behind that you realise just how much the ball dipped and swerved on its way into the net.

Now we were into the quarter-finals, and it was certainly starting to feel like it was going to be our year in the cup, as the draw for the sixth round had paired us with Norwich City at home. Not an easy game by any stretch of the imagination, but not the hardest either. We had also avoided local rivals Portsmouth, who had also made it this far, and now there was a real possibility of an all-south coast semi-final or even the final, imagine that!

Wembley

Saints 2 Nottingham Forest 3 (AET) Zenith Data Systems Cup Final
29 March 1992

As it transpired, the fifth round was where our FA Cup adventure ended, as after a dull 0-0 draw at The Dell in the original tie, we would go on to lose the replay in controversial circumstances at Carrow Road.

Southampton's record at Carrow Road is poor, and it is a ground where we usually struggle, so it came as a bit of a surprise when Neil Ruddock headed home to give us the lead early on.

The match was full of niggly fouls and Ruddock was involved in the next incident when he got away with a particularly nasty challenge on Norwich's Robert Fleck on the stroke of half-time.

Fleck, incensed by the challenge and the referee's decision not to see it as a foul, decided to put himself about at the start of the second half, and his first victim was Matthew Le Tissier, who lashed out after a robust Fleck challenge.

That petulant kick took place in front of the referee, and it was no surprise when he reached for a red card, which would be Matt's first for the club.

With only ten men on the field, defending a one goal lead was always going to be difficult, and so it proved when Norwich equalised a few minutes later. Saints were rocking now and coming under increasing pressure from a Norwich side that could sense a place in the semi-finals was theirs for the taking.

Prior to this replay, the draw for the semi-finals had paired the winners of this tie with Second Division Sunderland, whilst Portsmouth (who had shocked First Division Nottingham Forest in their quarter-final at the first attempt) had drawn Liverpool.

44

Therefore, there was a distinct possibility of both south coast rivals squaring off at Wembley, but before any of us could contemplate that, we had to fend off Norwich.

Fleck was still being a nuisance, and with just a few minutes left in normal time he riled up Neil Ruddock enough to lash out at the Scotsman, and he received his marching orders, leaving us with only nine men on the field.

It looked as though holding out for another penalty shootout was going to be the only way we could win this match, and even though we made it to extra-time, we couldn't hold out to take the game to penalties.

With just five minutes of the extra thirty to go, Norwich scored the winner to send them through to the semi's where they would lose to Sunderland. It was a cruel way to go out of a competition I felt we could have gone on to win, but at least Portsmouth faltered at the semi-final stage, when they lost to Liverpool in a replay, ironically after a penalty shootout.

Not all was lost on the cup front, however, as Saints made their first return to Wembley Stadium since 1979, in the Zenith Data Systems Cup tournament.

This tournament had come into being in 1986 as The Full Members Cup before succumbing to corporate sponsorship. Its introduction being seen as a way of adding extra fixtures to the calendar to replace those missing European matches that had been taken away because of the ban on English clubs playing in European competitions after the 1985 Heysel Stadium disaster.

The whole competition was a bit of a joke really, with the trophy being contested by teams in the top two divisions, with teams in the lower two divisions contesting their own competition. Several of the big clubs shunned the competition altogether, and during its seven-year existence Arsenal, Tottenham, Liverpool and Manchester United never took part.

The competition was split on a regional level – North and South –, which was probably to cut down on travelling for a competition that was solely played during midweek. This also meant that the final would be a North versus South affair, which added a little bit of extra spice, and it did give teams another route to the twin towers of Wembley Stadium.

The 1991/92 season was to be the last for this particular competition (although the tournament for the lower divisions has endured to this day) as the UEFA ban on English clubs in European competition had ended.

To get to the final Saints had to navigate tricky away games at Bristol City and Plymouth, before dispatching West Ham at The Dell in the regional semi-finals. The regional final would be a two-legged affair against Chelsea, who Saints beat 5-1 on aggregate. This set up a Wembley showdown with Brian Clough's Nottingham Forest, the same team we had faced in our last visit to the twin towers for the 1979 League Cup Final. Unhappily, for me and all the other Southampton fans, the scoreline on this day would be the same as it was in 1979.

Despite the pitiful attendances in the early rounds, a trip to Wembley unquestionably stirs the interest of the fans, and over 67,000 supporters filled Wembley for this final. I wasn't one of them, however, as I stubbornly refused to go on the grounds that I wanted my first trip to the national stadium to be for a "proper" cup final, not this insignificant tournament. It was an attitude that would change as I got older and Southampton's cup final appearances grew scarcer.

I did watch the final though, as the fledgeling BSkyB sports channel was broadcasting it live, and I watched us go two down before half-time with a certain amount of disillusionment and acceptance.

At 2-0 down I felt justified in not going to the match, and it looked as though Forest were going to win the trophy without too much trouble, but halfway through the second-half, the Saints players decided to make a fight of it.

Matthew Le Tissier's neatly headed finish gave us a way back into the match, and only a few minutes later it was 2-2 when Kevin Moore leapt highest to nod home to restore parity, and with no further scoring, we faced yet another period of extra-time.

During the extra thirty minutes, both teams squandered chances to take the lead, and it looked as though a penalty shootout was going to be needed to decide the winner. However, just like the Norwich FA Cup match, the Saints conceded a goal that turned out to be the winner with just five minutes remaining.

I remember being bitterly disappointed, despite my initial indifference to the competition. I guess no fan likes to see their team lose a Wembley final. If I had known that it would be the clubs last Wembley appearance for eighteen years, I may have made more of an effort to go, but hindsight is a wonderful thing.

With cup competitions finally out of the way, it was back to the league and top-flight survival. Our survival chances received a lift when we hit a run of six consecutive victories, which equalled the clubs record for consecutive wins in the top division, a run that ended when Nottingham Forest came to The Dell and left with all three points.

Nevertheless, that run of wins, as well as the trip to Wembley seemed to instil some much-needed confidence into the team, and we managed to avoid relegation, finishing a respectable (and highly unlikely back in January) 16th place.

This sparkling end of season form and surviving relegation when it looked like a certainty would become something of a leitmotif of

Saints during the nineties, as there would be even closer scrapes with relegation to come.

In spite of turnaround in form towards the end of the season, Rumblings of discontent from the terraces meant that it wouldn't be long before the knives were out for manager Ian Branfoot, and he was going to find it hard to change the overriding feeling amongst the supporters that he wasn't the man for the job.

A Whole New Ball Game But Same Old Saints

Saints 1 Q.P.R. 2   Premier League   12 October 1992

In the close season, all of the top-flight clubs resigned from the Football League en masse and the FA Premier League was born, backed up with a truckload of cash from Sky Sports. Sky had won the live TV rights from under the noses of ITV, and as an upshot of that, there was the welcome return of BBC's Match of the Day highlights programme on Saturday nights.

A comprehensive highlights programme was something that was sadly missing from the ITV schedules in the previous seasons unless you happened to live in London or Manchester. If you had the misfortune to live in an area covered by the rest of the ITV regions then you had to make do with a 30-second highlights package on your local news show, a sad indictment of the way ITV treated football fans back then.

For most Southampton fans, it was just a relief to be in the Premier League after all the tension of the relegation battle the previous season. The relief was to be short-lived, however when the announcement came that our top scorer from the previous season, Alan Shearer, had signed for newly promoted Blackburn Rovers for a British record fee of £3.6 million.

Blackburn had just returned to the top-flight after decades in the lower leagues, and in millionaire and lifelong supporter Jack Walker, they had a man to whom money was no object in the pursuit of the Premier League title.

For Southampton, the only cash injection we received always seemed to come from the selling of our star players, a business strategy that hasn't changed much through the years. Witnessing the sale of the club's top scorer for the second consecutive summer was a bitter kick in the teeth, and the fans only hope was that the club would spend most of the money on a decent replacement or two. How wrong we were.

As part of the Shearer deal, we would receive Blackburn's striker David Speedie in return. Now, Speedie was not a prolific striker, but he had had his moments and had played for both Chelsea and Liverpool in the past. However, by the time he signed for us, he was approaching the tail end of his career, and his signing looked to be a bit of a gamble by the manager.

Branfoot followed up this signing with a swoop for another former Chelsea striker Kerry Dixon. Dixon signed for £575,000 and the reasoning behind his signing was to reignite the partnership that Dixon and Speedie had forged at Chelsea in the 1980s.

Branfoot couldn't help but crow about his new strike partnership in his programme notes for the opening day game at home to Spurs. He talked about how prolific they had been for the Stamford Bridge club in the past, and how they would be just as productive for us this season. He even went on to make a prediction that they would score more goals than Alan Shearer would during the season, a prophecy that was about as wide of the mark as one of David Speedie's shots at goal.

The game against Spurs turned out to be a rather dull 0-0 draw and it was a sign of things to come. Neither Dixon nor Speedie could find

49

the back of the net, and by the time this match at home to Queens Park Rangers came about, only Kerry Dixon had found the net and only on one occasion. In fact, David Speedie only troubled the headline writers at the local newspaper's sports desk once during his time with the club, and that involved a drunken punch-up with Terry Hurlock on the clubs pre-season tour to Jersey.

The Dixon and Speedie experiment turned out to be a total disaster, and between them, they only made 16 first team appearances and scored only two goals (both by Dixon). Speedie found himself out on loan to various clubs before Christmas, whilst Dixon would also go out on loan, to Luton in February. Both players would eventually leave on free transfers, a piece of business that cost the club a fraction under a £1 million, a sum the club recouped with the sale of crowd favourites Neil Ruddock and Barry Horne. It showed that Branfoot was about as astute with money as he was with tactics and team management.

Now the managers' popularity rating was sinking lower than ever. The fans who had been so critical of his predecessor Chris Nicholl, had seen his talented players who he had nurtured, shipped out for big transfer fees only to be replaced by overpriced, over-the-hill flops, and many had to ask themselves, what had Chris Nicholl done that was so bad? Yes, we had stagnated a little, but under Branfoot we were heading in only one direction, and that was backwards.

Seven Goal Thriller

Saints 4 Ipswich Town 3   Premier League   13 March 1993

With Dixon and Speedie dropped, the manager switched to playing Iain Dowie alone up front with Le Tissier, and promising youngster Neil Maddison as attacking midfielders just behind him. The change worked, and for once Saints looked relatively comfortable despite dropping into the relegation zone on a couple of occasions.

At one stage, we even hit the dizzy heights of 9th place after winning this exciting match against Ipswich Town. Now the word "exciting" isn't one that usually springs to mind when describing matches played during Branfoot's reign of terror, but this was an absolute cracker, real old fashioned end-to-end stuff, with both teams throwing caution to the wind.

As this game was closest to my birthday, I had decided to treat myself to a seat in the upper west stand. After the Taylor Report into the Hillsborough disaster had deemed that all football grounds should become all-seater, I decided to see what sitting down at a football match was actually like.

Now, anyone who was a Dell regular will tell you that the upper west stand was the preserve of our more staid and elderly fans, and it did come as a bit of a culture shock to find myself sitting amongst people who seemed to be equipped for a picnic. They had blankets, boxes of sandwiches and flasks of hot soup, tea or coffee, and the obligatory half-time orange. With blankets on laps and provisions stowed safely under their seat, they proceeded to watch what was probably the most exciting 90 minutes of the season in almost total silence.

Apart from the odd heavy sigh when a pass went astray, the only sound they made was when we scored a goal, and even then, their celebrations seemed quite muted compared to what I had experienced on the Milton Road terrace.

It certainly came as a bit of a culture shock after spending so long standing on the terraces, or occasionally sitting on the bench seats under the east stand. Yes, bench seats in a football ground, like the bleachers in American sports grounds, and I think I am right in saying that they were a unique feature at any English football ground, and an odd feature that added to the character and distinctiveness of The Dell.

Ipswich started this match the brighter and deservedly lead 2-1 at the interval, and with less than half-an-hour remaining, they looked to be holding on for the win. That is until Stockwell's clumsy trip ended Neil Maddison's run into the penalty area, and Le Tissier coolly slotted home the resultant spot-kick.

The scoring was not over though, as with nine minutes remaining Jeff Kenna's tap-in from close range looked to have won the three points for us. However, in injury-time Ipswich's Chris Kiwomya made the most of some slack Saints defending to poke in what looked like the final goal of the game, to make the score 3-3.

Saints were not to be denied though, and deep into time added on, Le Tissier popped up unmarked in the six-yard box to slot home a dramatic winner, after Ken Monkou's far post header had come to him via the crossbar.

With eight games to go we looked all but safe after this result, but as I made my way home little did I know just how close we would come to throwing it all away.

Having looked so comfortable after the Ipswich win, we ended up just two places and one point above the relegation zone and many fans were convinced that if the season had been one or two games longer then we would surely have gone down.

The reason for this slide down the table was a horrendous run of results, the worst being a truly awful 5-2 defeat at Hillsborough against what was virtually a Sheffield Wednesday reserve side. Wednesday were looking forward to playing Arsenal in the FA Cup final a few weeks later, and their manager Trevor Francis had decided to rest a number of key players for what for them was a dead rubber league match. Yet somehow, just like that 6-2 loss at Derby that went some way to costing Chris Nicholl his job, we put in a performance of such ineptitude that many Saints fans wondered (and hoped) whether the same thing would happen again to Branfoot.

He Has Got To Go

Saints 0 Everton 2   Premier League   14 August 1993

For those of us hoping to see Branfoot leaving via the exit door in the summer, there was bad news. Instead of getting the sack, the club rewarded him for his ineptitude with a three-year extension to his contract. It was a move that angered even the most placid of fans, and now the pressure was on the manager, the chairman and the board of directors. Nothing less than a good start to the season would do to placate the ire of supporters who had had enough of Branfoot, his long ball tactics and the selling of star players.

The only major change during the summer came off the pitch when the Archers Road terrace was levelled, and replaced with a small, covered all-seated stand, that became affectionately known as the "bike shed" due to its compact size. Initially, this stand would house the away fans for the first couple of seasons of its existence, before housing home supporters. The lower east and west stands had also seen changes and my beloved bench seats/terrace combo was replaced by rows of normal red tip-up seats. This work was necessary due to the Taylor report into football ground safety after the Hillsborough disaster, which had recommended that all grounds in the top two divisions become all-seated.

These changes had the effect of reducing the capacity of The Dell to 19,000 from 22,000 for this season, and that total would come down to just over 15,000 when the Milton Road terrace became all-seater the following year. Mind you, despite the reduction in the capacity, it was still ample enough room for the size of the crowds we were now getting under Beelzebub Branfoot, as crowd numbers would plummet this season as fans voted with their feet.

A good start to the season was imperative but unfortunately, it was to be one of our worst starts to a season in decades, and this opening day defeat was the catalyst.

On paper, losing 2-0 to our bogey side Everton doesn't look too bad, but it was an appalling match where we offered nothing in the way of an attacking force, and Everton sauntered to a victory that was so easy it looked like a training match for them.

Two more defeats followed in consecutive away games to leave us pointless after our first three games, and despite some respite in our next home game, where we dispatched newly promoted Swindon Town 5-1, five consecutive defeats followed. The only reason that we were not anchored to the foot of the table was the fact that Swindon were fairing slightly worse.

In an attempt to find a solution, Branfoot does what any manager would surely do in this situation; he leaves out the one man who could turn a match in an instant. Ergo, he drops Matthew Le Tissier from the starting line-up. Firstly, for the visit of Shrewsbury Town in the first leg of the League Cup at The Dell, (fair enough, as most teams rotate their starting lineups when it comes to the League Cup), but then there is no sign of Le Tissier for the following three league games either. Then the return leg at Shrewsbury comes around and Le Tissier is still conspicuous by his absence. Not only has he dropped the previous season's top scorer, but also, in doing so, he had now completely lost what little support he had amongst the Southampton fans. It was an amazing faux pas confounded by the fact that Matty doesn't even warrant a place on the bench, and despite beating Shrewsbury 1-0 in the first leg, no one is left in any doubt that it will not be enough to see us through in the return fixture.

Some supporters hold a demonstration in the car park after the first leg match against Shrewsbury, and things are starting to turn ugly. There are whispers that some fans are going to form a pressure group to try to force the board into taking the only action that many see as the only way to save the season, namely the sacking of Ian Branfoot.

Despite the protests (banners sporting "Branfoot Out" and "Sack the Board" now start to appear at home games) either the club directors are not listening, or they are just too stubborn for their own good, and the protests seem to have no effect, meaning Branfoot remains in his job...for now.

Watching the Defectives

Saints 3 Sheffield United 3   Premier League   2 October 1993

Whilst some fans protested, others simply chose to stay away, and who could blame them? Crowds were falling fast, and I would soon join the ranks of the disenchanted, as this would be the last game I attend for three months. I point-blank refused to pay to watch the utter garbage the team served up week in week out, and this match against fellow strugglers Sheffield United was the one that did it for me, and I vowed never to return whilst the Beelzebub Branfoot was still in charge.

There were rumours pre-match that Matty was in line for a recall, but whether it was done out of spite or not, he was missing from the line-up once more, and I almost felt like going home there and then.

I remember that the weather seemed to match the downcast mood on the terraces as rain lashed down throughout the entire 90 minutes, and I got a thorough soaking, as did the rest of the pitiful attendance of 11,619 who had the misfortune to witness this latest shambles. Not only did we have to contend with Matt's continued absence, but also

Branfoot had replaced him with 37-year-old Peter Reid, a man who recently sacked as manager of Manchester City.

To be fair to Peter he did add some much-needed strength to the midfield, but he must have wondered what he had let himself in for such was the strength of ill feeling towards the manager.

Peter would make his debut in this match, and we actually started quite well scoring twice either side of half-time. A Sheffield United red card added to the feeling that this might actually be a hard-fought three points. Even the blades pulling a goal back didn't unduly worry us as we re-established our two-goal advantage with 14 minutes to go. No matter how bad we had been lately, surely even we could hold a two-goal lead against ten men. However, once Jostein Flo pulled one back in the 80th minute I just knew what was coming next, and sure enough in the 89th minute, Flo popped up again to grab the inevitable equaliser.

At the final whistle, the mood of the home supporters darkened considerably and the anger shown towards Branfoot was starting to get nasty. It was bad enough losing every week in the Premier League, but this result left no doubt in my mind, or that of my fellow supporters that the away match at Shrewsbury in the League Cup second-leg was going to be nothing other than an embarrassing defeat.

Such was the apathy amongst the fans that a tannoy announcement during half-time broke the news of the cancellation of the solitary travel club coach for the match at Shrewsbury. A cancellation due to lack of interest, which surprised nobody. I had never known things so bad that we couldn't even fill a solitary coach for an away match.

The only surprising thing about the feeble collapse in this match was that United didn't go on to score a winner in injury-time, but by then I was past caring and like thousands of others, I was already making my way to the exit.

The only thing that Saints fans agreed on was that either Branfoot went or we did.

Magical Man

Saints 2 Newcastle United 1   Premier League   16 October 1993

As expected, the match at Shrewsbury ended in a 2-0 defeat, a result that knocked us out of the competition 2-1 on aggregate to a side in the bottom tier of English football. Not that the result came as a surprise to anyone, and it was getting to the point where people actually wanted us to continue losing just so the board would have to act and axe this fool Branfoot once and for all.

I watched this game against Newcastle live on television on a dank and dreary Sunday afternoon, as a test of my self-imposed exile. Afterwards, I wish I had been there to witness the return of Le Tiss, but that said, the crowd was only a couple of thousand up from the Sheffield game so I probably wasn't alone in feeling that I had missed something magical.

Tuning in, I was shocked to discover that Matty was back in the starting lineup, a move that at least went some way to subduing certain sections of the crowd, but not all of them.

With the Sky TV cameras in attendance, this match was the perfect way for those embittered fans to make their feelings known to a much wider audience. In the lower East Stand (the stand opposite where the main television camera gantry was situated at The Dell) a few supporters unfurled a banner bearing the words "Branfoot and Askham Out" (Guy Askham was the clubs chairman who had recently given an interview to the local press supporting Branfoot and dispelling any notion of sacking him). Other banners proclaiming "Branfoot Out," and "Sack the Board" appeared in other areas of the stadium too, and it seemed as though to some, the match was actually a secondary consideration.

The general mood of ill feeling that permeated those on the terraces meant that home games were now being played against a backdrop of minacious malice, something that wouldn't help the Saints players to perform. Yet, somehow, they managed to find enough spirit and tenacity to win this game against one of the Premier League's up and coming teams.

Newcastle were riding high on a crest of a Kevin Keegan wave, as the former Saints captain had taken his beloved Newcastle from the foot of the old Second Division to the Premier League, and he was starting to build a team that would challenge for the title in coming seasons. It would be a fascinating contest in many ways, and with Newcastle having such a poor record at The Dell and with the Saints in such poor form, there was a genuine belief amongst the Southampton fans that the Geordies would get their first win at The Dell since the early 1970's.

The first half was as dreary as the weather, and after a quarter of an hour of the second, it looked as though Branfoot was getting ready to replace Matty with striker Paul Moody, who was energetically warming up on the touchline. Then, just as Branfoot seemed to be signalling Moody back towards the bench to get ready to come on, Matty conjured up a moment of magic that still makes the hairs on the back of my neck stand on end whenever I watch it.

He was 35-yards from goal when he controlled Dowie's flick header from behind him with a flick of his boot over his own head. He controlled the dropping ball expertly before proceeding to dash past Newcastle's Barry Venison with a right foot stab of the ball. Now he was bearing down on the penalty area, but there was still another Newcastle defender between him and the goal. No problem for Le Tissier, as he lobbed the ball over the static United defender and sauntered past him all in one movement, before sublimely side-footing the ball past the advancing keeper with a first time shot on the half-volley. It was a breathtaking goal to watch, which was almost balletic in its beauty and swiftness. Matt would later admit that he mishit the finish, as he wanted to blast the ball into the top corner, but he scuffed it and it bobbled into the bottom corner instead. Either way, it was still a joy to behold.

As the rest of his teammates joined him in celebration the Sky cameras zoomed in on the Southampton bench, where Branfoot (arms folded and a look of cold indifference on his face) appeared to turn to Paul Moody and say, "sit down Moods." Matt really had been just seconds away from being substituted. What that would have done to the already dark mood of the crowd we will now never know of course, but suffice to say it wouldn't have been pleasant.

Matt wasn't finished yet either, as after Andy Cole had equalised for Newcastle, and with the game looking like it was going to peter out to a tame 1-1 draw, he conjured up yet another breathtaking moment of skill to win the match for the Saints.

With just two minutes of normal time remaining, another piece of Matty magic lit up The Dell and everything around it. As the Newcastle defence failed to clear a cross, the ball fell invitingly to Le Tissier on the edge of the penalty area. There seemed to be no other choice but to lift the ball back into the box in the forlorn hope that one of his teammates could find enough time and space to get a decent shot on target. Not a bit of it, as Matt controlled the ball nonchalantly on his thigh before swivelling in one movement and unleashing a dipping 20-yard volley into the top corner. The crowd erupted in an explosion of joy and hysteria, only matched by Sky Sports commentator Martyn Tyler, who almost ran out of superlatives to describe what he had just seen.

When the final whistle went soon after, those fans that had been planning on demonstrating against the board of directors and club manager had all but forgotten their protests, and instead, they were all in awe of a man who had just won a game almost single-handedly.

As for Branfoot, well in the days that followed, the cretin even tried to claim credit for Matt's display that afternoon, saying that dropping him had spurred him on to produce a much better performance. Arrogance that was typical of the man, especially as he had been seconds away from substituting Le Tissier.

Finally, Matty had given us something to cheer rather than jeer, but there was no doubt that it was going to take more than one win to placate the supporters.

Nothing but Blue Sky

Saints 1 Coventry City 0   Premier League   15 January 1994

That win against Newcastle was just papering over the cracks, and although we followed it up with wins at home to Tottenham and away at Villa, another run of poor form would follow. Five consecutive defeats through December included losing 2-1 at Swindon the only team below us in the table, which did nothing to lighten the ever-darkening mood amongst the supporters.

Things weren't much better on the transfer front either, as the exodus of our star players continued. These were still the days before the transfer window, and transfers would take place until March. Therefore, it came as no real surprise when our England international goalkeeper Tim Flowers followed his old roommate Alan Shearer to Blackburn for a fee in the region of £2.4 million.

The fans had had enough now. Not only of the poor on-pitch performances but the club seemed intent of selling our diamonds and replacing them with lumps of coal. The result of all this anger and frustration culminated in the formation of a pressure group called the Saints Independent Supporters Association or SISA for short. Their sole aim to rid the club of the Beelzebub Branfoot, and they produced fanzines to help raise awareness of their cause.

At first, it seemed to be sincere but light-hearted enough but then one publication went a bit too far over the boundaries of bad taste. The fanzine entitled On the March went over the top with its front cover picture of Branfoot accompanied by the headline "Hope you die soon!" A repugnant statement that left a bad taste in the mouth and its distasteful statement was singled out by certain football pundits as an example of why fanzines were a bad idea.

Although it was wrong, it did rather sum up the feeling among the supporters of just how detested Branfoot really was. He had pushed the loyalty and the sanity of the supporters to breaking point, and he really was the most hated man in Southampton.

Despite events off the pitch making more headlines than the teams' performances on it, there was the odd glimmer of hope, and the losing run ended with a 3-1 win over Chelsea at The Dell just after Boxing Day.

I have to admit that I attended the game, thus breaking my boycott, and I wasn't the only person to decide to come back to The Dell either, as former manager Lawrie McMenemy also returned to the club as a Director of Football. Now, Director of Football is a rather unusual term that seemed to spring up during the 1990s. It was a position that was popular on the continent, where the Director of Football would be the link between the manager or head coach and the Chairman and directors. Lawrie's job seemed to be the same, to act as a link, but was it necessary? Hadn't the Chairman fully backed his manager numerous times in the past few months? Most fans wondered whether there was more to this appointment than met the eye.

The answer would come a few days after the appointment of McMenemy when after another insipid FA Cup display against lower league opposition (a 1-1 draw at home to Port Vale) Branfoot was gone.

I almost cried tears of joy and relief when I heard the news that his reign of terror was finally over, the most detested manager in our history up to that point had never endeared himself to the supporters, and he paid the price.

The final protest against Branfoot came at that Port Vale game, where thousands of people waved giant red cards at him as he made his way along the touchline to the home dugout, just to show him he wasn't welcome anymore and he should do the honourable thing and resign.

To everyone's dismay, one of the early frontrunners for the vacant manager's job was Peter Reid, according to the press at least, but he quickly ruled himself out of the job, as Branfoot brought him to the club, and he didn't want to jump into his job. Cue a huge sigh of relief from every Saints fan around the world.

Now managerless, the Saints crashed out of the FA Cup in a replay at Port Vale, under the temporary stewardship of Branfoot's two assistants, Lew Chatterley and Jon Mortimore. However, with just under half of the league programme still to come, and with the right appointment, avoiding relegation was still a realistic possibility.

Before the Port Vale defeat, we hosted fellow strugglers Coventry at The Dell, and we won a tight tense affair thanks to a solitary Matt Le Tissier penalty just before half-time. The result wasn't the main thing I remember about this match, but rather the lighter happier atmosphere in the stands and on the terraces. It was refreshing to witness the fans get behind the players once again, and for the players themselves to dig deep and grind out a vital victory, in stark contrast to the caustic atmosphere of previous home games.

Now we just had to wait and hope that the board that had made such a pig's ear of the previous managerial appointment could now partly redeem themselves and get this one right.

The fans man of choice was former Saints player (and former Portsmouth boss) Alan Ball, who was now plying his trade at lowly Exeter City, and it wasn't long before he announced that he would certainly be interested in the vacancy. However, would the board of directors listen or would they go against the flow again and pig-headedly appoint another unpopular manager.

Having a Ball

Saints 4 Liverpool 2   Premier League   14 February 1994

For once (and probably for the only time) the board of directors had taken notice of the fans feelings, and the day after the Port Vale defeat, Alan Ball was confirmed as the new manager at a Dell press conference. He stated that he had always wanted to return to Southampton as manager, and although there were a few people who disliked the fact that he had managed Portsmouth, I think most people were happy with the appointment.

His first game in charge wasn't going to be an easy one, however, as he had to take his new charges to Newcastle, a ground where Saints had a very poor record.

I remember listening to the game on the radio and not giving us much of a chance, yet amazingly, we took the lead after only five minutes thanks to a Neil Maddison header. Andy Cole's 38th-minute equaliser looked like the precursor to another defeat at St. James Park, but as the match entered the final ten minutes, we seemed to be holding on for a valuable point. The game still had one final twist though, when a lackadaisical lunge of the leg from a Newcastle defender ended Matt Le Tissier's mazy run and dribble about 25-yards from goal. Matt took his time positioning the ball and as the ref blew the whistle, he somehow slammed the free-kick over the wall into the top corner of the net past the statuesque Newcastle goalkeeper to silence the St. James' Park crowd. It was the first of many amazing free-kicks he would score over the next few games and indeed the following seasons, and it was enough to ensure a winning start to Alan Ball's reign.

Mind you, some of that good work was spoilt with a 2-1 defeat in the next game at fellow strugglers Oldham, despite us taking the lead with Le Tissier's second in as many games, and it was typical that we were brought right back down to earth after that Newcastle result.

Ball reacted to this loss by dipping into the transfer market, bringing in striker and Saints old boy Craig Maskell, and midfielder Jim Magilton prior to this game against Liverpool.

Switched to a Monday night for live coverage by Sky, the game now fell on St. Valentine's Day, and there must have been many irate wives and girlfriends of Saints fans across Hampshire and beyond who had to postpone their romantic evening so their partners could watch the match.

Being single, I didn't have that problem and I was free to spend my evening in the company of about 18,000 others who braved the bitingly cold wind to cheer on their beloved Saints.

It was a freezing night and we all needed something exciting to happen early on to warm us all up, and boy did we get it. There was just 28 seconds on the clock when Le Tissier latched on to a half-hearted Liverpool defensive clearance to rifle a low shot past a startled Bruce Grobbelaar at his near post from 20-yards. If that had us all stunned with disbelief then we were pinching ourselves eight minutes

later when Le Tissier's corner was flicked on at the near post by
Dowie, and Maskell rose unchallenged 4-yards out to nod home a
debut goal.

Two goals up against Liverpool inside ten minutes had everyone
comparing this match with that 4-1 win back in 1989, although
admittedly, this Liverpool side was not a patch on that one, but we
had been so awful for so much of this season, that this was probably
more of a surprise to us than the result that day. With half-time
approaching, Liverpool's Julian Dicks' cumbersome challenge on
Maskell in the penalty area set Le Tissier up for our third goal from
the penalty spot.

Despite being 3-0 up at half-time there were one or two clouds on
the horizon, namely the snow bearing clouds that were now
congregating over The Dell. The light snowfall soon turned into a
mini blizzard, and as the green grass disappeared under a white
blanket, there seemed to be an increased risk that the match may be
abandoned.

Even the lesser seen orange ball made a rare appearance such was
the state of the pitch, and I remember thinking that an abandonment
could have a real negative impact on our season.

Not that switching to the orange ball seemed to help Liverpool
much, as another penalty-area mishap (this time a handball by former
Saint Mark Wright) gave Le Tissier a chance for a hat-trick from the
spot. A chance he took with his customary nonchalant ease.

It was a strange feeling, knowing that your team was 4-0 up on
Liverpool but not actually knowing if the result would stand as the
snow continued to fall. Even from where I was standing on the
terraces, it was plain to see that some of the Liverpool players were
having passing words with the referee in the hope of trying to
convince him to abandon the game.

To his credit, the referee was having none of it, and thankfully it stopped snowing with about 20 minutes left to play, and despite Liverpool pulling a couple of goals back, Saints saw out a rather comfortable and surprising win.

We had certainly shown the rest of the teams down at the bottom of the table that we were not going to go down without a fight, and with the boost that a new manager often brings to a club in trouble, there were plenty of reasons to be hopeful that avoiding relegation was a distinct possibility.

The Last Stand

Saints 3 Blackburn Rovers 1   Premier League   16 April 1994

New boss Alan Ball had certainly made an impact on the team, but especially on Le Tissier who had scored five goals in three games for his new boss, and he would hardly stop scoring for the rest of the season. That crushing victory over Liverpool had the effect of lifting us up to 17th in the table but only one point above the drop zone. A solitary Le Tissier goal saw off a stubborn Wimbledon side in the next match, and it was another stunning free-kick that settled it, as Matt flicked the ball up and smashed the ball into the top corner all in one movement.

Sadly, not even Le Tissier's ability could prevent Saints decent run of form from hitting the buffers and after two draws in our next two games a 4-0 drubbing at home to Arsenal followed. It was a devastating blow to the morale of the fans and the players, and we now had three out of our next four games against our fellow relegation candidates. The first of these was a gutsy and hard-fought goalless draw at Sheffield United that prevented them from leapfrogging us in the table. However, the second of these vital six-pointers against Oldham Athletic at The Dell would prove to be a disastrous evening, as we lost 3-1 on a foggy night in a match we couldn't afford to lose.

The situation was becoming critical, and from looking as though we were going to escape relegation, this rather unexpected dip in form had us fighting for our lives once more. Then fellow strugglers Manchester City came to town, a team also fighting to stay in the Premier League, and who were three points ahead of us in the table. A draw would be a bad result whereas a defeat would spell disaster.

With so much riding on the result, the match was never going to be a classic, and with neither side capable of creating any clear-cut chances, the match seemed to be petering out to a dull and lifeless goalless draw. Then with just two minutes to go, the match was to take a late dramatic twist when out of nowhere City created a chance from nothing and the ball fell kindly to substitute Steffen Karl who blasted a low shot to snatch all three points for City.

That blank against Manchester City was our fifth in seven games, and we had only scored two goals in that time. Little did I realise, that we were just saving them up for the trip to Norwich the following week. I toyed with the idea of undertaking the long trip to Norfolk before the defeat to Manchester City, but as relegation seemed nailed on I decided against it.

A draw was the barest of bare minimums that we needed to come away with from Carrow Road, and then only if other results went our way, defeat for us, and wins for everyone else around us would have the press writing our Premier League obituary.

For that reason, I stayed at home at contented myself with listening to the match on the radio. The first half hour was fairly even with Saints playing some neat football but without making the crucial breakthrough, but on 37 minutes, Mark Robbins scored to give Norwich the lead.

Just as it looked like we were heading into the break demoralised and a goal down we had a huge slice of good fortune when Norwich's Robert Ullathorne deflected Neil Maddison's wayward shot into his own net. One-all at half time and we're still in with a shout of coming away with a much-needed three points.

Then at the start of the second-half came an extraordinary spell where six goals were scored in just fifteen minutes. By the 55th minute, Norwich had stormed into a 3-1 lead thanks to goals by Jeremy Goss and top scorer Chris Sutton.

As each goal went in it felt like they were hammering another nail into the coffin of our Premier League existence, and I felt angry at our players for putting in, what I perceived to be a lack of effort against a team that had nothing much to play for. It was a vital match for us, and here we were, losing 3-1 and looking as if we were going to surrender our top-flight status with nothing more than a whimper.

Anger getting the better of me, I switched off the radio in disgust at this pathetic capitulation, and instead switched on the television in order to watch the closing stages of the Grand National.

After watching the horse I had chosen but neglected to back with cold hard cash win the race at a canter, my afternoon was taking on a very depressing air, although all that would change in the next twenty minutes.

For some reason, I switched the television over to Sky News, where after a couple of minutes they ran through the latest Premier League scores, and there on screen was Norwich 4 Southampton 3. My jaw nearly hit the floor at the news that we were actually making a fight of it after all, compelling me to switch the radio back on for the last twenty minutes of the match.

As the radio crackled into life, I realised from the commentators frenzied ranting, that we had in fact just levelled the scores at 4-4. Apparently, we had pulled it back to 3-3 earlier only in typical

Southampton style to let Norwich retake the lead straight from the kick-off, before a Le Tissier header had completed a perfect hat-trick (a goal scored with the left foot, right foot and head) to set up a nail-biting finale.

With both sides squandering chances to take the lead the game entered stoppage-time, and deep into that added on time Saints earned a corner-kick, and one last opportunity to take all three points.

Le Tissier took the kick and with his customary accuracy, finding the head of the centre-back Ken Monkou, whose late run into the box wasn't picked up by the Norwich defence, and he rose majestically to thunder a header into the net to give us an improbable 5-4 win!

Watching the highlights that night on Match of the Day I couldn't believe how many chances were created by the two sides in the ninety minutes. I can honestly say that it could have quite easily ended up as any score up to about nine-all. It was an immense victory and it lifted the spirits of players and fans alike, and with Oldham and Sheffield United not playing, we were back from the dead, and now both Everton and Tottenham found themselves involved in the relegation scrap.

The following Saturday we hosted title-chasing Blackburn Rovers, who arrived at The Dell in second place behind Manchester United only on goal difference. This was another massive match in a month that seemed to be chock-full of must-win games, and it really did seem that every game we played in the spring of 1994 felt like a cup final.

I had decided to go back onto the Milton Road terrace for this our penultimate home game of the season, as it was due to be bulldozed during the summer months, and replaced with a brand new all-seater stand that would slash the capacity to little over 15,200.

Thoughts of how we would cope with Blackburn's attack meant that I took my place on the terracing hoping that we could maybe scrape a narrow win, but I need not have concerned myself as we took the

---

game by the scruff of the neck from the first whistle. Our cavalier opening to the match was finally rewarded when in the 28th minute, Le Tissier's perfect chipped cross found an unmarked Iain Dowie to nod us into the lead.

If that wasn't enough, then ten minutes later Le Tissier was instrumental in setting up our second as midfielder Paul Allen latched onto his clever through ball and held his nerve to score with an angled shot past Flowers.

So, two up and looking comfortable, that was until three minutes into the second half when Stuart Ripley's weak long range effort somehow went through keeper Dave Beasant to put them right back into the game. Rovers were on top now and having their best spell of the match and an equaliser was looking like a distinct possibility. Yet, with a little over twenty minutes to go and on a rare foray into the Rovers penalty area, Rovers midfielder Tim Sherwood inexplicably handled a Le Tissier cross. Penalty!

Both Shearer and Flowers had words with Le Tissier as he placed the ball on the spot, but their attempts to psyche Matt into missing his spot-kick were futile, and he kept his cool to slot home, 3-1.

Rovers looked a beaten side from then on, and we held on to dent their title chances whilst simultaneously dragging ourselves out of the bottom three for the first time in a month.

London Calling

West Ham United 3 Saints 3   Premier League   7 May 1994

Suddenly, those two back-to-back victories gave us all a newfound belief and confidence that we could beat the drop, but that newfound confidence did take a bit of a dent when on the following Saturday we lost horribly at Tottenham 3-0. That result all but sealed their safety but kept us right in the mix with only three games to go, and with only one of those games at The Dell, I knew we still had our work cut out if we wanted to beat the drop.

The next "must win" game would be Aston Villa and our last home game of the season. Just as against Blackburn, we tore into them from the off and our attacking play earned us a deserved 4-1 win.

A few days later, we played our game in hand at Old Trafford but lost 2-0 to a Manchester United side celebrating their title victory. A win would have been nice, as would a draw, but with such an horrendous record at Old Trafford, most Saints fans had written this match off anyway.

With only one game to go, everyone from the players and the fans knew that a win would guarantee Premier League survival, but anything other than that meant that results from matches elsewhere would have a big say on whether we stayed up or went down.

The team in most jeopardy going into the final round of matches was Everton. They occupied the last remaining relegation place, whilst just above them, both Ipswich Town and Sheffield United also needed to get a positive result. We were three places and one point above Everton, so a draw or defeat could spell disaster if the three teams below us all won. It was going to be a tense afternoon.

My grandfather had managed to get a couple of tickets for this vitally important match early enough before our allocation was sold out, and we decided to utilise the travel club coaches for the trip to London's east end as we didn't fancy trying to find our way via public transport.

As we made our way up the M3 motorway to London, there was a tangible sense of foreboding about what was to come. Yes, we were in the driving seat as far as safety was concerned, but if we lost and the other three results went against us then we were down.

On the way to the capital, we pulled into Fleet services to pick up more fans and have a quick rest stop. Quite a few fans took this chance to stretch their legs or go and purchase some overpriced food and drink. I was content with just milling around in the parking area along with a couple of dozen other Saints fans.

It was whilst stretching my legs that I first noticed that parked next to us was a coach full of Taunton Town fans that were on their way to Wembley for the FA Vase final. For those you who don't know, the Football Association runs two knock-out cup competitions for semi-professional and amateur clubs. The larger clubs contest the FA Trophy, whilst the smaller clubs compete for the FA Vase, and these clubs are ones that count their attendances in dozens rather than thousands.

Anyway, some of the Tiverton fans noticed us, and couldn't help but make some snide comments.

"Oh there's going to be some tears tonight!" said one fan whilst grinning and pointing us out to his mates. He looked exactly like the comedian Jethro and spoke with a heavy West Country burr. This was how low we had sunk thanks to Beelzebub Branfoot, having the piss taken out of us by fans from a team so small I had never even known they existed up to that point.

After suppressing the urge to shout some derogatory comments back at them, I climbed back aboard the coach for the rest of the journey to East London, to the background noise of more catcalls and jibes about our survival chances.

Due to heavy traffic, we arrived only forty minutes or so before kick-off, not ideal as with so many Saints fans in attendance, it was going to take some time to get into the ground, especially as the police were insisting of frisking every Saints fan as they approached the turnstiles.

Now I know you shouldn't believe everything you hear from the media, but I would just like to lay one myth to rest, and that is the one about the cheerful cockney copper. I can tell you now that it is a load of old tosh! What a sorry morose lot they were, herding us into the ground like cattle and they must have been expecting trouble, as there were plenty of mounted police and some in full riot gear. Mind you, the natives weren't much better, there always seems to be an aura of menace from West Ham fans which makes for a rather unpleasant trip to this part of London, and I have to say that it isn't one of my favourite away days.

Now the match itself was a cracker, although the first real buzz of excitement came early on when the people with radios reported that Wimbledon had taken the lead at Everton, and this sparked a mini celebration amongst our fans as the good news filtered through the crowd.

Then disaster, as we went behind ourselves on eleven minutes thanks to some shambolic defending. Worse news followed as Sheffield United took the lead at Chelsea, and with Ipswich still 0-0 at Blackburn, we had slipped two places to just above the relegation zone inside half an hour.

An equaliser for Everton now would really be bad news, but thankfully, news of a second Wimbledon goal sparked another more raucous celebration amongst our fans. On the pitch, the players were huffing and puffing but not making much headway against a stubborn West Ham defence.

Then in the 44th minute, we won a free kick about 20-yards from the West Ham goal, almost dead centre, just perfect for Matthew Le Tissier to hit one of his trademark specials. Now Matty had come in for a bit of stick from opposition supporters over the seasons due to his looks, mostly to do with the size of his nose, and the West Ham fans were no exception as he lined up to take the free-kick.

"Big nose, he's got a f**king big nose!" came the cry from thousands of hammers fans stood on the terracing behind the goal their team was defending. What did Matty do in response to these insults? He just took a couple of steps and side-footed the ball around the

73

defensive wall and straight into the top right-hand corner of the net. It was the perfect riposte to their insulting chants and after we had all finished cavorting up and down in celebration we gave them a chant back of "Good goals, he scores some f**king good goals!" and it soon became the standard response to any group of fans who started up with the "big nose" chant.

We made it to the half-time interval all-square, and everyone needed to take stock of what was happening in the other games up and down the country. That goal put us up one place above Ipswich Town who were still deadlocked with Blackburn. Elsewhere, Sheffield United still held a lead at Chelsea and looked comfortable, and Everton were still losing 2-0 at home to Wimbledon and they looked doomed.

Now our entire season came down to just forty-five minutes of football, and it looked likely that only a freak set of results could relegate us. Relegation looked even more unlikely when after seven minutes of the second half we took the lead. We were now attacking the goal at our end of the ground and Matty found himself with the ball, wide left, facing West Ham's Tim Breacker. Le Tissier tantalised and toyed with Breacker, not unlike a cat playing with a mouse, before launching a pinpoint cross onto Neil Maddison's head, whose downward header bounced past the Hammers goalkeeper and into the net, 2-1.

Our joy was short-lived, however, when ten minutes later Dave Beasant fumbled Trevor Morley's shot and Martin Allen tapped the loose ball into the empty net, 2-2.

The match was now back in the balance, but just three minutes later we were back in front when Le Tissier's exquisite through ball put Dowie in behind the Hammers defence and his run was ended by Tony Gale's tug on his shirt in the penalty area.

Le Tissier dispatched the resultant spot-kick with ease, 3-2!

Better news followed as news of a Chelsea equaliser against Sheffield United filtered through, although with fifteen minutes to go Everton had somehow pulled level in their game at 2-2, which meant we were back to where we had started the day, 17th place.

Then with four minutes to go there was a slight melee in one corner involving a couple of players from each side, which prompted the referee to run in their direction blowing his whistle like a 1950's police officer on an emergency call. Some West Ham fans took this as the final whistle and on they came in their hundreds onto the pitch as the players ran for the safety of the tunnel. Ten minutes and countless appeals over the tannoy later, the pitch was cleared and the match was ready to restart.

The delay in our game meant that all the other matches had finished, so we knew we were safe unless we conceded three goals in the remaining four minutes of normal time and whatever the referee added on for stoppages.

Someone near me who had a radio glued to their ear informed everyone around them of Everton's unlikely comeback to win 3-2, and Sheffield United's defeat at Chelsea and Ipswich's draw at Blackburn. That meant that Sheffield United had fallen into the relegation zone for the first time that day, thanks to a stoppage-time Chelsea winner, and all we had to do was not to lose 5-2.

Even with our record of conceding goals in quick succession that was never a likely outcome, although a Ken Monkou own goal in the last minute ensured a point apiece.

That goal signalled another pitch invasion of West Ham fans and as they made their way down the pitch towards us, only a thin line of police prevented a major crowd disturbance from taking place.

The referee knew that getting the pitch cleared a second time in order to complete the added on time would be almost impossible, and that is where the match finished, 3-3.

Sheffield United went down with Oldham and Swindon, although there were rumblings of discontent from the United management in the following days as they stated that our game against West Ham was finished before the 90 minutes were up.

Thankfully, both the match referee and the Premier League stated that the entire 90 minutes were completed, and there was no need for West Ham and us to play out the last few seconds in an empty stadium.

Despite taking ages to get through the gridlocked London traffic, the mood on our coach was a mixture of joy and relief at yet another relegation battle successfully negotiated. We had survived against all the odds really when relegation seemed a certainty at so many stages during the season.

There would be other last day escapes from relegation to come in the next few seasons of course, but for now, all I wanted to do was savour the feelings of relief and schadenfruede.

Do you remember those gobby Taunton Town fans mocking us about tears at the end of the day? Well as it turned out, the only tears shed were theirs, as news came over the radio that they had lost their FA Vase final 2-1 to Diss Town thanks to a goal in the final minute of extra-time. Karma? I love it!

The Sorcerer's Apprentice

Saints 2 Everton 0   Premier League   8 October 1994

After that nail-biting end to the previous campaign, everyone was looking forward to seeing how the team would progress now that Alan Ball had a full pre-season to get the team organised.

The only major addition to the squad in the summer was Liverpool's veteran Zimbabwean goalkeeper Bruce Grobbelaar, who had arrived on a free transfer, and he would contest the goalkeeping duties with Dave Beasant.

After a slow start that saw us draw the opening two games and then lose the next two, which included a 5-1 mauling at Newcastle, Alan Ball announced the signing of Danish midfielder Ronnie Ekelund from Barcelona.

It was a strange signing that came out of the blue, with Alan Ball using his friendship with the then Barcelona manager Johan Cryuff to arrange the season-long loan with the option to buy at the season's end should we want to.

Ronnie breezed into the club like a breath of fresh air, and he soon struck up an instant rapport with Matthew Le Tissier, and with the two of them firing on all cylinders our results started to improve. One game in particular at Coventry – which was Ronnie's full debut – he scored a wonderful goal after exchanging a couple of one touch passes with Jim Magilton.

In the next game at home to Ipswich, he scored again in a 3-1 win and many fans were wondering what the catch was. Why had Barcelona let this little diamond go so easily? That question wouldn't be answered for a few weeks, but for now, he was a perfect foil for Matthew Le Tissier's mercurial talents. Such was his impact, John Motson and the Match of the Day cameras arrived for this game against last season's fellow escapologists Everton, who were once again struggling at the wrong end of the table.

The match didn't start well for the Saints however, as goalkeeper Bruce Grobbelaar had to go off with a fractured cheekbone after a nasty-looking collision with a couple of Everton players.

Despite that early setback, we soon settled into our rhythm and with Matty and Ronnie pulling the strings in midfield we began carving out numerous chances that Neville Southall in the Everton goal did well to repel.

In spite of Southall's heroics, Everton were powerless to resist, and the breakthrough came in the 18th minute when Le Tissier's volleyed through ball set Ronnie away down the inside-right channel. He shook off his marker but in doing so, he left himself a tight angle from which to shoot, but he finished with aplomb past a stunned Southall with a fierce drive.

We should have won this game by a hatful really, and it was a total contrast to that awful two-goal defeat to Everton on the opening day of the previous season. We secured a well-deserved three points when Le Tissier scored midway through the second half with a low rasping shot from the edge of the penalty area.

On Match of the Day that night, John Motson enthused about the Saints performance, and Ronnie Ekelund in particular, as well as his partnership with Le Tissier. With the pair of them in fine form, the season seemed to be shaping up to be anything but another depressing relegation battle. For me personally, it felt as though we had done nothing but fight against relegation for the past five years or so, and it felt great to be looking at the top half of the table rather than at the bottom three. However, as is typical when things seem to be going swimmingly, controversy and scandal were waiting around the corner.

Notes on a Scandal

Saints 1 Arsenal 0   Premier League   19 November 1994

In true Southampton style, it wasn't long before a crisis reared its ugly head, not only for the club but for me also, as I faced a spell of unemployment and I found myself on a government sponsored IT training course. It was whilst on this course that I heard the news about the match-fixing allegations made against goalkeeper Bruce Grobbelaar.

When I arrived at the office, I knew something was up straight away as my fellow students who had no interest in football were talking about it and awaiting my arrival. I was completely unaware of the breaking news story, having not seen or heard the news that morning. Nor had I purchased a newspaper. I had to borrow a copy of The Sun newspaper to find out that Grobbelaar along with Wimbledon goalkeeper Hans Segers and Aston Villa's John Fashanu (who had just completed a transfer from Wimbledon) had found themselves caught in a sting operation, where they had admitted fixing matches in order to help a Far Eastern betting syndicate.

The evidence looked convincing enough on the face of it, The Sun newspaper had a secret videotaped recording of Grobbelaar accepting money to let in goals, but also admitting that he had deliberately let in goals in other matches for Liverpool and for us.

The game in question was that 3-1 victory over Coventry at Highfield Road earlier in the season where Ronnie Ekelund had made his debut. Coventry had taken the lead in that game after two minutes with a looping shot from Dion Dublin that Grobbelaar got a hand to but couldn't keep out. On the tape, you can hear him say that he purposely palmed the ball into the net. Later on, he jokes about accidentally saving a goal-bound shot in another match for his former club Liverpool that cost him money.

I was stunned and I could not believe that a player who must have earned a fair amount of money, if not with us then certainly at Liverpool, would want to throw games just for the sake of a few thousand pounds. All three denied the charges and played on, their respective clubs all standing by them, and Alan Ball announced publically that Grobbelaar would be starting in goal for the next match at home to Arsenal. The news had come out on a Thursday before a break in the league programme for a round of international matches, and the story was never off the back pages of the national and local newspapers for the next nine days.

I arrived at The Dell for the match and it seemed like there were as many news reporters around the ground as fans. I had never been to a match where the performance of one player would come under such scrutiny as this, and I kept hoping that he would not make any harebrained mistakes that would cost us a goal.

Bruce had always been an eccentric character and I remember as a young boy watching some of his antics early on in his career at Liverpool. Those mistakes had cost them matches, and the stick he took at the time was probably justified before he went on to prove himself as one of the best goalkeepers in the world during the late 80s.

If anyone had any doubts about how he would handle the situation, then his larking about before the kick-off dispelled any fears that he might crack under the media spotlight. Arsenal fans had come down armed with bundles of fake cash that they had mocked up, with the words "Bank of Brucey" emblazoned on them, which they intended to throw at him during the pre-match warm up.

Playing along, Grobbelaar walked over to one particular steward who was wearing a flat cap, and after taking it off his head, he proceeded to walk over to the Arsenal fans and hold it out towards them like a man collecting for a whip-round. The Dell erupted in hysterical laughter as both sets of fans enjoyed the moment, but the real test for Grobbelaar would come during the match itself.

It certainly wasn't a classic match and to be honest, neither goalkeeper had much work to do throughout a dour 90 minutes. We eventually took the lead in the 60th minute thanks to a fine Jim Magilton effort, but just six minutes later the referee awarded Arsenal a rather soft penalty.

This is what all the reporters had come for, a moment like this, Bruce Grobbelaar facing a penalty just days after accusations of match fixing surfaced. The crowd quietened to an apprehensive hush as they awaited the outcome of the spot-kick.

Arsenal's diminutive Scottish striker Paul Dickov stepped up to take the kick on a rather short run up, and he somehow skewed the ball wide of Bruce's left-hand post, and it seemed as though lady luck was smiling down on Brucey after all. After that penalty miss, Arsenal looked a beaten side and as the final whistle signalled our 1-0 win, Bruce found himself mobbed by his teammates and even his manager Alan Ball who had run onto the pitch to congratulate him.

The match-fixing saga would rumble on for years, and after being charged and pleading not guilty, the defendants would finally be cleared in 1997 after two trials (the first of which the jury could not agree a verdict), before the three defendants were acquitted at a retrial.

Grobbelaar would sue The Sun newspaper for libel, win damages, but lose all but £1 of it when the case ended up in the appeal court. Added to which, Grobbelaar was ordered to pay The Sun's court costs of £500,000, a sum that later forced him to declare bankruptcy.

Was he guilty? Well, the acquittal wasn't a "not guilty" verdict; it just meant that the jury couldn't reach a conclusive decision. In having his £85,000 libel award against The Sun newspaper reduced to £1 by the House of Lords, Lord Bingham of Cornhill observed:

"The tort of defamation protects those whose reputations have been unlawfully injured. It affords little or no protection to those who have, or deserve to have, no reputation deserving of legal protection. Until 9 November 1994 when the newspaper published its first articles about him, the appellant's public reputation was unblemished. But he had in fact acted in a way in which no decent or honest footballer would act and in a way which could, if not exposed and stamped on, undermine

81

the integrity of a game which earns the loyalty and support of millions."

The majority of Saints fans wanted to believe that he wouldn't dare do such a thing, especially with matches involving our club, and I was also in the "innocent until proven guilty" camp, however, his performance in the match that follows even tested my faith in him.

Throwing it all Away

Saints 2 Tottenham 6 (AET) FA Cup 5th Round Replay 1 March 1995

Whether it was the all the hullabaloo over the bribery scandal or the fact that Ronnie Ekelund was out with a long-term injury but our form worsened during the weeks that followed that win over Arsenal.
The answer to the question of why Barcelona had let Ronnie Ekelund go out on loan was due to a persistent back problem that our club doctor said required an operation, but Ronnie wasn't having it and he eventually returned to Barcelona in a huff. It was a sad end to a career that seemed to promise so much in the early days, and although he would play a few games on loan at Manchester City and Coventry he would eventually leave English football altogether.
Our poor form meant that we would only win once in our next sixteen league games and that was thanks to an injury-time winner from Matthew Le Tissier against Aston Villa in front of the Sky Sports cameras. We just couldn't find a win, and at one point we even broke the club record for the number of consecutively drawn games with seven stalemates in a row.
We had found some form in the FA Cup though, and after seeing off second-tier opposition in the shape of Southend United 2-0, we dispatched Luton 6-0 at The Dell in a replay in Round 4.

That win over Luton set up a fifth round tie at fellow Premier League side Tottenham, who had been expelled from the competition for financial irregularities, only to be re-instated on appeal. Most Saints fans knew soon as they heard the news that Spurs were to be let back into the competition that our paths would cross at some point, and so it proved.

We actually played well at White Hart Lane in the first tie, and despite going a goal down to a Jurgen Klinsmann strike, a Matthew Le Tissier penalty gave us the draw our adventurous play deserved. A few days later, it was back to The Dell for the replay and despite our recent awful league form, there was a real sense of optimism around the ground pre-match that we could progress to the sixth round.

We started the game like a team that meant business, and we duly scored in the 5th minute when Neil Shipperley diverted a Jason Dodd shot into the net. With Neil Heaney's pace down the left causing the Spurs defence all sorts of problems, it looked like it was just a matter of time before we scored again, but we had to wait until just before the break.

Again, Neil Heaney's pace caused panic at the back for Spurs, and Dean Austin's clumsy challenge ended his run just inside the penalty area. Matty duly slotted home the penalty, and as the players walked off for the interval I thought that we thoroughly deserved our two-goal lead, and perhaps should have had more.

Despite our seemingly comfortable lead, I wasn't going to take victory for granted, as Saints have often imploded when trying to hold on to what should be a comfortable win. All it usually takes is one incident to turn a game on its head, and this time it was to be a substitution made by the Tottenham manager Gerry Francis ten minutes into the second-half.

The substitutes name was Ronnie Rosenthal, an Israeli striker whose only real claim to fame was to miss an open goal at Villa Park when he

83

rounded the Villa goalkeeper, only to contrive to hit the bar from 12-yards out, whilst under no pressure. He had been playing for Liverpool at the time, and he now found himself at Spurs where he found it difficult to hold down a regular first-team place.

It seemed like one last desperate throw of the dice by the Tottenham boss, but within three minutes of coming on, Ronnie had levelled the scores. His first came from what must have been his first touch of the match, and he followed that up with a 25-yard screamer into the top corner that flew past a static Grobbelaar.

Whilst the Tottenham fans celebrated, the rest of The Dell sat in stunned silence. All of that hard work to establish a two-goal lead wiped out in less time it takes to boil an egg. Our players visibly took on the appearance of a side that had lost their momentum, and they were now desperately clinging on to make it to full-time and the chance to regain their composure in time for the extra thirty minutes.

They did hold out, and they did manage to regain a foothold in the match at the start of the first period of extra-time, but in the 101st minute, Rosenthal hit another 25-yard effort that flew in to give Spurs the lead for the first time and also complete his hat trick.

In a desperate bid to salvage a match we had looked comfortable in for 55 minutes, we threw everyone forward, but in doing so we left ourselves completely open to the counter attack, a situation that Spurs took full advantage of. As goals, four and five went in before the break, I, and quite a few others couldn't bear to watch the slaughter any longer and we made our way to the exits. Spurs would add a sixth before the end, and in doing so become the first team to put six goals past Saints in an FA Cup match.

As for me, I had to endure the taunts of my fellow students the next day in the office, and I can say that as a football fan you have to get used to fans of other clubs taking the piss out of you when your team does badly. However, when non-football fans start taking the piss then you know it's bad. This result was going to take a lot of living down.

Fool if You Think it's Over

Saints 3 Newcastle United 1   Premier League   22 March 1995

Out of the cup, Saints needed to move on and quickly, especially as league games were running out and yet another relegation battle loomed large on the horizon. This wasn't how the season should be panning out in most fans eyes; nothing seemed to be going to plan on the pitch or off. News had come through that the club's bid to move to a new stadium at Stoneham Lane looked to be dead in the water, as Hampshire County Council rejected an application to buy the land needed. Whilst on the pitch, two more draws and a heavy 3-0 loss at Nottingham Forest followed the Spurs disaster, and that had stretched our winless streak in the league to twelve games.

To help bolster the forward line, Alan Ball signs Gordon Watson for £1.2 million from Sheffield Wednesday, a signing funded by the sale of defender Jeff Kenna to Blackburn Rovers for £1.5 million. Watson would make his debut in that Forest game, but that loss puts us into the relegation zone for the first time this season, and there were four relegation spots this season too, as the Premier League looked to reduce the number of clubs from 22 to 20.

As this match was the closest to my birthday, and to celebrate the fact that I had finished and passed my IT course, I decided to buy a ticket even though I was ambivalent of whether it was the right decision as money was tight.

Remembering that Newcastle had a terrible record at The Dell, I thought it was worth the risk, yet for 86 minutes of this match, it looked as though I had made a bad mistake. We were woeful yet again, and when Newcastle's Kitson put them ahead in the 18th minute with a cheeky overhead kick, it looked like the best we could hope for was yet another draw.

With four minutes left and after a couple of Newcastle near misses, we finally got the equaliser we probably didn't deserve in all honesty. Neil Heaney, who had come on as a substitute for Francis Benali, was the quickest to react when Srnicek in the Newcastle goal palmed away Gordon Watson's diving header to prod the ball home. Relief at last, and although another draw was not going to do us any favours, it was preferable to a loss.

What happened next has become one those incidents where you look back in later years, and you say to yourself, "I was there, that night!" and it brings a little smile to your face and a warm glow somewhere deep within your soul.

As the clock hit 90 minutes, and with some of the crowd filtering away towards the exits, from somewhere the players suddenly found an extra gear.

Attacking the Archers Road end, where I happened to be sitting (well standing by now because everyone else was, despite the desperate calls of the tannoy announcer for us all to sit down), we were about to witness what was about to be the turning point in our season.

Firstly, we took the lead as Srnicek again fumbled, this time from Dodd's cross from the right, and Gordon Watson was on hand to stab the ball home. Cue pandemonium in the stands and I nearly went flying over the row of seats in front of me as I was clattered from behind by one of our more burly supporters.

The resultant celebrations hadn't even had time to die down when from the kick-off Newcastle gave the ball away, and all of a sudden Neil Heaney was sprinting down the left touchline once more. Closed down by a couple of shell-shocked Newcastle defenders, Neil cut inside before unleashing a rasping low shot at the Newcastle goal, and yet again Srnicek couldn't hold it, and he took on the appearance of a man trying to find a slippery bar of soap in the bath as desperately clawed at the loose ball.

Unfortunately, for Srnicek, the ball fell kindly for Neil Shipperley to snaffle up the rebound to make it 3-1, and now the pandemonium in the stands had turned to full on hysteria. I don't think I had ever heard the crowd at The Dell so deafeningly loud, despite the fact that the attendance was well below 15,000. It was a frantic finish to a match that was dour and flat for most of its life, yet somehow we had managed to grasp a victory from the jaws of defeat and had for once acted in a typically un-Saints-like fashion by actually scoring goals late in a match rather than conceding them.

I awoke the next day to find my shins covered in bruises where I had smashed them against the back of the seat in front of me, such was the force of the celebrations, and I wore those bruises as a badge of honour for days afterwards.

Complete Balls Up

Saints 3 Nottingham Forest 4   Premier League   18 August 1995

That win against the odds seemed to inject a new found belief and determination in both the fans and the players, as in the next game we won a seven-goal thriller against Spurs to gain revenge for that cup defeat a month earlier.

It was shown live on Sky and couldn't be faulted on entertainment value as the lead changed hands three times before Jim Magilton scored what proved to be the winner in the 62nd minute for a valuable 4-3 win. I was in the Archers Road end again, sans bruises, and with a front row seat, which gave me a perfect view of a match where the lead changed several times.

Despite losing the next match at Liverpool 3-1, we hit a mini six-match unbeaten run that consisted of four wins, and included a 2-0 win at Chelsea, a 2-1 win at Wimbledon and a 3-1 win over Crystal Palace, a match where Matt Le Tissier scored after just 45 seconds!

Even though we didn't win any of the last three games of the season, which included losing a 2-0 lead at home to Leicester City in the final game, Saints actually finished in a healthy tenth place, their highest final placing since 1990.

On the back of that decent second half to the campaign, there was real optimism that we could possibly improve next season with the addition of a couple of decent signings during the summer. However, that newfound optimism would be short-lived, when in the summer, the club announced that manager Alan Ball was in talks with Manchester City about their vacant managerial position.

The news was a bolt from the blue, but it later transpired that Alan was good friends with City's Chairman, and former England teammate, Francis Lee who was keen to take Alan to Maine Road. The club had agreed to let City talk to Ball and for him to decide where his loyalties lied, but Ball seemed to take that decision as a sign that the Southampton board no longer wanted his services. Fuming, he retaliated by stating that he didn't want to be somewhere where he felt he wasn't wanted.

Within days, he was gone, and the fans of both clubs were not happy. Our fans didn't want him to go, because despite that slump the previous season, he had managed to get the best out of Le Tissier, and the football was certainly more entertaining than the garbage served up under his predecessor. Whilst City fans didn't want him at all, and when a manager is not well received by the majority of the fanbase, he is always going to find it hard to turn the tide of opinion, just ask Ian Branfoot.

Most Saints fans were shocked that the club could let a manager go so easily and there was a feeling among some sections of our fanbase that Ball had somehow engineered the move, turning him into public enemy number one, meaning there would be added spice to the two league encounters between the clubs during the forthcoming season.

The man that Saints chairman Guy Askham turned to, to replace the departed Ball, was long-serving coach Dave Merrington, the man who had been in charge of the youth team and had brought through players like Alan Shearer, and Matthew Le Tissier.

The only doubts that myself and other Saints fans had at this appointment was that as good a coach as he had been at youth level, could he cut it with the first team?

The answer to that question was a resounding "no", and he soon took on the appearance of a man so out of his depth, that I'm surprised the club didn't hire a couple of lifeguards to sit in the dugout with him.

We lost this game (his first in charge) 4-3, a match played in a rather hostile atmosphere resulting from some sections of the Forest fans disrupting the minute silence before kick-off.

During the summer months, the club had lost two of its former stalwarts, namely Ted Drake (no relation) and the scorer of the winning goal in the 1976 FA Cup final, Bobby Stokes. Crass whistling and shouting from a large section of the Forest support marred the minute of silent reflection, which elicited a chorus of boos and shouts of "scum" from the Saints fans at the end of the period of silence.

The nasty atmosphere seemed to spread to the players, as Forest's Colin Cooper had a few choice words to say to Matt Le Tissier after Le Tiss had "won" a couple of penalties.

After that opening day reverse our results started to mirror those of the Branfoot era, namely, low scoring and usually ending up in a defeat or at best a draw. In addition to which, just like at the start of Branfoot's reign of terror, after that opening day goal fest, the goals soon dried up (well for us but unfortunately not for the opposition) and we would not match that opening day triumvirate of goals again in the league until April.

It was going to be another long hard season.

Technical Difficulties

Wimbledon 1 Saints 2   Premier League   28 October 1995

We gained our first point of the season in our next home match when midfielder Tommy Widdrington bagged an equaliser against Leeds with his chin whilst lying prostrate on the ground. Actually, the ball hit him in the face after a goalmouth scramble and a Leeds defender cleared the ball off the line straight at Tommy who had fallen over in the mêlée. It was a comical way to score, yet it seemed very appropriate for the way we had started the season.

For some reason we started the season with three home games out of four and next up was Newcastle United, a team that was probably still smarting from our great comeback in that 3-1 win in March.

This time there wasn't to be the fireworks and excitement of that match, and a single Jim Magilton goal gave us our first win of the season. That win would be our last for six games though and that included a goalless draw on a Monday night against West Ham that Sky Sports had picked for live coverage. It was a match so devoid of any entertainment value that the Sky TV executives must have been wishing for a power failure or for the satellite to fall from space.

I have seen a few shocking 0-0 draws in my time both as a neutral and in games involving Saints, but this ranks as one of the worst, I don't think either team actually had a shot on target during the whole ninety minutes.

If that was bad enough, on our next appearance on Sky at home to Liverpool three weeks later, we lost 3-1 after taking an early lead, but I will remember the match for a red card for Matthew Le Tissier.

For some mad reason that only he knows, Dave Merrington seemed to be playing Matthew Le Tissier in some sort of deep midfield role. Not only did this nullify Matt's attacking threat, but now he was expected to tackle as well, which was certainly not his strong point. He had already been booked in this match when he went in late on Liverpool's John Barnes midway through the second half, and despite the howls of protest from the stands, he probably deserved his second yellow. I then had to sit and watch, as any hope we had of salvaging anything from the match, trudged off disconsolately towards the changing rooms for an early bath

It was a poor start to the season again, although we did have the consolation of the awful start that Alan Ball had overseen at Maine Road. Ball had failed to muster a win in his opening eleven league games with his new charges, and in fact, on the same day that we were winning this match at Selhurst Park against Wimbledon (our first away win of the season), City were being thrashed 6-0 at Liverpool. How we all cheered as we left the stadium and that result came over the tannoy, a result that kept them rooted to the foot of the table a clear seven points adrift of us.

Mind you, our away form would be nothing to boast about either, and it was nothing short of a disaster all season long. We wouldn't win away from home in the league again until late April, although one loss in particular still sticks in my mind to this day because it was just so typical of all things Southampton FC.

One thing you learn early on as a Saints fan is that trips to Old Trafford don't usually bear fruit. Our record there is terrible, and a draw there feels like a win anywhere else. This particular trip took place three weeks after our win at Wimbledon, and due to rebuilding work at Old Trafford lowering the capacity, it meant that away fans found themselves persona-non-gratae for the entire season. However, in order to appease those supporters who have to watch every match home and away, several clubs decided to relay live coverage of their visits to Old Trafford onto giant television screens back to their own stadiums.

Saints also decided to do this and proudly announced in the programme for the home game prior to our Old Trafford trip that they would be charging £10 for adults and £5 for children to sit in the Milton Road stand, where we could watch the game live on a giant screen.

Just for the novelty value, I decided to buy a ticket, and I took my seat just before kick-off to find that the screen wasn't working properly. It appeared as though the screen was suffering from some form of technical glitch, as large sections of the screen were just blank, whilst two men in overalls seemed to be frantically pulling and pushing wires in order to get the thing working correctly.

Just as the match was about to start it seemed as though the technical difficulties had been fixed, although, twelve seconds into the match, I and many other Saints fans were wishing it hadn't.

Twelve seconds was all it took for United to take the lead from the kick-off, and to make matters worse, it was our kick-off. Going a goal behind after a mere 12 seconds is embarrassing, but going behind after 12 seconds when it is your team that starts the match is taking it to another level.

Three minutes later it was 2-0, both goals coming from Ryan Giggs, another five minutes passed and we were 3-0 down when Paul Scholes tapped in a simple goal. That is when the screen started to play up again, and after a few minutes of waiting for it to clear, I followed the hordes of other people who had had enough and headed for the exit. Apparently, the screen didn't work properly for the rest of the match, resulting in the club announcing through the local press the following Monday morning that anyone who still had their ticket stub could claim a refund.

Oh, and we lost 4-1 in the end, so at least it wasn't the cricket score I thought it might have been after being three down inside ten minutes. On the plus side, at least everyone who was at The Dell that afternoon didn't have far to get home!

The Phantom Phone Caller of Old Reading Town

Reading 2 Saints 1   League Cup 4th Round   28 November 1995

For all our bad league form, at least we had picked up a couple of wins in the League Cup. After dispatching Cardiff City 5-1 over two legs in the second round, we faced fellow Premier League side West Ham, and thankfully, this game was a bit more exciting than that dismal 0-0 draw a few weeks previously. In addition, we had a new signing in the shape of Barry Venison who we signed from Turkish side Galatasaray for £850,000.

Barry was a tenacious midfield battler who had played at the highest level with Liverpool and Newcastle after starting his career with Sunderland, and he added much-needed backbone to a mellifluous midfield. He made an immediate impact, making his debut in that 2-1 victory at Wimbledon. He also set us on our way in the League Cup match against West Ham when his wayward shot hit Gordon Watson on the heel, which caused the ball to spin off at a weird angle and past the wrong-footed West Ham goalkeeper.

93

Despite a Tony Cottee equaliser, Neil Shipperley ensured our passage into the fourth round when his bullet header from the edge of the penalty area flew in with eleven minutes remaining.

The draw for the next round gave us a tricky tie at First Division Reading, and I queued up in the pouring rain on a Saturday morning to secure my ticket and place on the travel club coach for the short midweek trip to Berkshire.

The autumn of 1995 was probably one of the wettest on record, as it never seemed to stop raining. It poured down when I purchased my ticket, and it never seemed to let up at all in the days prior to the match.

The amount of rain that fell over those few days meant that I had serious doubts as to whether the match would actually go ahead. Happily, the torrential downpour had diminished into a light but persistent drizzle by the time I made my way to The Dell through the evening rush hour traffic to meet the coach. Yet, when I arrived at the stadium there wasn't a coach to be seen, and quite a few fellow Saints fans seemed to be milling about aimlessly wondering what was going on. One fan I spoke to said that he had overheard someone saying that the match had been postponed, and going by the severity of the recent weather that wouldn't have been a surprise. Despite this, I decided to hang around and wait for official clarification, and after a few minutes of waiting, I recognised one of the travel club stewards who told me that the match was on and that the coaches were on their way.

It later transpired that earlier that afternoon the club officials had received a telephone call from someone purporting to be the club secretary of Reading FC. That person then proceeded to tell someone at our club that the referee had no option but to postpone the game due to a waterlogged pitch. Taking this news at face value and without confirming it, the club officials decided to send the players home and to cancel the travel club coaches. What happened next I'm not sure about, but obviously, someone at the club must have been suspicious and called Reading to confirm the postponement, only to be told that the match was actually on and that no-one from the club had called earlier in the day. This meant a frantic few minutes as the club officials had to call all the players and staff and all the travel club coaches back to the stadium at short notice. This being in the days before mobile phones became ubiquitous, that was probably a lot more difficult to do than it would be now.

Eventually, we set off for the match, albeit nearly an hour later than planned, and to make matters worse the traffic on the A33 into Reading was horrendous. In the end, we made it to the outskirts of Reading but then we hit another problem, namely Thames Valley Police. They insisted that all the coaches needed to arrive at the stadium together under escort and that we had to wait for the other delayed coaches to catch up.

We waited and waited and waited and as the clock ticked ever closer to the 7:45 kick-off time, tempers started to become frayed. There had been no notification from the police about a delay in the kick-off time in order to give us time to enter the ground, and people were starting to lose patience and their cool, as the police came in for some justifiable criticism.

Finally, and with less than half an hour to the official start time of the match, the last remaining coach arrived, and we snaked our way slowly through the gridlocked traffic towards Elm Park.

We arrived at the ground with less than ten minutes until kick-off, and outside the turnstiles, chaos had broken out as thousands of Saints fans tried to get into the ground in time for the start of the match. I remember being concerned about the crush of bodies outside the turnstiles. This feeling soon turned to anger thanks to two Thames Valley Police officers stood just to the right of me. The cause of this anger came with their response to a valid question asked by the man stood in front of me, who enquired as to whether there was to be a delay to the kick-off due to the congestion outside the ground.

The response from one of the police officers was "No and you'd better hurry up the match is about to kick-off!" It was a stupid answer in a situation that was concerning enough to worry a mounted policeman so much that he began to shout at people to stop pushing and shoving as the crush of bodies got worse.

There were still thousands of fans trying to get through only six turnstiles (four for the terracing and two for the seats in the main stand) and in the narrow street outside, and with half a dozen coaches taking up valuable space, there was limited room to move. As the crush got worse people started to look worried, and I couldn't help but think about the people who lost their lives in the Hillsborough disaster a few years previously, and although this was no way near as bad as that, it was still the worst crush I had been in at a football match. Ultimately, common sense prevailed and when the announcement came over the tannoy that the kick-off was now subject to a 15-minute delay, everyone seemed to calm down. I was just glad to get into the ground in one piece, as well as being able to draw breath properly, and it was frightening to experience how difficult it is to inflate your lungs fully whilst being crushed by other bodies.

Reading now play at the brand new (and often two-thirds empty) Madjeski Stadium, which is a few miles away from Elm Park in distance, but a million miles away from it in facilities, not that I would call what I saw in the away end at Elm Park facilities as such.

I had opted for a ticket on the terracing, as having the option to stand was becoming limited due to the Taylor Report into the Hillsborough disaster that advocated that all stadiums in the top two division of English football now needed to be all-seater. The terracing itself was fine; however, the facilities were not. The gents' toilet was literally a brick wall to piss up against, and it appeared that for many years, this "facility" had been open to the elements, although the addition of a roof that didn't quite sit flush with the walls was a nice touch. Moss and lichen grew in the gaps where the roof and walls didn't quite meet, giving the place a rustic feel it didn't deserve.

People who criticise the facilities at modern-day football grounds are probably people who never had the pleasure of urinating in what was essentially a medieval outhouse, whilst simultaneously hoping that your shoes don't get splashed by the guy standing next to you.

I don't know how much that hoax phone call had affected the players' pre-match preparations but collectively they had an awful match, and on a damp and miserable night (it was still raining) we succumbed to a 2-1 defeat, and to be fair to Reading they deserved it. The only consolation for me was winning the raffle on the coach on the way home and becoming the proud owner of a pennant signed by the first team, but I would have happily swapped it for a victory or at least a replay.

Cup of Cheer

Saints 3 Portsmouth 0   FA Cup 3rd Round   7 January 1996

If being knocked out of a cup competition by Reading was hard to take, then a few days later the draw for the third round of the FA Cup paired us with Portsmouth at The Dell, and a proper local derby. The Reading match had been more important to them than to us as we don't really see them as local rivals, but now we had the real thing to look forward to in the New Year.

Our league form leading up to this match had been poor to say the least, and we failed to win any of the six league encounters we had faced, although we did well to get a 1-1 draw at Liverpool the weekend after the Reading defeat.

My own life had also taken a bad turn and after a 2-1 loss at West Ham nine days before Christmas. My girlfriend, who was also a fellow Saints fan and had actually travelled with me to Upton Park for the match, dumped me after we got back to Southampton. Being dumped by letter - a letter she had handed to me when she got off the coach with the strict instructions not to open it until I got home – was hard to take and was probably the mid-nineties version of being dumped by text message today. I knew something was up as she had been frosty towards me all day but to be honest it did come unexpectedly and hurt like hell. We had already purchased our tickets for the Portsmouth game together and with the match completely sold out, I was not looking forward to spending my first local derby and the tensest 90 minutes of my football supporting life so far, in the company of someone that I loved but didn't love me back.

Mercifully, when I arrived someone else was in her seat so I guess she had managed to swap her ticket, and now I could just concentrate on the match.

Feeling as low as I had ever been in my life up to that point hadn't exactly put me in the mood for my first Saints versus Pompey match. I was more desperate for a victory than I would normally have been; losing to our hated rivals at home in the cup would have been the rotten cherry on top of a very stale cake.

Our form had been wretched and we were languishing in 16th place, although thankfully Portsmouth were themselves floundering in 17th place in the division below, however, this was the cup and league form counts for nothing in these games.

I believed that they were capable of getting a draw and finishing the job at Fratton Park in the replay, and given our awful away form and the hostile atmosphere that we would encounter at Fratton Park, that scenario was a distinct possibility. In addition, Pompey's form had picked up recently with four wins in December, and they were in confident mood when they arrived at The Dell for the Sunday lunchtime kick-off.

There were plenty of "High Noon" style headlines in both cities local newspapers and a succession of players from both camps gave interviews. One particular interview saw Portsmouth's ex-Arsenal winger Jimmy Carter, give an exclusive to the Sun newspaper. Jimmy, who was a self-confessed curry lover, was boasting about how he was going to be "too hot for the Saints defence to handle." Although for me, their main threat would come from veteran striker Paul Walsh, who always seemed to have a good game when playing against us for the likes of Tottenham and Liverpool in the past. For us, defensive lynchpin Richard Hall missed the match through suspension, whilst Matthew Le Tissier had been firing blanks since the League Cup match against Cardiff back in September.

The players entered the field to a crescendo of noise from both sets of fans, with the 1,500 or so Portsmouth supporters and their mournful "Pompey Chimes" song, drowned out by a rousing chorus of "Oh, when the saints go marching in." It seemed everyone in the stadium was singing or cheering and clapping, even the older supporters in the upper west stand seemed to be in high spirits and joining in.

The match itself was a tense nervy, scrappy affair early on, which derby games usually are, with both sets of players fearful of making that first crucial mistake that could lead to a goal.

Matthew Le Tissier whizzed a 25-yarder just over the bar early on, and then in the 12th minute came two incidents that changed the game. Firstly, Portsmouth's danger man Paul Walsh went over in the Saints penalty area under an innocuous challenge, his protestations, and the cries of their fans failed to convince the referee that he should award the spot kick. With Walsh still picking himself up off the ground, Saints broke down the right and Gordon Watson's cross from the by-line found the head of Neil Shipperley. His tame header rebounded off a combination of goalkeeper and post, and Jim Magilton was on hand to slam the ball home from almost under the crossbar. It could have been a much different scenario had the referee been conned by Walsh's swallow dive just a few seconds earlier.

That early goal was just the start we needed to settle the nerves, but despite having a couple of good chances to increase the lead, we had to be content with a solitary goal at the break.

Some people still hadn't taken their seats for the second-half, when Saints doubled their advantage within sixty seconds of the restart. Le Tissier found acres of space on the right and ran or rather jogged (as Matty never ran if he could help it) half the length of the pitch before cutting inside and letting fly with a stinging left-footed shot. Alan Knight in the Portsmouth goal could only parry the ball into the path of Jim Magilton, and Magilton gratefully slotted home whilst the Pompey defenders stood still appealing for a non-existent offside.

Magilton nearly grabbed his hat-trick a few minutes later, when put clean through by Neil Shipperley, but a moment's hesitation allowed Knight to smother the ball at his feet. With a two-goal cushion, Saints could now relax and sit back whilst hitting Portsmouth on the counter-attack, and in the 80th minute, that's exactly what they did.

Le Tissier's trickery again on the right set up Neil Shipperley to score from close range with almost nonchalant ease to make it 3-0, and chants of "easy, easy" were directed towards the Portsmouth supporters who looked on with glum faces. The icing on the cake was to come in the final minute when Portsmouth "hot shot" Jimmy Carter rounded a prostrate Dave Beasant, after seizing onto Jim Magilton's suicidal back-pass.

Surely, the red-hot striker that was Jimmy Carter was going to salvage a consolation goal? With an empty goal at his mercy, and from about 6-yards out, Jimmy somehow managed to hit the base of the post, and he watched as the ball rebounded out for a goal kick to the background noise of 14,000 Southampton fans laughing hysterically.

The match never lived up to all the pre-match hype, and despite our poor performances in the Premier League we had proven once again that we were still a class above Portsmouth, a team now left with trying to avoid relegation from the First Division, a feat that unfortunately they managed.

For us, we had a cup run to look forward to, as well as trying to preserve our Premier League status, so our season was still very much alive on two fronts.

Nearly All Change at Crewe

Crewe 2 Saints 3   FA Cup 4th Round Replay 13 February 1996

Fourth Tier Crewe were pulled out of the velvet bag in the fourth round draw, and they were not to be underestimated as they were flying high in their division and looking good for promotion.

The original tie at The Dell had succumbed to the severe cold snap that had hit the country, and in typical Saints style, there was a touch of farce about our postponement. Whilst most matches had fallen foul to frozen pitches, the reason why our tie couldn't go ahead bordered on the ludicrous.

The reason why our game was postponed was due to frozen water pipes, which meant that the toilets and the fire hoses couldn't be used, and as they couldn't be defrosted in time, this meant that both clubs would have to wait another ten days before finally playing, you couldn't make it up.

When the tie did go ahead, it was full of attacking fast-paced football, as Crewe belied their lowly status and came out all guns blazing, and their attacking attitude bore fruit as they took a shock early lead.

An innocent looking cross from Crewe's Darren Whalley, sailed in past our own wally Dave Beasant in goal, as somehow he totally misjudged the flight of the ball, and he ended up sitting on his arse with the ball in the net behind him.

That setback certainly wasn't in the script, and Saints dominated from then on in search of an equaliser. We must have wasted six or seven good chances in the first half, with the Crewe keeper Gayle in inspired form whilst also benefiting from huge slices of luck.

The second half was end-to-end stuff, with us laying siege to their goal, whilst Crewe tried to hit us on the counter-attack, and it was from one such counter attack that Crewe nearly extended their lead.

It came about when Beasant rushed out of his penalty area to clear the ball, but this being Dave Beasant, he skewed his kick, and it fell to Crewe's Edwards who hit it straight back on the volley from fully 40-yards. The ball sailed over the head of the quickly retreating Beasant and seemed to be destined to ripple the net of the unguarded goal, yet somehow, from somewhere, Beasant managed to leap like Superman leaving via a window, to paw the ball away from goal with one hand from almost on the goal line. It was one of those incidents that always seem to play out in slow-motion, but Beasant had done enough to stop the ball crossing the line, and it was cleared away, to a collective sigh of relief from around the ground.

We eventually found a way past Crewe's stubborn resistance when Matt Le Tissier ended his goal drought in dramatic style, as his beautiful curling shot beat the keeper and flew into the top corner of the net from 20-yards out.

Despite some late pressure, the winner would elude us, and a pulsating cup-tie finished all square, meaning we had to do it all again at Crewe in the replay a week later.

Still suffering from being dumped by my girlfriend, I decided to fill my life with as much football as possible to alleviate the gloom, so I did not have to deliberate too long about going up to Crewe for the replay the following Tuesday evening.

It was the first time I had travelled such a distance mid-week for an away match and I hoped that I wasn't about to witness another cup humbling by a lower league side, albeit a fairly good one. It felt like Crewe's manager, Dario Gradi had been in charge of Crewe since the dawn of time. He was the league's longest serving manager of the same club at the time, and he liked his teams to play good attractive, fast-paced one-touch football, not the usual physical style of play you tend to find in the lower reaches of the Football League. A tactic that suited us perfectly, as more often than not, it was the more physical and direct teams that we usually had problems playing against.

There was to be no repeat of the sluggish start in the first encounter though, as we wasted no time in piling on the pressure early on. Our reward for this attacking start was a succession of corner kicks, and it was from one of these that we took the lead in the eighth minute.

Le Tissier's in-swinging corner found Neil Shipperley, who controlled the ball expertly on his chest before turning past his marker Barr, and faced with what looked like an impossible angle, he somehow squeezed the ball between the goalkeeper and the near post.

Then just a few minutes later Gayle in the Crewe goal had to react smartly to deny both Matt Le Tissier and Mark Walters's shots, but even he was powerless to stop Richard Hall's towering 15-yard header after another succession of Southampton corners.

We were so on top that it looked as though we were going to run up a huge score, and we made it 3-0 inside thirty minutes when full-back

Jason Dodd tried his luck from distance (and on his weaker left foot) to curl a 25-yard beauty into the top corner. We were coasting now, and we even had the luxury of seeing Neil Shipperley's goal-bound shot cleared off the line just before half-time.

Job done? Well no, this is Southampton and one thing that Saints fans know all too well is that our players never make things look easy when they can make things look difficult. The second-half had started pretty much as the first had done with us dictating play and creating chances, and almost straight from the kick-off, we were denied what looked like a stonewall penalty, for a foul on Watson in the box.

Still, when you are three up away from home against lower league opposition, you don't feel unduly worried when those sorts of decisions go against you. In spite of this, on 52 minutes Crewe gave themselves a glimmer of hope when Edwards was given too much time and space to plant a free header past Beasant. Now the tables had turned, and it was all Crewe as they started to play more direct.

Crewe's big powerhouse of a striker Dele Adebola twice went close, before Ashley Westwood rose highest in the penalty area to loop a header over Beasant to reduce the arrears to 3-2 with fifteen minutes left. We were now in serious trouble and in danger of throwing away a three-goal lead to a team who had looked dead and buried thirty minutes ago.

Crewe now threw everything they could at us, but somehow they couldn't force the equaliser, similarly with their defence wide open we had chances to kill the game off, but our two best chances, from Walters and Widdrington, were saved and scrambled off the line respectively. The biggest drama took place during injury-time when Adebola beat Beasant to a cross and just as it looked like his header was going to loop in, Simon Charlton managed to head it off the line from virtually under the crossbar.

104

The referee blew the final whistle just as a Crewe player went down in the penalty area, and for a split second, it seemed as though he had awarded the spot-kick. Much to the relief of those around me, the whistle had indeed signalled an end to the match, and now we were through to face Swindon away in round five.

Emotionally exhausted, I arrived back at The Dell at around 2 AM, and with no taxis in sight, I made the decision to take the hour-long walk home. Highlights of the match had been shown on the BBC's midweek sports show, Sportsnight, and I sat up to watch the twenty minutes or so of highlights there and then (I had recorded it but couldn't wait to watch it again) but it was a decision I would regret in the morning. Because of the postponement of the original tie and then the replay, the Fifth Round game at Swindon was only four days away, and the tickets went on sale to season ticket holders the morning after the Crewe replay. Unfortunately, I had overslept, and by the time I made it to the ticket office, it was too late to secure a ticket. Therefore, instead of cheering the team on from the terraces, I had to content myself with listening to the next chapter of our cup run on the radio.

Silly Little Machines

Saints 1 Coventry City 0   Premier League   25 March 1996

Missing out on that trip to Swindon was annoying, especially after all the effort I had put in travelling all the way to Cheshire and back midweek, but in the end, I didn't miss much and a Gordon Watson header in the 77th minute cancelled out Kevin Horlock's first-half opener. This meant another replay at The Dell eleven days later, and this time there was no problem getting a ticket.

Just like against Crewe in the previous round, we struggled to find a breakthrough against a lower league team. A resolute Swindon defence held firm until just past the hour mark when Watson seized onto an under hit back-pass, and although Fraser Digby in the Swindon goal managed to block his shot, the ball ricocheted to Matt Oakley (who had replaced the flu suffering Le Tissier) and he steered the ball in neatly from the edge of the penalty-area. Saints sealed their passage into the quarterfinals, and a trip to Manchester United when Shipperley pounced on a defensive lapse to score from 12-yards a few minutes later.

I had to be content with watching the United match on television due to not being able to get the time off work to make the trip to Old Trafford, and despite my fears of another thrashing (remember we had been comprehensively beaten 4-1 there earlier in the season) we actually made it to half-time, goalless.

However, there was one incident in the first-half that would be talked about for a long time afterwards, and if it had gone our way, it would have made a big difference to the result. The incident happened when Neil Shipperley rose above United's Lee Sharpe to head home an excellent cross from Jason Dodd, only for the referee Steve Dunn to disallow it. The commentators assumed it had been a push by Shipperley on Sharpe when jumping, but the television replays showed that it was a perfectly good goal. Even Sky Sports' Andy Gray commented during the half-time interval that the goal should have stood. You don't often get the chance to take the lead at places like Old Trafford and inevitably in the second-half, United asserted their dominance and took their place in the semi-finals with goals from Cantona and Sharpe.

It was a fine performance and despite the outcome and we could take a lot of pride from the way we took the game to them and actually dominated for long periods. How might things have been different if the referee had not disallowed that Shipperley header?

Some clubs find that a good cup run can have a positive effect on their league performances too, but this was not the case for us and after a 2-1 home win over Middlesbrough midway through January we failed to win our next six games.

One particularly depressing result happened on my birthday when we lost 1-0 at home to Sheffield Wednesday. Wednesday took the lead in the very first minute of the match, and I naively assumed that at least we had 89 minutes to do something about it. Not a bit of it, as what followed was 89 minutes of the worst football I had the ever seen; on par with that 0-0 home draw against West Ham earlier in the season. We huffed and puffed but couldn't create one decent goalscoring opportunity against a side whose away record wasn't much better than our own.

After that defeat to Wednesday, we didn't play again until the following Monday night and the visit of fellow strugglers Coventry City for a televised game, and a massive 6-pointer.

Led by the charismatic Ron Atkinson, Coventry were only two places and two points ahead of us in the table (that loss to Wednesday had sent us back in the drop zone) and this game would have huge significance for both clubs, hence why it was broadcast live by Sky Sports.

In complete contrast to the Sheffield match, the atmosphere at The Dell was loud and proud, as the Saints fans got behind the team right from the first whistle.

The mood of the fans was helped when Jason Dodd swooped in low to head home Matthew Le Tissier's fizzing in-swinging corner kick in just the second minute.

So now, it was our turn to hold onto the slender one-goal advantage. A feat we accomplished with more than a little bit of luck at times, as Coventry threw the proverbial kitchen sink at us.

Nonetheless, hold on we did, and in doing so, we climbed above them and out of the relegation zone. As was my custom, I had recorded the match in order to watch it all over again when I got home, and in doing so I was fortunate enough to witness an on screen barney between Coventry City manager Ron Atkinson, and the Sky Sports presenters, Richard Keys and Andy Gray.

Richard Keys never hid the fact that he was a massive Coventry fan, and this defeat to a relegation rival had hurt him greatly. Prior to the kick-off, Richard asked Ron what he thought City would get from the game, to which Ron replied, "We'll get what we deserve." In the post match interview, Richard Keys reminded Ron of what he said pre-match and this is how the conversation went:

Richard: The bottom line is you lost. You're running out of time, what next for Coventry City, how can you get out of it?

Ron: Tottenham on Saturday, that's next.

Richard: But surely, you'll have to show a little bit more than was evident tonight?

Richard was making a point that Andy Gray in his post-match analysis had pinpointed the fact that in his opinion one or two of the Saints players wanted it more and had put in more effort and more passion than the Coventry lads had. You could see Ron struggling to keep his cool and he hit back.

Ron: You may say that but we don't think so Richard!

Then he lost it and came out with this immortal line, "I'm sorry, you can sit there and play with all your silly little machines as much as you like! I'm manager of a football team, I'm experienced, yeah if the boys haven't done enough I'll whip 'em, I ain't whipping them for that tonight!"

It was totally unexpected and delivered by a man who looked to be at the end of his tether. To back up his argument he then went on to ask who had won the man of the match award. An equally annoyed looking Richard Keys then had the dubious pleasure of telling him that in fact, the Saints goalkeeper Dave Beasant had won the award, and this pushed Ron even further over the edge.

"Oh sorry, so he mustn't have played too badly then, thank you very much lads see you later!" Ron snapped back, and he threw his microphone and headphones away before apologising to someone off camera who he hit by the flying sound equipment, before storming off.

It sometimes still appears on television every now as an example of when football managers lose the plot, typically coming a close second to Kevin Keegan's meltdown that occurred a few weeks later.

You can relive it on YouTube by typing in "Ron Atkinson v Richard Keys," and it is well worth two minutes of anyone's time.

The Wrong Kind of Shirts

Saints 3 Manchester Utd 1   Premier League   13 April 1996

Our hopes of an improvement in form after that narrow win over Coventry were quickly dashed when we were humbled 3-0 at Q.P.R the following Saturday, this was quickly followed by a 1-0 loss at Leeds a few days later

We did manage another tight 1-0 win in our next home match against Blackburn Rovers; a solitary Matthew Le Tissier penalty ten minutes from time was enough to give us the three points needed to keep ourselves above the relegation zone. However, with such wretched away performances we had to be thankful that the other teams below us had also been dropping points, if any of them suddenly found some form then we were in serious trouble.

A week after that win over Blackburn at The Dell, we were soundly beaten 3-0 at Villa Park by a very ordinary Aston Villa side. It was our sixth consecutive away league defeat stretching back to New Years Day. In fact, we had mustered only seven points from our tally of thirty-one away from the comfortable confines of the Dell, but things weren't going to get any easier as our next two matches were against the top two teams.

Manchester United and Newcastle were in first and second respectively, and league leaders Manchester United were first up. They arrived at The Dell for what everyone thought would be an easy three points for them. United were six points clear of Newcastle, after being so far behind at one stage that it seemed impossible for them to catch up, but catch up they did as Newcastle started to crack under the weight of expectation. This led to Kevin Keegan's infamous on-air emotional meltdown, where he lost his cool in response to some gibes by United boss Alex Ferguson.

Just like Ron Atkinson's outburst at the end of our 1-0 win over Coventry, Keegan's was during a live interview on Sky Sports and was headline news the following day. His words of "I will love it if we beat them [United], love it" will probably be on his headstone when the time comes. The reason United were six points clear was that whilst Newcastle's form had dipped, United had gone and won ten of their previous eleven matches in the league, and they had four games to play (Newcastle had a game in hand) and if they beat us and Newcastle lost then the title would be all but theirs.

Yet this match wouldn't just be remembered for what happened on the pitch, but what also happened off it. This happened to be another match where I could say, "I was there, I was at that game!"

110

In the early to mid-1990s, football shirts (and away shirts in particular) seemed to go through a phase where each manufacturer and shirt designer seemed to be trying to come up with the most abhorrent designs imaginable. Migraine inducing zigzag patterns and colour combinations that could make a person's eyes bleed if they looked at them for too long seemed to be the norm, and it was United's very own away kit monstrosity that would make this game hit the headlines for more than just its unexpected result.

Manchester United are famous for changing their kit style nearly every year, and this season they sported a shirt that can only be best described as looking like an out of tune television set. The top half, the sleeves, and the back were a light grey with a fuzzy pattern, the bottom half of the front was a darker grey with even darker grey vertical pinstripes, the two halves were separated by two horizontal lines of another shade of dark grey edged with red. It was truly hideous even by the standard of football kits of that time, and it was about to become headline news around the world!

Now the great thing about sporting contests and football, in particular, is that when you take your seat, you have no idea what is about to happen in the following 90 minutes, unlike a trip to the theatre or cinema where you will have a rough idea of what is going to happen. There are no reviews, no trailers, and no spoilers', just pure unscripted drama. Okay, most of the time, it can be mundane and boring, but just occasionally a match takes place that will have people talking about it for weeks or years afterwards.

As I have mentioned in previous chapters, the atmosphere at The Dell at times during this season had been less than impressive, but on this day as is usual for the visit of any of the Premier League's big guns, the atmosphere was electric, and everyone from the fans to the players seemed to be up for it.

111

We steamed into them from the kick-off, harrying and hustling and closing down the United players all over the pitch, and it was no great surprise when Ken Monkou put us in front after 11 minutes. Matthew Le Tissier free-kick was only parried out by Peter Schmeichel, and Monkou was the quickest to react to slam the ball home at the second attempt.

Things got even better 12 minutes later when Neil Shipperley expertly guided in Alan Neilson's low cross from the right at the near post.

Both sets of fans were almost unable to believe what they were seeing, with the United fans who had arrived expecting to all but seal another title triumph, to us Saints fans who weren't really expecting to get much out of the game at all. The consensus amongst my fellow supporters before the kick-off was that a draw would suffice, what with United in such red-hot form of late.

Now that we were two goals to the good, I was expecting a United onslaught, but although they looked dangerous when going forward, it was the Saints who scored the next goal.

This time it was Neil Shipperley who crossed a high floating ball into the United penalty area, where Peter Schmeichel flapped at it and palmed it down. The ball fell invitingly to Matt Le Tissier, and he nonchalantly flicked the ball over the prostrate keeper with his left foot, before coolly slamming the ball in with his right foot via the far post.

Three goals up at half-time against the runaway league leaders and everyone at a stunned Dell is expecting to wake up from this wonderful collective dream (or nightmare if you are a United fan). Let's not forget that this is the same Saints team who hadn't scored three goals in a league match since that opening day 4-3 loss to Nottingham Forest back in August, and now they had scored three in the first forty-five minutes against the champions elect.

112

You can never rule anything out of course, and if we could score three goals in one-half of football, then I was sure that United could score at least three in the second. However, it was what took place within the walls of the United dressing room at half-time that would have people across the world talking about this match for years to come.

I can't speak for the people who were seated nearest to the tunnel entrance, but from my vantage point in the Archers Road end it took me a while to cotton on to the fact that the United players had come out wearing a completely different strip. Those of us still engrossed in reading our programmes or chatting to mates suddenly found ourselves getting a tap on the shoulder and urged to look towards where the United players were running onto the pitch. Incredibly, the Manchester United team who were now wearing a blue and white striped kit instead of the grey one they had worn in the first half, a change that caused bemusement amongst my fellow fans.

The second forty-five minutes didn't live up to the high drama of the first-half, and with many fans still murmuring about United's change of kit, Ryan Giggs' consolation goal for United in the last minute almost went unnoticed.

After the match, the reason for the change of strip became headline news, when in his post match interview, United boss Alex Ferguson explained that his players had complained about not being able to "pick each other out against the crowd in the background". Apparently, United had worn the grey kit on four previous occasions and had failed to win any of them, and now being humbled by a very poor Saints side meant that despite obligations to the manufacturer Umbro, the kit would not be worn again.

At the time, everyone seemed incredulous that a kit supplier could make a strip that rendered the players invisible to each other. Would this mean that governments from around the world would contact Umbro to make their armies camouflage for them?

Looking back, it may well have been a masterstroke by Ferguson in deflecting the blame for such a humbling defeat from his players and onto the kit. It certainly seemed to help, as United wrapped up the title a couple of weeks later, for us, however, this win was a massive shot in the arm for our survival hopes, but could we carry it through to the next match at Newcastle?

Land of Confusion

Saints 0 Wimbledon 0   Premier League   5 May 1996

Sorry, Newcastle, we really did try to help you win the Premier League but in the end, you just weren't good enough! After our win over United helped keep the Geordies slim title hopes alive, we did them another massive favour a week later when we travelled to St. James Park and lost 1-0. This kept them in the hunt for the title (albeit still hoping for a monumental collapse by United), whilst doing nothing to help our cause at the other end of the Premier League table.

Losing by a solitary goal meant that our goal difference was still superior to Manchester City and Coventry, and kept us just out of the relegation places, but games were rapidly running out.

Next up was our last away game of the season, a trip to Bolton Wanderers, who themselves were struggling at the foot of the table and all but mathematically relegated. This game was too important to miss and I decided that if we were about to join them then I wanted to be there to share the pain with my fellow supporters.

After attending a family celebration the night before, and consuming way too much alcohol, my hangover and me made our way to The Dell to meet the coach for the long journey north. It probably wasn't very wise of me to consume so much alcohol when faced with a six-hour coach journey to Bolton, and to say it was an uncomfortable trip would be an understatement; still, a win would make me feel better.

Unlike that Norwich match a couple of seasons back, when I decided not to travel as I didn't think we had any chance of avoiding relegation, I fancied our chances at Bolton. Also in making the trip, I would get to see one England's oldest and well-known football grounds before it would be lost for good, as Bolton were due to move to a brand new stadium in a few months time.

Burnden Park had become a bit of anachronism by the time of my visit. Unloved and undeveloped, it suffered from one major problem, namely the fact that a rather large supermarket literally cut the terracing in half at one end. Such was Bolton's financial problems back in the 1980s that they sold part of their ground to a local supermarket chain that had demolished a large section of terracing and built their supermarket on the site. The terracing that was still in situ had been reserved for visiting supporters, and with a giant tin shed in the way, the view was predictably horrendous.

To the right-hand side of the terracing the outer brick wall of the supermarket restricted the view of the right-hand side of the pitch, so much so, that if you stood at the back, you could just about see the near goal. In fact, even though I was stood fairly near to the front, I still could not see the right-hand corner flag, that's how bad the view was.

Burnden Park was once immortalised on canvas by the great L. S. Lowry with his painting entitled, "Going to the Match," showing people flocking to the stadium to a backdrop of dark satanic mills, their chimneys belching smoke across the town. Completed in 1928 he failed to capture the ground's greatest quirk at the time, which was the railway line that actually ran across the top of the terracing at one end of the ground. This strange arrangement was partly responsible for the Burnden Park disaster of 1946 when 33 fans lost their lives due to overcrowding. A number of fans managed to enter the ground by crossing the railway line and then clambering over the fences in order to circumvent the now closed turnstiles. In a sickening turn of events, that defies belief nowadays, they placed the deceased along one touchline whilst the match played on regardless!

Mercifully, those days are gone and although the view was terrible, Saints performance was not, and they produced a hard-fought win thanks in part to a huge faux pas from a Bolton defender.

Rule one of the defender's code is, never pass the ball across your own penalty area, but this is exactly what happened about midway through the first half, thus presenting Matt Le Tissier with a simple side-foot finish from 12-yards. From then on, it was a case of holding on, and without too much effort, we did just that thus confirming Bolton's relegation whilst giving us a priceless away win in our quest to avoid the drop. And, what a crucial win it turned out to be, as our euphoria at witnessing a rare away win was tainted somewhat by the news filtering through that both of our rivals in the relegation scrap, namely Manchester City and Coventry had also notched an away win. Now, everything came down to the last game of the season.

This is how the table looked going into the final round of matches:

	Pld	Pts	GD
15. Sheff Wed	37	39	-11
16. Coventry	37	37	-18
17. SAINTS	37	37	-18
18. Man City	37	37	-25
19. QPR	37	33	-16
20. Bolton W.	37	29	-31

With Bolton and Q.P.R. gone, four teams had a realistic chance of taking that last unwanted relegation place, with Manchester City in the mire courtesy of their significantly worse goal difference. Sheffield Wednesday's superior goal difference meant that all they required for safety was a point, failure to get that point at West Ham would mean relegation if all three teams below them won, so the odds were in their favour, but relegation was not entirely beyond the realms of possibility. All Saints had to do was to match Manchester City's result against Liverpool at Maine Road to be sure of safety.

Although at the start of the season the majority of Saints fans hoped that Alan Ball would get Manchester City relegated, no-one could have imagined how it would come down to almost a straight fight between us and them. For our final game of the campaign, we welcomed Roy Kinnear's Wimbledon to The Dell. Known across the football land as "The Crazy Gang" I knew that they would not be taking it easy against us, as they were not mathematically safe from the drop themselves. Despite being in 14th place and three points better off, they weren't mathematically safe from the drop, although it would take a freak set of results to send them down. Either way, that gave them something to fight for, and the statistics pointed to this match ending in a draw as there had only been three victors in the previous nine league meetings between the two teams at The Dell. We had two of those wins, but Wimbledon's solitary success had come the previous season.

I was feeling less than optimistic when I took my place in the Archers Road end for what was going to be another nail-biting 90 minutes of football. I looked around me and it seemed as though almost everyone had an ear pressed to a radio listening to the Manchester City game broadcast live on BBC Radio Five Live.

117

A few minutes into the match, and there were mutterings from the people around me that City had fallen behind in their match, and not wanting to celebrate prematurely, I asked the guy next to me if it was true. Before he could respond an enormous roar erupted in the Archers Road end as confirmation came through that City were indeed a goal down.

Our match was another nervy tepid affair with neither side having the flair or endeavours to create a clear-cut chance, but it seemed as though we didn't need to, as City were too busy shooting themselves in the foot.

Four minutes prior to the break, another spontaneous celebration broke out as news spread of another goal for Liverpool, and surely, there was no way back for City now.

At the half-time break, with both ourselves and Coventry being held to goalless draws, City looked all but doomed, but as with that final day at West Ham two seasons before, the second-half would have a sting in its tail.

There was twenty minutes to go when we heard that Manchester City had pulled a goal back, via a Uwe Rosler penalty kick, but despite the fact that neither team looked likely to score we still looked to be safe.

Then disaster, as former Portsmouth player Kit Symons scored an equaliser for City with little over ten minutes remaining. Now our nerves were jangling again, as another goal for City (who according to those with radios, were throwing everything at Liverpool in the search of a winning goal) or a goal for Wimbledon would mean that we slipped into the relegation zone instead.

Despite the odd rumour that City had taken the lead, those with radios announced that the final whistle had blown in Manchester, with the match ending 2-2 and we all breathed a sigh of relief. Nevertheless, we still had to hold on for a few more minutes, and a goal for Wimbledon now would be enough to send us down. The only brief moment of worry came when Wimbledon's Efan Ekoku hit a long-range shot that was a little too close to the goal for my liking, but in truth, was always going wide of the goal.

At the final whistle, the celebrations were on par with winning a cup final, such was the relief and the release of tension, mixed with the feeling of schadenfreude at Alan Ball's demise with City. In the end, all four clubs involved in the relegation scrap had drawn their matches and City were down on goal difference, seven goals had cost them, and ironically, that six-goal loss at Liverpool on the same day as our 2-1 win at Wimbledon was what cost them.

It wasn't until I got home that I learned that in fact the match at Maine Road had descended into farce in the last few minutes, and it turned out to be one of the most comical incidents of the entire season.

Just as rumours had circulated around The Dell that City had taken the lead, a similar falsehood regarding Wimbledon taking the lead in our match had reached the ears of Alan Ball in the City dugout.

This happened a few minutes after City had levelled the scores in their match, and believing what he had heard without double-checking, Ball barked at his players to sit back and hold on for the draw that would guarantee their Premier League status.

By the time those in the know had related to manager and players alike that the score at The Dell was still 0-0 it was too late, and when City's match finished before ours, their only hope of avoiding the drop was for Wimbledon to score. They didn't, and Ball and his City team were relegated, whilst Saints fans celebrated justice being done.

Alan Ball had done much for Saints as a player and during his brief stint as manager, but he had left us under a cloud. The directors may have given him permission to talk to City about their manager's job, but he didn't have to take it. The way I saw it was that karma had come back to bite him on the backside, and now he had to face life as

119

a First Division manager, not that he would be in the job for much longer. Three winless games into the following season he resigned.

Where I Find My Heaven

Saints 4 Middlesbrough 0   Premier League   28 September 1996

Dave Merrington's reward for keeping us in the Premier League on a shoestring budget was the sack, which was not a great way to treat such an honourable and long-standing servant of the club. His replacement turned out to be former Liverpool, Sampdoria and Glasgow Rangers midfield hard man Graeme Souness.

Souness forged a reputation as an uncompromising midfield battler in his playing days; however, his managerial record was not particularly great. Although he had had moderate success with Rangers and with Turkish side Galatasaray, his return to Liverpool in a managerial capacity had ended in abject failure, due in no small part to their poor league form. He did win an FA Cup as well as bringing through several promising youngsters who went on to greater things. Players such as Steve McMananman and Robbie Fowler would go on to play for England, but in a results-driven business, he had failed to deliver the goods to a club and set of fans who demand success.

For a club the size of Southampton, the appointment of Souness had the feeling of being a bit of a coup. Dave Merrington whose reputation was largely limited to the borders of Hampshire wasn't the right man for the job, and I felt that the appointment of a world famous manager could only help the club to attract better players.

Even so, there was more than a sense of disappointment when his first two signings turned out to be Graham Potter and Richard Dryden. Potter was a left-sided midfield player signed from Stoke, who would never make it at Premier League level, and he would leave at the end of the season after only a handful of appearances in the first team.

On the other hand, Richard Dryden stayed for five seasons and played regularly under Souness, but he would later fall out of favour under a succession of different managers, and he would only play 47 games during his five-year stay.

The new season started in the same way as the old one had finished with a goalless draw at The Dell. This time Gianluca Vialli's Chelsea were the visitors, and by the time this match against Middlesbrough came around at the end of September we found ourselves in our now customary place in the bottom three, without a win and after having lost all four of our away games. In fact, our only victories had come in both legs of a League Cup second round tie against lowly Peterborough United.

For this match though, everything seemed to click into place, despite the fact that Middlesbrough arrived sporting two big new signings in Italian international Fabrizio Ravenelli, who they signed for a club record £7million and Brazillian midfielder Emerson. He joined fellow compatriot Juninho who had signed the previous season and all of a sudden the football backwater of Middlesbrough had a team that was an attraction, instead of one that was about as an exciting as the town of Middlesbrough itself.

I wasn't too hopeful of a victory, considering that all three of Middlesbrough's big money signings started this game. They lined up with, Juninho, Emerson and Ravanelli on their teamsheet, whilst we had Robbie Slater, Neil Shipperley and Graham Potter!

Yet despite the perceived gap in on field talent, we tore into them straight from the off and after Juninho missed an early chance to give 'Boro the lead, Matthew Oakley scored to put us in front.

With Matthew Le Tissier pulling the strings in midfield, we grabbed the match by the scruff of the neck, and we extended our lead in the

29th minute when Le Tissier struck to put us 2-0 up. Le Tissier scored again, three minutes into the second half and by now Middlesbrough were beat, and we wasted several good chances to increase the lead until Gordon Watson rounded off the scoring to make it 4-0 after 82 minutes, the icing on the cake coming three minutes later when Ravanelli missed from the penalty spot.

This match acted as a catalyst for a mini revival through the month of October and after the Middlesbrough game Saints travelled to Coventry for a live Super Sunday game.

The game was average fare but a piece of brilliance from, Matt Le Tissier, lifted this particular match out of its mediocre malaise.

When Matt received the ball 35-yards out from the Coventry goal, it appeared as though it was too far out for even his mercurial talents, but he took a couple of languid steps forward, and with no City defenders closing him down, unleashed a wicked 30-yard curling shot into the top corner of the net. It was a goal good enough to win any match, but we had to be content with a 1-1 draw.

A week later Sunderland visited The Dell only to leave on the wrong end of a 3-0 scoreline, but if things were looking up on the pitch, then off it things were about to become a lot more complicated.

Rupert the Share

Saints 2 Lincoln City 2   League Cup 3rd Round   23 October 1996

Rupert Lowe arrived at The Dell on the back of a motorbike, although it would have been more fitting if he had arrived in the back of a hearse, such would be his impact on the football club, but more on that later.

This League Cup tie against League Two Lincoln City was apparently the first professional football match he had ever attended, and

122

unfortunately, for the majority of Southampton fans, it wasn't to be his last. The reason why this rugby, hockey, and duck-hunting lover became involved in the club is not easily explainable.

The board of directors had been looking to float the club on the stock exchange for some time, mostly as a way of financing their plans to move the club to a new stadium. Acquiring the preferred site was turning into quite a saga, but they needed the funds to be in place when the long sought after planning permission was granted.

To avoid an expensive and long drawn out floatation the club needed to find a company that was already a public company and take them over but who in reality would actually take us over, a process that is known in financial circles as a "reverse takeover". Rupert Lowe's company Secure Retirement owned a number of care homes across the country. The Southampton board of directors saw them as the perfect company to float the club on the stock exchange.

As a result, a new company was formed, to be known as Southampton Leisure Holdings Plc, with Rupert Lowe as chairman, and Andrew Cowan his business partner at Secure Retirement becoming vice chairman. The existing chairman Guy Askham would step down and become a director. The idea behind this seemed to be that having a man with a history of working within the banking system, would help the club to gain the finance it needed to move to a new multi-purpose arena.

I can only wonder what the new chairman and board of directors thought when they watched a Saints team huff and puff their way to a 2-2 draw against a team from League Two, which meant a replay at Sincil Bank a couple of weeks later. We won the replay only to draw another lower league side in the next round, Oxford United away.

October was also a month where Graeme Souness decided to go to work in the transfer market, no doubt spurred on by having watched the players he inherited struggle to find any kind of consistency.

123

The signings came thick and fast, with striker Egil Ostenstad signing from Norwegian side Viking Stavanger, and a young up and coming Israeli playmaker Eyal Berkovic joined the squad from Maccabi Haifa.

Dutch international defender and man mountain Ulrich Van Gobbel signed from Souness' previous employers Galatasaray and Norwegian centre-back Claus Lundekvam who would become one of our longest serving players, joined soon after these three. All four players would make their debuts in that 3-0 win over Sunderland, but their biggest impact would be in our next home game against Manchester United.

The Joy of Six

Saints 6 Manchester Utd 3   Premier League   26 October 1996

United arrived back at The Dell for the first meeting between the two clubs since that humiliating 3-1 defeat in the "wrong kind of shirts" match, and on the back of another humbling defeat.

Their 5-0 thrashing at Newcastle less than a week before had been broadcast live to the nation, and there seemed little chance of us repeating our 3-1 win back in April, as I was in no doubts that the United players would be desperate to put things right. Not only did they need to get that 5-0 loss out of their systems, but they would also want retribution for our surprise win the previous campaign.

I was convinced that we were in for a caning and that we would be lucky if we didn't shift three goals or more by the time the final whistle blew. I was right of course, we did concede three goals, although, amazing as it seems even now when I look at the scoreline, we managed to bag six ourselves.

What started out as a day full of fear and trepidation, turned into one of total disbelief, as we witnessed the total humiliation of the reigning Premier League champions.

124

United had not had a great start to the season, yet they still arrived with a team capable of inflicting some serious damage, with the likes of Jordi Cruyff, Roy Keane, a young David Beckham and mercurial Frenchman Eric Cantona in the team. In short, a team crammed full of talented internationals, and with Alex Ferguson's words of fury still ringing in their ears from the previous week's embarrassment, they were sure to be in the mood to put things right.

In fact, some of their players seemed more fired up than was probably necessary, as Roy Keane received his marching orders in only the 21st minute of the game for two bookable offences. He only had himself to blame too, after receiving a caution for dissent early on, he followed that up with a lunging tackle on Claus Lundekvam, picking up a second yellow in the process.

By the time of his dismissal, United had already fallen one goal behind, thanks to a stunning half-volley from 12-yards out from Eyal Berkovic. His neat back heel had given Ostenstad the opportunity to shoot, but Schmeichel parried the shot back into Berkovic's path and he hit a sweet strike past the stunned Danish keeper.

Berkovic seemed to be all over the pitch, and he was almost single-handily running the show from midfield ably supported by Matthew Le Tissier.

Not to be outdone, it wasn't long before Matt got in on the goal-scoring action with a sublime chip of the highest quality. Thirty-five minutes were on the clock when he received the ball on the edge of the United penalty area. With no-one open to pass to, he decided to try an audacious chip shot that at first sight seemed to be going over the crossbar. Yet, just as it passed over the helpless Schmeichel's head, it dipped just enough to drop underneath the crossbar and into the net. I remember there seemed to be a second of silence before the Saints fans started celebrating; it was if our brains couldn't believe what the eyes had just witnessed. In a later interview, Matt said that he had seen Schmeichel beaten by a lob from Phillipe Albert in that 5-0 loss at Newcastle the week before, and he had decided to take a chance on the Dane being slightly off his line. He was, and what we saw that afternoon was, by his own admission, one of the top five goals that Matt ever scored for the Saints.

The cheers had hardly died down when it appeared that the United fight back was on as David Beckham scored a direct free kick from the edge of the area to reduce the arrears. Nevertheless, right on the stroke of half-time, Egil Ostenstad somehow squeezed the ball between Schmeichel and his near post from an almost impossible angle to restore our two-goal advantage. Three-one to the good at half-time against ten men, and it felt as though history was repeating itself.

For United, there could be no blaming of the colour of their shirts this time, as ironically, they had started the match in the blue and white striped kit they had finished the game in back in April.

No doubt spurred on by a half-time rant from Ferguson, the United players did start the second period on the front foot. They had already wasted a couple of decent chances to score before David May bundled the ball home on 56 minutes, to reduce the areas to a single goal.

We responded by pouring forward once more, and now the match was pure end-to-end stuff, but my overriding fear was that if United were to equalise, then they would also inevitably go on and find a winner.

Despite playing against ten men, our attacks on the United goal became more infrequent, but as the game wore on and the equalising goal never came, the United attacks became more desperate. This left them wide open to a pacy counter-attack, and that's exactly what we hit them with on 83 minutes.

A Le Tissier corner wasn't cleared properly, and the ball fell to Berkovic on the edge of the area and with no hesitation, he smashed a right-foot volley past a stunned and stranded Schmeichel to make the score 4-2.

For all of United's possession and pressure, they now found themselves two goals behind once again, and they threw everyone bar the goalkeeper forward in the last six minutes in a desperate bid to salvage something from the game. We took full advantage of their gung-ho play, and we hit them with another classic piece of counter-attacking play when Ostenstad was played in by Berkovic's exquisite through ball, and he had no difficulty in sweeping the ball home for his second goal of the match.

Ostenstad's hat-trick goal came four minutes later after Paul Scholes had reduced the deficit to 5-3 when Ostenstad again got in down the left and this time he rounded Schmeichel to slot the ball in despite a last-ditch sliding attempt to stop it by Gary Neville. The goal was later given to Neville as an own goal by the Premier League's dubious goals panel, which seemed a little harsh as there was no doubt in my mind that the ball was going in without Neville's intervention. I still consider it a hat trick for Ostenstad no matter what the Premier League statisticians say.

When the referee ended the proceedings, a breathless Dell crowd tried to take in what they had just seen. To use a baseball term, it was a result totally out of left field, it sent shockwaves around the football world, hitting the headlines on the national news, and forcing statisticians to look up the last time United had conceded six goals in a match.

This result made us the toast of English football, and for a few weeks football fans talked about little else, but in true Southampton style what happened a few weeks later would turn the club (and Souness in particular) into a laughing stock.

The 53-Minute Career

Saints 0 Leeds United 2   Premier League   23 November 1996

Two more signings arrived after that United win, with Souness signing his former goalkeeper from his Glasgow Rangers days, Chris Woods, and although his first couple of performances were okay, Chris was part of a team that lost 7-1 at Everton, just weeks after that 6-3 thrashing of United. Remarkably, it could have been a lot worse, as we found ourselves 5-0 down inside 35 minutes of the first half. It was a match I had toyed with going to and not going turned out to be one of my better choices that year.

The other new signing turned out to be an unknown player called Ali Dia, and he signed just days after that 7-1 loss to the Toffees. Whether that thrashing on Merseyside had impaired Souness' judgement, no one other than Souness will know, but what happened next has gone down in football folklore.

Souness had received a telephone call purportedly from the African Footballer of the year George Weah, who was touting his cousin Ali Dia around as a free agent. Souness thinking that he could find himself with a quality player who had slipped under the radar of some of Europe's biggest clubs signed Dia up on trial.

By the Friday before the Leeds match, Dia had signed professional terms, and he found himself named amongst the substitutes for this match. The club announced the signing to the press, as well as the story about how he came with George Weah's personal recommendation.

Not only was Dia on the bench amongst the substitutes, but he would also get an early chance to impress everyone when on 22 minutes, an injury to Matthew Le Tissier gave Dia his first taste of top-flight football.

128

It took, I don't know, ten minutes or so before I could tell that this guy wasn't actually very good, and I wasn't the only one who noticed, as the rumblings of discontent increased in intensity every time he gave the ball away.

Despite taking a shot that was easily saved at the near post by the Leeds keeper, he soon took on the appearance of someone who had been plucked from the crowd, thrown into a football strip and asked to play in a professional match. In short, he was bloody awful. He seemed to have no clue what he was doing, or where he should be, and he rushed around the pitch in all directions like the proverbial headless chicken. He was so bad that after 53 minutes on the pitch (and I'm surprised he lasted that long) he was replaced by Ken Monkou to much relief and even cheers from sections of the Saints support.

The match itself was not much better, and with a goalless draw looking likely, Leeds secured a 2-0 win with goals in the final ten minutes, but all the talk post-match was about Ali Dia.

Once the full story came to light, the phone call from George Weah, the fact that Dia was supposed to be his cousin, the fact that he had supposedly played for Paris St. Germain in France, and in the German second division, most people were incredulous that none of this fantasy had actually been checked out. It also transpired that several of the squad had expressed their concerns about Dia's ability during his trial, yet the manager and his coaching staff dismissed their concerns.

It was soon apparent that the phone call Souness received hadn't been from George Weah, and may have actually come from Dia himself, but whoever made the call had managed to convince the Saints boss to give Dia a chance.

After the Leeds match, Dia actually had the gall to turn up at the club's training ground seeking treatment for an injury, before disappearing altogether, with the club releasing him two weeks later.

Dia would eventually show up at non-league Gateshead FC, and he played a few games for them before they let him go, so he wasn't even up to non-league standard.

Souness would never live the episode down, and even now, when I see him employed by Sky Sports as a pundit, I feel like screaming at the television, "don't listen to him, he was the man who signed Ali Dia for goodness sake, he knows nothing!"

Ali Dia, the man who managed to con his way onto the pitch to play in a Premier League match. As brazen bluffs go, it's right up there with Hitler's diaries and the Turin shroud.

Another Close Shave

Saints 2 Blackburn Rovers 0   Premier League   3 May 1997

Those defeats to Everton and Leeds sparked a run of five straight league losses, which dropped us back down to the relegation zone, and yet another battle against the drop loomed large on the horizon.

The only highlight had been a run to the quarter-finals of the League Cup, helped by not having faced any top-flight opposition in the competition's earlier rounds.

After winning that replay at Lincoln City, I travelled to Oxford United's Manor Ground for round four.

To describe the Manor Ground as a dump would be the ultimate understatement. Upon arrival, the ever-lovable Thames Valley police unceremoniously herded us into the stadium. Well, I say stadium, at first viewing it looked more like a Second World War internment camp. The away terracing had been separated into pens, and these pens were surrounded by 7-foot high barbed wire-topped security fencing and more CCTV cameras than I'd ever seen in one place in my life up to that point.

From my vantage point, I struggled to follow the action, especially when it took place at our end of the ground, and I don't even recall seeing our goal from Richard Dryden hit the back of the net. That goal seemed to be more than enough to see off this Oxford United team, but on came a striker that the majority of Saints fans there that night knew was going to score against us as soon as he stepped foot onto the pitch, Paul Moody. The very same Paul Moody who we had signed from Waterlooville just as Ian Branfoot was taking over as manager. The same Paul Moody, who couldn't hit a barn door from 2-yards out when wearing a Saints shirt, the same Paul Moody who duly popped up with an injury-time equaliser to force a replay back at The Dell a week later.

We made hard work of the replay before eventually winning 3-2, which set up a trip to Stockport County in round five. Stockport under the stewardship of Dave Jones were flying high in Division 2 (the third tier) and looked odds on for promotion. They had already disposed of Premier League Blackburn Rovers and West Ham in previous rounds, and now they had us firmly in their sights.

The game at Stockport started well with Ostenstad opening the scoring on 16 minutes before Stockport roared back with two goals in two minutes midway through the second-half. It looked as though we would be the latest top-flight victims to succumb to Stockport, and it took a scrambled and deflected Egil Ostenstad effort late on to restore parity, and give us another chance back at The Dell.

With home field advantage, I was in no doubt that we would reach our first League Cup Semi-Final since 1987, and I took my customary place in the Archers Road end fully expecting us to do just that. With the draw for the Semi-Finals already made, we knew that we would face Middlesbrough in a two-legged affair, and after our 4-0 thrashing of them earlier in the season, I fancied our chances in that one too.

We started the match well and our superiority was duly rewarded when Matt Le Tissier chested down an Alan Neilson cross to slam home left-footed to give us the lead, a lead we held until half-time.

The longer the game went on, however, the more likely that Stockport looked capable of grabbing an equaliser, and sure enough just past the hour mark, Brett Angel pounced to level the scores once more.

With our players seemingly tiring, and the Stockport players encouraged by that goal and roared on by a very vocal travelling support, it appeared that the game was swinging in their favour.

With all the pressure now coming from Stockport, I clung to the hope that we could snatch a goal on the break. It wasn't to be though, and with extra-time looming, Stockport sealed their passage into the semi-finals thanks to Andy Mutch's low drive with little over seven minutes left.

To be honest, they fully deserved it, and they deserved the generous round of applause that the majority of Saints fans afforded their players whilst they applauded their travelling fans, leaving us to wave goodbye to another chance to make it to a Wembley final.

With our cup run over (our FA Cup campaign ended on a frozen pitch at Reading's Elm Park in the third round), all our attention could now be focused on guaranteeing our Premier League status, but with our poor form, that was going to be a monumental challenge in itself.

By the time I made my way to Stamford Bridge on a cold March evening for an away game against Chelsea, Saints once again found themselves anchored to the foot of the table after a shocking run of just three wins from 18 games. With drawn matches, that meant a return of just 14 points from a possible 54, and things needed to improve dramatically if we were going to avoid the dreaded drop.

We lost the Chelsea match 1-0, and the following Saturday's game at home to Leicester ended in a 2-2 draw. This meant we had garnered a grand total of 15 points out of a possible 60, not the sort of form you want to take into the next match, which just so happened to be a massive 6-pointer away at fellow strugglers Nottingham Forest. However, we had an ace up our sleeve.

That ace came in the form of striker Mickey Evans, a bushy sideburn-sporting Devon lad with a West Country accent so thick it could clot cream. Souness signed him in order to enhance the Saints attack, and Mickey's beef and brio certainly made an impact, scoring two goals in the 3-1 defeat of Nottingham Forest.

Mickey followed that brace up with two more goals. One in a 2-0 home win against West Ham and the other helped secure a point in a 2-2 draw at home to Coventry, as we hit a run of form that kept us unbeaten for five matches.

With Rovers safe in mid-table, this match turned out to be a straightforward 2-0 win, and it looked to have been enough to secure our safety, but Middlesbrough's stoppage-time penalty at Aston Villa, gave them the three points they needed to keep things interesting, especially as they had two games-in-hand. The only saving grace was the fact that the win against Blackburn propelled us up to 14th in the table, and with so many teams below us, it would take an improbable set of results to send us down. We could even afford to lose our final game at Aston Villa and survive.

The match at Villa Park was a bit of a damp squib, a solitary Richard Dryden own goal meant a 1-0 defeat, though defeats for Sunderland and Middlesbrough meant that relegation was not a possibility. In fact, we actually finished as high as 16th, a position we could only dream of when we were bottom of the table in March.

So more relief at another close shave and another relegation battle successfully negotiated, but things were about to change for both the club and me in the summer months ahead.

The Managerial Merry-go-Round Continues

Saints 0 Bolton Wanderers1   Premier League   9 August 1997

The evening after our Premier League status was confirmed, I went out to celebrate and ended up meeting a woman who would have a big impact on my Saints supporting life over the next few months.

Mandy had no interest in football whatsoever, but when I met her she told me she wasn't averse to going to a match, and with Francis Benali's testimonial only a couple of weeks away, I thought it would be a good match for a first timer to experience.

The match was one of those fun games where nobody tends to stick to the rules and anything goes, and the match between the current Saints side and a team made up of ex-players ended in a final score of 8-7 to the ex-Saints.

Being an odd-numbered year, there was no summer football to fill the void, so I spent most of my spare time that summer with Mandy, and it was whilst travelling back from a day at the beach that I learned of the departures of both Graeme Souness and Lawrie McMenemy.

Picking up a newspaper on the way back from the station, it was obvious that there were problems concerning the reverse takeover and the appointment of Rupert Lowe as chairman, and Both Souness and McMenemy spoke candidly to the press about their concerns as to which way the club was heading.

Southampton have always been seen as a family club, where the players and the fans were part of a close-knit setup, but this was now a publicly listed company, and let's be honest, most publicly listed companies are only interested in one thing, and that's profit. Both Souness and McMenemy stated that they thought the men now in charge of the day to day running of the club (Rupert Lowe and Andrew Cowan) were not "football men" and that they could see only one outcome from this appointment, that the club was on a slippery slope to oblivion. In hindsight, they would be correct in their assumptions, even if it did take nearly a decade to happen.

A large number of fans were now beginning to have their fears realised, that the men running the club were not up to the job and that the reverse takeover was bad news. Some were more sceptical of Souness and the reasons for his departure, as only a few weeks later he joined Italian side, Torino. It was a move that annoyed some fans, who suggested that the Souness had already agreed his move to Italy before resigning as Southampton manager and that the impetus behind the move was our old friend, money.

If that was the case, why had McMenemy walked also? Something did not add up, and this was just the start of the backroom disagreements and cloak and dagger shenanigans that would affect the club on and off for the next ten years or so.

For now, though, we needed another new manager and the new appointment when it came turned out to be a familiar face.

Dave Jones had been the man in charge of Stockport the previous season when they knocked us out of the League Cup quarter-finals at The Dell. He had also taken them to promotion to the First Division, which was enough to convince Rupert Lowe to make him the first of what was to become a long line of managers under his leadership. Jones brought with him his namesake Paul Jones, a Welsh international goalkeeper, as well as winger Lee Todd.

I must admit that the appointment of Jones left me feeling underwhelmed, as I feared that his lack of top-flight managerial experience could be his undoing. Getting success with a Third Division club is one thing, but in the Premier League, where every defeat is analysed and dissected in every conceivable way, there is immediate pressure to get results. It was going to be an interesting season, and I was willing to give Jones the benefit of the doubt, after

135

all, he was a young manager who was hungry to succeed in the top flight.

Alas, things didn't start well, and he was in for a rude awakening as Bolton came to The Dell on a hot August afternoon and left with all three points, in what was a fairly dire match. Losing at home on the opening day of the season was becoming a nasty habit for the club, but this defeat to a newly promoted side was right up there with that awful 2-0 loss to Everton on opening day in 1993.

Two more losses followed although they were against Manchester United at Old Trafford and Arsenal at The Dell before we eventually got off the mark in our next home match against Crystal Palace, a scrappy affair won thanks to a solitary goal from Kevin Davies.

Signed by Graeme Souness at the tail end of the previous season for £700,000 from 3rd tier Chesterfield, Kevin would go on to be sold a year later for £7 million. In the meantime, he would be banging in the goals for us in his first ever season in the top-flight and a number of crucial goals in 1-0 wins helped to stave off the threat of relegation, especially in the second half of the season. The win over Palace though did not set us on a long unbeaten run as we'd hoped, and we proceeded to gain just one point from the next five games. An improvement was needed, and quickly.

Rules of Engagement

Saints 2 Leicester City 1   Premier League   13 December 1997

Francis Vincent Benali. A local Southampton lad who had come through the clubs youth system and had made nine appearances for the England schoolboys side, where he scored on his debut. He started out as a striker as a youngster and was quite prolific in front of goal, however, when he signed schoolboy forms for Saints in 1985 he was seen by the then youth team coach, Dave Merrington, as having better prospects as a defender. From that moment on, he became a solid fullback rather than a striker

He would make the left back slot his own during his professional career, but it soon became a running joke that he had never scored a goal in a professional match. His only real claim to fame was his reputation of being one of football's hard men, a reputation he earned early on in his Saints career thanks to one match in particular at Wimbledon in the late 80s.

Wimbledon had their own reputation as a team of hard men with the likes of Vinnie Jones, Dennis Wise and John Fashanu in their ranks, and it was the aforementioned Fashanu who felt the full force of a Benali tackle one sunny Saturday afternoon at Wimbledon's old Plough Lane ground.

As Fashanu galloped up the wing towards the halfway line, the ball got away from him slightly, just as Benali was steaming towards him at full speed. Although Benali was aiming for the ball, Fashanu made the mistake of toe poking the ball forward just as Benali committed himself to the tackle. The resultant lunge saw Fashanu launched nearly three feet into the air as he pirouetted and landed with a thud on the turf. Benali earned himself a straight red card, and legend status amongst Saints fans and those who detested Fashanu, a man who liked to dish out similar tackles on a regular basis.

Despite his cult hero status, the fact that he had never scored a goal for Saints in a competitive match caused many Saints fans to say that if they ever missed a game after attending dozens or hundreds of matches in a row, that that would be the match that Franny finally broke his duck.

On the subject of missing games, my decision to give up my season ticket for the woman I love meant that I was now beginning to miss games, and it's an unusual feeling knowing that there is a match going on and you're not there to see it. Missing away games was one thing, but being out shopping on a Saturday afternoon when your team is playing a home match was a strange feeling. If I missed home games before it was because I couldn't go, now I could go but I decided not to in order to spend time with my fiancée.

Our engagement took place in October, and quite by accident as it turned out, but not the type of accident that typically springs to mind when the words accident and engagement end up in the same sentence.

Mandy received an invitation to one of her friend's birthday parties, and she took me along as her "plus one." It was a standard party, lots of drinking and dancing and she introduced me to several of her friends and work colleagues, and her friends would play a big part in our eventual engagement.

Knowing that Mandy had been engaged before and that it had ended on a sour note (ironically to someone who I had gone to school with) I just happened to casually mention to one of her friends whether she knew if Mandy would ever get engaged again.

I was not planning to ask her to marry me at that point in our relationship, as we had only known each other for about five months, and it was just a question born out of curiosity, but boy, did it backfire on me.

Her very inebriated mate took this question as a sign that a marriage proposal was in the offing, and she quickly rushed off to spread the news to the rest of her mates. I hadn't asked Mandy the question directly, as I didn't want her to get the wrong end of the stick, but now that was exactly what was happening now, and the news of my supposed marriage proposal quickly found its way to Mandy's ears.

To save face, I told her that I was thinking of asking her to marry me and that we should talk about it later between ourselves, but her friends had already begun making a fuss of us, and I could see that backing down now would put the entire relationship at risk.

A few days later and somehow, I found myself in a jeweller's shop buying a moderately priced engagement ring for a woman I loved, but one I certainly hadn't considered running up the aisle with, although I made it clear to Mandy and anyone who listened, that even though the announcement was swift, the engagement would be a long one.

As it turned out it wasn't, and even though we had started looking at buying a flat together, the relationship was starting to show signs of breaking up, and it would all be over by the new year.

The reason for this dramatic downturn in our relationship had to do with my continued interest in Southampton Football Club. I *had* made sacrifices, giving up my season ticket, and not going to so many away matches so we could spend more time together, but this wasn't enough, and she seemed to want me to give up attending matches permanently. She worked shifts, which often meant that we did not spend every weekend together, and in her mind, she wanted to spend the ones she did have off, with me. Fair enough, but when she began complaining that I had the audacity to listen to matches that I did not attend on the radio, then it began to get too much for me.

One Saturday in particular sticks in my mind, we were out shopping in the afternoon and I was listening to the Saints game on the radio, she referred to my radio as "the idiot box" for some reason best known to her, but as far as I was concerned I had met her halfway. If she couldn't stand me listening to 90 minutes of football on the radio well then that was her problem. Just who was the selfish one in the relationship? After all, here was someone who couldn't go without her weekly Saturday night fix of those television stalwarts, Blind Date, and Gladiators. In a few weeks, the relationship had gone from engagement celebration to breaking point, and it wasn't helped further when we had a blazing row one night after a particularly bad Saints performance.

It was a home game against our bogey side Sheffield Wednesday, a team we hadn't beaten at home in the league since the early 1970s, and despite falling behind early on we came roaring back to take a 2-1 lead only to throw it away and lose 3-2 in the last few minutes.

That late collapse put me in a foul mood, and all I wanted to do was to go out in the evening, have a few drinks, and forget about it. Unfortunately for me, all Mandy wanted to do was sit at home and watch her low brow television programmes, something I had no desire to do whatsoever. A blazing row ensued, resulting in me storming out of her flat, although after a couple of drinks I returned and we smoothed things over. Nevertheless, in my mind, this felt like the beginning of the end of our relationship.

Thanks to Mandy working on this particular Saturday, I was able to make my way to The Dell and be in place to witness the miracle of a Francis Benali goal. It came thanks to a Matthew Le Tissier free kick that eluded everyone in a crowded Leicester City penalty area, and Franny thumped home a free header from about 16-yards out that flew into the top corner.

It was one of those "I was there" moments and I am proud to say I was one of the fans who can lay claim to witnessing the only goal scored by Francis Benali in a competitive match.

Unfortunately, it would be the only bright light in a dark and wretched December and January for both the club and me.

Cheated

Derby County 2 Saints 0   FA Cup 3rd Round   3 January 1998

With our indifferent league form, I was hoping that the FA Cup would give us something to cheer about, but the draw gave us a tricky looking trip to Derby, where we had already been comprehensively beaten 4-0 in a league match earlier in the season.

I really wanted to go to this match and after a particularly straightforward festive season with Mandy, who had made it quite clear that we should spend Christmas Day itself with our own families, I'd taken the plunge and got myself a ticket. The match was due to take place a couple of days into the New Year, and when Mandy found out that I had booked the trip, she went ballistic. A very nasty argument took place and despite the fact that we were about to sign a mortgage application for a flat we both liked, our relationship was all but over. Once again, I found myself single, but hey, I had a football match to look forward to right?

Thanks to Mandy and her determination to turn me away from all things Saints and football related, this would be only my third away trip of the season. I had taken Mandy to an away game at Blackburn in October; she wanted to experience an away game so I picked one that would be okay for a first timer. Blackburn fans are a decent bunch, and there was likely to be very little trouble between the two sets of fans. However, she hated it and wasn't shy about telling me when we got home. Apparently, being surrounded by Blackburn fans was too intimidating for her (what she expected from an away match I wasn't sure) and so she vowed never to go to another away game again. However, reading between the lines, it looked as though I wasn't allowed to either.

Breaking up with someone is tough, but when it happens between Christmas and New Year it seems to multiply the pain. I did try to patch things up after leaving her alone for a couple of weeks, but she had already met someone else. Something that I thought was a little too quick for my liking and it was evident to me that she had been seeing this other guy behind my back.

Anyway, the trip to Derby gave me a chance to leave Southampton behind for a few hours, and concentrate my mind on football. In times of personal crisis, I always find that football becomes something of a security blanket, something I can embrace to help me take my mind away from my troubles. The only problem was that the coach journey to Derby was a long one (most away games are long trips when you live in Southampton) and that gave my brain plenty of time to replay the disastrous last few weeks of my relationship with Mandy.

So, for most of the trip to Derby, I was in a melancholy mood, and only a win would help to lift the gloom. Okay, I would take a draw and a replay back at The Dell too!

The match was a rather drab affair played in near freezing conditions. Back then, Pride Park had one corner that hadn't been built, and the freezing cold wind blew straight through the gap. It was a miserable dull overcast day, the slate grey clouds threatening snow, the weather totally suiting my wretched mood.

With Claus Lundekvam missing through injury, Dave Jones had to reshuffle the side putting Carlton Palmer into defence thus weakening the midfield, and it was to be a costly mistake, as Derby's midfield totally dominated the game.

Despite the amount of possession Derby enjoyed, the Saints defence easily dealt with Derby's early efforts, but our attacks were rare, and our best effort was a long-range shot from Kevin Davies that stung the hands of Derby's goalkeeper Mart Poom.

The second half saw us pinned back into our own half and we seemed more than content to hang on for a 0-0 and bring them back to The Dell for a replay. There was to be no second match though, thanks to the cheating antics of one or two of the Derby players.

Derby had two Italian players on their side in the form of Francesco Baiano and Stefano Eranio, the latter had already "won" Derby a penalty in the league match earlier in the season that set us on the way to that 4-0 defeat. This time the cheat was Baiano, whose swallow dive in the penalty area with just over 20 minutes left earned Derby the most outlandish penalty I had ever witnessed given against the Saints.

The incident happened at our end of the ground and the nearest Saints player to Baiano, Carlton Palmer, hadn't even attempted a tackle, yet Baiano's theatrical dive and subsequent appeal earned him the spot-kick from a referee who was not actually in a position to see the action. The assistant referee on that side had not flagged for the penalty but the referee gave it anyway despite the assistant having a clearer view of the situation. It was an outrageous travesty of justice and Baiano duly slotted home the ill-gotten spot-kick, and from then on there was only going to be one winner.

That horrendous decision seemed to knock the stuffing out of the Saints players, and five minutes later, some slack defending let Derby in for a second goal, but my misery wasn't complete, not a bit of it.

Morose and despondent at the end of my relationship with Mandy, this defeat did nothing to help my mood, and I sat there as the cold wind blew, and it got colder and colder and it began to snow and my misery deepened. Here I was miles from home, depressed and freezing cold watching my team surrender timidly in the FA Cup. It was a thoroughly wretched and dismal day, and I couldn't wait to get home.

Our Cup Runneth Over

Saints 0 Fulham 1   League Cup 2nd Round 2nd Leg
                                                  23 September 1998

The clubs fortunes did improve after the cup exit at Derby, with a 1-0
win against Manchester United at The Dell and an amazing 3-2 win
against Liverpool at Anfield, our first win there since 1981.

   In the end, relegation was not as much of a threat this season as it
had been in the previous years, thanks in no small part to the goals of
Matthew Le Tissier and Egil Ostenstad. The pair had scored 15 goals
in total between February and the end of the season, which was
fortunate as we had lost Kevin Davies to a long term injury in that 1-0
win over Manchester United. All in all, a 12th place finish was very
respectable, considering our poor start to the season, and the fans
were just relieved at not having to endure yet another last day
relegation battle.

   The close season had seen Kevin Davies sensationally sold to
Blackburn (yes them again) for £7.25 million, a club record, and
although there was no David Speedie making up part of the deal, we
did receive Stuart Ripley in return, as well as a promising young striker
James Beattie.

   Beattie would go on to great things, whilst Ripley tried his best to
emulate the aforementioned Speedie by contributing sod all to the
club. He scored a solitary goal in 53 appearances before eventually
leaving on loan to Barnsley and Sheffield Wednesday.

   Manager Dave Jones seemed to be turning into another Ian Branfoot
with his less than inspiring signings, and as if to reinforce this he
signed another veteran who just happened to be looking for one last
payday.

You can't knock Mark Hughes' career stats from his time at Manchester United, Barcelona and Chelsea, but you can certainly knock his stats from his time with us. Mark was 34 when he joined us and well past his best, and in the 52 matches he played for us he only found the net twice, putting him on par with Kerry Dixon and only slightly better than David Speedie. His biggest tally came in the cautions department, where he racked up 14 yellow cards in just one season, which I believe is still a Saints Premier League record.

Off the pitch, and the continuing saga of the proposed new stadium at Stoneham that had dragged on for years rumbled on with no resolution in sight. There was talk of the club abandoning the project altogether, and this was not entirely unexpected due to the level of opposition to the project by local residents and county councillors alike. However, not all was lost as the city council had a Brownfield site that was ripe for redevelopment in the St. Marys area of the city.

A return to the clubs spiritual home, where it was founded back in 1885 got the fans excited, but after so many false dawns over the Stoneham plans, nobody was betting their mortgage on the new stadium actually coming to fruition.

The start to the 1998/99 season saw us facing Liverpool at home on the opening day, then we had to play Leeds, Newcastle, and Arsenal away, and Tottenham and Manchester United at home all before the middle of October. If I thought last season's start had been terrible it was nothing compared to this season, and we failed to win any of those games, which left us rooted to the bottom of the table with a meagre two points.

This League Cup second round second leg tie against Fulham came in the middle of that awful run of league games. Fulham were then in the second division (the 3rd tier) and were red-hot favourites to be promoted. Backed with Harrods owner Mohamed El-Fayed's millions and with former Saint Kevin Keegan at the helm, they had assembled

a team that was more than a match for us. In the first leg at Craven
Cottage, we were lucky to come away with a draw that set up a
delicately poised second leg at The Dell a fortnight later.

Fulham's German striker Dirk Lehmann scored the only goal after
10 minutes, and I spent the next 80 minutes watching us labour
towards trying to find an equaliser. Fulham carried more than enough
threat on the counter attack and in the end, we were lucky not to
concede more, and it was a straightforward victory for the Londoners.
As I left the ground, I couldn't help but think that we may very well
be meeting again in the same division next season.

Actually, we didn't have to wait that long because in December the
draw for the third round of the FA Cup paired us with Fulham at The
Dell. In a reverse of the League Cup results, we drew 1-1 at home and
lost the away match 1-0, so that was both cup adventures over before
they had really started. My opinion of Dave Jones, which was never
high in the first place, was starting to fall quite quickly, and I was not
alone in my thinking that here was another Saints manager who
appeared out of his depth in the Premier League.

Many Happy Returns

Saints 1 Sheffield Wednesday 0   Premier League   20 March 1999

We eventually registered our first win of the season in the league at
the tenth attempt when we scraped past Coventry 2-1 at The Dell, but
things were not improving as they had done the season before. With
Davies gone and Le Tissier constantly struggling with a succession of
niggling injuries, we just didn't seem to have enough punch up-front.

To combat our poor form Dave Jones dipped into the transfer
market continually during this season, and next to arrive was
Moroccan midfielder Hassan Kachloul, although he came on a free

transfer after his release by French side, Metz, and he would make his debut coming off the bench in a crucial 2-0 away win at fellow strugglers Blackburn Rovers. It had only been four years since Rovers had won the Premier League title, but now here they were keeping us company in the relegation zone, a startling reminder of how quickly fortune can change in football. Our victory at Ewood Park ended the managerial reign of their boss Roy Hodgson, a man who had only been in charge since the summer, and the welcome three points allowed us to leapfrog them and off the bottom of the table.

The expected rise up the table failed to materialise though, and more losses followed, the worst being a 7-1 loss at Liverpool.

Thankfully, that result coupled with one or two new faces seemed to galvanise the team into action, and eventually our home form picked up with five consecutive home victories at the turn of the year, of which this win over Sheffield Wednesday was the last (a 0-0 draw against Arsenal in our next home match ended our run). In fact, this was our first home league win against the Owls since the 1969-70 season which was a run of 14 winless matches, our only two victories in that time against Wednesday had come in cup competitions. Moreover, as this win took place on my birthday, it turned out to be the perfect present.

It was a hard fought victory, and a single Matthew Le Tissier goal settled the match two minutes before half-time, it was also my new girlfriend Ruth's first match. So dire was the clubs situation that despite five consecutive home victories we were still not out of the relegation zone, having been bottom of the table for the entire season up to this point.

Two defeats to Coventry (1-0) and Aston Villa (3-0) followed that draw with Arsenal, and our next match at home to fellow strugglers Blackburn Rovers would be a massive 6-pointer.

It was a match that neither side could afford to lose, and the reward for the fans who attended that day was a match packed with goalmouth action, as both sides threw caution to the wind in a desperate search for three points.

Saints nearly took the lead early on but Hassan Kachloul's saw his effort well saved, and a few minutes later Rovers went up the other end and took the lead through Ashley Ward.

Despite that setback, it was another of our recent signings who restored parity after 23 minutes, as bald-headed Chris Marsden thumped in Jason Dodd's lovely chipped cross from 7-yards out. Game on? Well not quite as within three minutes, Darren Peacock found himself unmarked from a Blackburn corner to slam home unchallenged to put Rovers back in front. Then the same Peacock cleared off the line minutes later when Hassan Kachloul beat the goalkeeper to Le Tissier's cross and his looping header was hacked clear.

Two minutes into the second-half the game looked to be up and Blackburn Rovers seemed to be about to get revenge for that 2-0 defeat at Ewood Park earlier in the season, when they extended their lead to 3-1, thanks to a powerful looping header by Jason Wilcox.

Unperturbed by this setback we surged forward, and the reward was a goal back on the hour mark when some good work down the right by Kachloul set Beattie in and his low drilled cross was met on the slide by Mark Hughes from two yards out. It was Mark's first goal for the club in his 33rd appearance and gave us the momentum we needed to claw our way back into the game with just less than thirty minutes left. Now, it was all Saints and in a desperate bid to salvage something from the match, Dave Jones decided to throw everything at Rovers, replacing defender Scott Hiley with another of his new signings, Latvian striker Marian Pahars, a player we had signed from Skonto Riga. It was his first outing at The Dell having only made a solitary substitute appearance two weeks earlier at Coventry, and we didn't have to wait long for him to make his mark. With nine minutes left on the clock, he bagged the equaliser. A leaping header from James Beattie on the edge of the area dissected two Blackburn defenders and fell perfectly for Pahars to nod home with a precise downward header.

There was still time for someone to score a winner, and it was looking more likely that it would be us as our fast attacking play had Rovers pinned in their own half. In spite of our best efforts, we just couldn't quite force the ball in, with both Peacock and Jason McAteer making last ditch blocks on or near the goal line.

It was a pulsating game for the neutral, but the 3-3 draw didn't really do either side any favours, and with matches running out, it looked as though another last day battle for survival was on the cards.

The Great Escape

Wimbledon 0 Saints 2   Premier League   8 May 1999

After all the excitement of coming back from 3-1 down to grab a precious point against Blackburn, myself and Ruth travelled to Pride Park for our penultimate away game at Derby County.

It was certainly a different atmosphere for me compared to my previous visit to Derby for that FA Cup match 16 months previously, and the weather was a lot warmer too! In the end, though there was nothing for either side to cheer about and the match finished as a tame goalless draw.

Our next league match was at home to Leicester, and it was Chris Marsden who secured another crucial three points as despite going a goal down early on, his and Beattie's goals in each half helped to drag us out of the bottom three for the first time that season, aided in part to Blackburn's draw with Charlton.

So, on to our last away game of the season, and a tricky looking trip to Wimbledon and their adopted home Selhurst Park for a game that no one was in any doubts would be a tough test. Such was the interest in this match that over 14,000 Saints fans made the trip to South London for the most important game of the season.

Our recent recovery, coupled with the fact that we had now clawed our way out of the drop zone, meant that this match had suddenly become the hottest ticket in town. Thanks to Wimbledon's minuscule home attendances (they usually peaked at around the 7,000 mark), there was plenty of room for thousands of Saints fans, although we probably could have taken double the amount we did, such was the demand for tickets.

For this trip to London, Ruth and her dad accompanied me, and the three of us boarded one of the many coaches to London that the travel club had laid on for this match. In fact, as many as 100 official travel club coaches were booked for this trip and it felt as though we were going to a cup final at Wembley rather than a league match at ramshackle Selhurst Park.

The match kicked-off to a cacophony of noise from the thousands of travelling fans but Wimbledon started the brighter and Paul Jones made a smart early save to tip an Efan Ekoku shot around the post.

Whether it was nerves or just Wimbledon hoping to be the party poopers, but we just could not get a foothold in the game, and Robbie Earle somehow managed to hit the legs of a prostrate Paul Jones from 6-yards out when it looked easier to score.

Our first opportunity to take the lead came when David Hughes (who had replaced the not fully fit Le Tissier) pounced on a mistake at the back by Chris Perry, but when one-on-one with the goalkeeper, he blasted the shot straight at him.

150

It was end-to-end stuff now, but Wimbledon should have been in front minutes later when Francis Benali cleared Robbie Earle's shot off the line with his chest.

When the half-time whistle blew and with the game still goalless, the consensus amongst the Southampton fans was that we could win this, fate appeared to be on our side.

The first chance of the second-half fell to Hassan Kachloul but his sliding effort went agonisingly inches wide. Minutes later, it was our turn to have an effort scrambled away off the line when Kachloul's cross deflected off a Wimbledon defender and was palmed away from goal by goalkeeper Neil Sullivan. As good as his save was, the ball fell invitingly for Pahars two-yards out, who sliding in under a challenge failed to get a telling touch to force the ball over the line.

With time running out the momentum was with us but we just couldn't find that all-important breakthrough. That was when Dave Jones made a telling substitution when replacing the hard working David Hughes with the guile and silky skills of a fit-again Matt Le Tissier for the last twenty minutes.

Matt had only been on the field for just over a minute when we were awarded a free-kick on the left-hand side about 40-yards from goal. Le Tissier stepped up with his usual confidence and delivered a peach of a cross into the box that found the head of James Beattie who only had to guide the ball in. As Beattie's head made contact with the ball, time seemed to stand still. Thousands of pairs of eyes watched transfixed as the ball sailed past the static Wimbledon goalkeeper before rippling the back of the net. Cue mass bedlam amongst the away fans, where people hugged friends, family or even total strangers.

All we needed to do now was to hold on for an important victory, but we went and doubled our lead a few minutes later when a Matt Le Tissier corner seemed to go straight in for 2-0.

Raucous celebrations ensued at the final whistle, although, the celebrations were tempered somewhat as news filtered through that our nearest relegation rivals Charlton had won their game at Aston Villa in stoppage-time. This meant that we had gone from certain safety to needing something from our final game against Everton at The Dell.

The equation was simple, Nottingham Forest had already succumbed to the drop, and there were two relegation places left to avoid. We were one place above the relegation zone, with Charlton just below us, 2-points behind but with a much better goal difference. Below Charlton were Blackburn, who despite being 5-points behind us, still had to play two more games, although their game in hand was away at Manchester United, a game they duly lost.

So going into the final game of the season, it was a straight fight between Charlton and us to avoid the last relegation spot. Thanks to their superior goal difference, a draw for us and a win for Charlton would send us down, so all that was required of us was to match or better Charlton's result.

My lack of foresight (and lack of faith in our ability to escape the drop) meant that by the time this game became vitally important to our survival chances, getting hold of a ticket was impossible, so it was time to dust off my trusty radio for another nerve-jangling ninety minutes.

In the end, the match was a straightforward victory with goals in each half by Pahars and Beattie securing our place in the Premier League for at least another season. Charlton actually lost at home to Sheffield Wednesday, which meant that we actually finished five points ahead of the relegation places. Anyone glancing at the league table for that season would assume that it was a more comfortable season than it actually was, but in truth, our poor form had seen us anchored in the relegation zone for 35 out of the 38 league games we played.

We'd had close calls before in some of the previous seasons, but having been nailed on certainties for relegation for most of the campaign, this season became known as "The Great Escape", although to me it was the greatest of great escapes.

Sexy Football

Saints 4 Newcastle United 2   Premier League   15 August 1999

If any Saints fans were looking forward to a nice stress-free close season, then they were going to be disappointed, as a disturbing news story broke concerning manager Dave Jones.

In between retiring from playing to becoming a coach and manager, Dave Jones worked for a few years in children's care homes on Merseyside, and all kinds of allegations began flying around about child abuse in the homes he worked in. Some of the former residents had come forward and had accused Jones of being one of the culprits, and it wasn't long before he found himself being questioned by the police, before eventually being released pending further enquiries. It was obvious that the case was going to drag on for quite some time, and most talks amongst the Saints fans was about how this was going to affect the club and Dave Jones' position as manager.

For the time being, the club stood by their man, and he took his place in the dugout for the start of the season. With all the money spent before the transfer deadline the previous March, the only signing of note was centre-back Dean Richards, who arrived from Wolves on a free transfer, replacing the departing Ken Monkou.

Mark Hughes decided to stay on despite becoming the Welsh national team manager, so despite the upheaval off the pitch, on it, there wasn't much change at all.

Another thing that didn't change was our form, as we carried our good form from the end of the previous season into this one, and we even managed to win our first game of the season, at Coventry, a match I attended more in hope than in expectation.

My last visit to Coventry was on a cold and bleak New Years Day in 1996, and although the August sunshine shone down on the place this time, the city still had a horrible bleakness to it. We all know that the Germans levelled the city during World War 2 but in their haste to rebuild after hostilities ceased, the authorities seemed to have come up with the idea of smothering everything in concrete. Everywhere I looked was dreary and cheerless grey lumps of concrete, which gave the impression that you have somehow stumbled into a 1950 town planner's wet dream. The city was famously the home of the band, The Specials, whose 1981 hit, Ghost Town, was a song about urban blight, deindustrialisation, unemployment, and disaffected youth. The drummer, John Bradbury was quoted as saying that when he thinks of the song Ghost Town he immediately thinks of Coventry, it's a suitable analogy.

The match itself was as uninspiring as the surroundings, Coventry's Highfield Road ground at the time was a confusion of stands assembled in different decades. The view of the pitch obscured by view impeding pillars and struts and the facilities for away fans were minimal.

For over 80 minutes, both teams huffed and puffed in the August humidity and the match looked to be petering out to a goalless draw. Then on 84 minutes, Matthew Le Tissier played an exquisite through ball for Egil Ostenstad to run on to and slot the ball past the advancing goalkeeper to secure our first opening day win since 1988.

154

Three points on the board early on made such a difference from our usual slow start, and now with two home games coming up, there was a real chance that we could keep that winning run going.

My new found optimism lasted until the following Wednesday when Leeds United rolled into town for our first home game of the season and left with all three points in a 3-0 win. The match was only memorable for the goal that never was. Leeds were still leading by a solitary goal when Mark Hughes hammered a low shot into the net so hard it rebounded back out in a flash. For some reason, both the referee and the linesman on that side thought the ball had hit the post and so the game carried on, whilst those Saints players who had seen the ball clearly enter the goal chased the referee whilst Leeds launched a counter attack.

Thankfully, Leeds didn't score whilst our players continued their protests, and the ball was cleared out for a throw, but the atmosphere around The Dell was a mixture of bewilderment and anger. No one near where I was sat had any idea as to why the referee had not given the goal, and even more perplexing was the fact that he hadn't whistled for an infringement either.

Leeds would eventually go on to win the match 3-0, thanks to a Michael Bridges hat-trick, but that non-goal would have levelled the scores at the time, and the final result could have been quite different.

The following Sunday Saints returned to The Dell to face Ruud Gullit's Newcastle United, for a Sky Super Sunday encounter. Gullit had come to England at the tail end of his career in 1995 when he signed for Chelsea and had coined the phrase "sexy football" during his stint as a pundit on the BBC's coverage of Euro '96. The term described teams that played attractive fast-flowing passing football, and the term followed him around during managerial stints at first Chelsea then Newcastle.

This match didn't seem to have the potential for too much "sexy football" with it having to be played in non-stop torrential rain, but it turned out to be a cracking match filled with numerous chances.

Newcastle were first to break the deadlock when they were awarded a very soft penalty for Claus Ludekvam's nudge on Kieron Dyer in the box, and former Saint Alan Shearer had no problem in doing the honours from the penalty spot.

The score stayed that way until thirteen minutes into the second half, when Saints finally got the reward their pressure deserved. Some neat play down the right set Stuart Ripley free and his cross from the goal line fizzed low and fast across the penalty area. The Newcastle defenders let it go, afraid that even the slightest touch would divert the ball into their own net, and with the goalkeeper static on his line, Hassan Kachloul nipped in unmarked at the far post to level things up.

Spurred on by that equalising goal we then went goal crazy, scoring another three in 12 minutes. First to get in on the goal scoring action was Marian Pahars, who nipped in between a defender and a static goalkeeper to latch onto Stuart Ripley's angled ball (Ripley was having his best, and only, decent game for us), and he volleyed it home from eight yards out.

Three minutes later Hassan Kachloul grabbed his second when he darted onto Soltvedt's knock down to slam home unmarked from just inside the penalty area. Mark Hughes scored twelve minutes from the end to complete the rout. This time there was no doubt as to the validity of Hughes's strike, and although Gary Speed pulled a goal back late on, the Saints emerged as clear winners.

Ruud Gullit was coming under fire from sections of the Newcastle fans, the media and players and after having public disagreements with both Alan Shearer and Captain Robert Lee, he dropped the pair of them for the local derby against Sunderland at St. James Park, a match they lost 2-1 and he was fired days later.

Six days after this match, Saints were thumped 4-1 at Everton, a result that brought us right back down to Earth, but despite that loss, things were looking a lot better on the pitch than they had at the same point the previous season.

Off the pitch, and Ruth and I were married at Southampton registry office in mid-September after a short engagement, and once again football took something of a back seat in my life, but not for long.

In Birmingham City Centre No-One Can Hear You Scream

Aston Villa 4 Saints 0   League Cup 4th Round   1 December 1999

Prior to that humbling at Everton, the club welcomed back striker Kevin Davies, who rejoined after a nightmare season at Blackburn. He suffered from poor form and illness during his stay in the north-west and we swapped Egil Ostenstad for him. Other new signings coming in were Norwegian midfielder Trond Soldvedt a £200,000 capture from Coventry City and Luis Boa Morte, a striker from Arsenal who joined on a curious appearance related fee. I guess we must have paid Arsenal a few quid for every game he played for us, which sounded like a football equivalent of a hire purchase agreement. It was a shame we didn't agree to pay Arsenal per goal scored, then we would have owed them virtually nothing.

On the pitch, our league form remained patchy, with too many points dropped from winning positions. Even so, one highlight was a 3-3 draw at Old Trafford against Manchester United that saw us take the lead and then battle back twice from 2-1 and 3-2 down to grab a share of the spoils. The match was also memorable for the goal that made the scores 2-2 when Le Tissier's scuffed long-range low shot somehow crept through the legs of United's goalkeeper Massimo Taibi and into the net. It was one of those goalkeeping howlers that often appear on videos of goalkeeping gaffes, and Taibi never really recovered from it, he didn't play for United for much longer, and after a 5-0 humbling at Chelsea a few weeks later, he was dropped, before eventually returning to Italy.

Off the pitch, manager Dave Jones is devastated to discover that he will face charges over those child abuse allegations, and the whole case may take up to twelve months to complete. Nevertheless, Rupert Lowe reaffirms the clubs position on the saga by saying that Jones has the full backing of the club, with no plans to replace him.

There was other good news though, relating to the building of a new stadium in the St. Marys district of the city when in September the club announced that the funding for the new 32,000 all seater stadium was now in place.

If our league form was up and down then our league cup campaign was starting to show signs of promise. In the second round, we dispatched Manchester City (then newly promoted to the second tier after a season in the third) 4-3 on aggregate, where all the goals came in a frantic 2nd leg tie at The Dell after a 0-0 draw at Maine Road.

As with the Manchester City match, Sky Sports chose our next match in the competition at home to Liverpool for live TV coverage, and it was to be another thriller.

Prolific Liverpool striker Michael Own put the Merseysiders ahead midway through the second-half, but just a few minutes later, Dean Richards powered in a header from a Matt Le Tissier free-kick to level things up. With the game seemingly heading towards extra-time, Trond Soldvedt nipped in quickest to a loose ball to score the winner in the last minute, which set up a fourth round trip to Aston Villa.

I wasn't going to go to this match originally, although I had toyed with the idea for a couple of weeks, but mid-week away games can be a pain to get home from if they are not local, and travelling up to the second city on a Tuesday night in December didn't exactly "float my boat" as it were.

However, my indifferent attitude changed when a work colleague offered me his spare ticket. He had originally planned to go to the match with his younger brother and his flatmate, but the flatmate couldn't make it, and he was desperately trying to find someone to take the spare ticket off his hands. After securing a half-day holiday from work, I decided to take him up on his offer and paid him for his ticket.

One of the factors that swung it for me was that my work colleague Keith was planning to drive all three of us up to Birmingham, so I didn't have to worry about getting home afterwards.

Our plan was to get up there a couple of hours before kick-off, park the car and head for the nearest away fan friendly hostelry for a few pre-match pints, before making our way to the ground. An idea that was straightforward in its planning but problematical in its implementation.

The first problem arose when we reached the outskirts of Birmingham before discovering that Keith had forgotten to bring his road map with him.

"No problem," said Keith's brother (whose name I can't remember), "I've got the programme from our last home game here, and it has directions to the away supporters allocated car park printed in it."

Brilliant, I thought, what could be easier than following a few simple instructions?

That was when the second problem arose.

Anyone who has driven from Southampton to Villa Park will tell you that as soon as you get on the Aston Expressway you only need to take the first exit and turn right and you are almost within sight of the ground. Now Keith's brother blamed it on a missing comma or full stop in the programme he was reading from, but somehow we missed the first exit off the Aston Expressway and instead we found ourselves heading towards the centre of Birmingham.

"No problem," says Keith, "we'll just get off at the next exit and double back!"

Therefore, we kept driving whilst looking for another exit, we kept looking and looking, and soon it was evident that that wasn't another exit, and in fact, we were heading miles out of our way.

Our planned pub visit was now in serious jeopardy as we travelled deeper into the urban sprawl of Birmingham city centre, but Keith was still hopeful that we would make it back in time for at least one drink. I didn't share his optimism.

Another quarter of an hour or so and we were hopelessly lost, although, ironically we did manage to find West Bromwich Albion's ground, The Hawthorns, that was of little use other than telling us that we were in the west of the city when we should be in the north of it.

Then just as we had given up on making it in time for kick-off, I spotted a beacon of hope in a desert of despair, a postman emptying a post box, so I get Keith to pull the car over to allow me to ask him directions.

I wind down the window and I ask him if he can tell us how to get to Villa Park.

"Villa Park?" he says back at us in a kind of strangulated voice, at least I think that's what he's saying. Determined to get us back on the right track I repeat myself a bit louder, only to get the same response. That is when I notice the two hearing aids he is wearing, and now the penny drops, he's severely deaf, and by the sound of it a bit mute too. Of course, he could be playing up to it just to wind up these three southern idiots who have somehow can't find one of the easiest football grounds to get to in the country.

160

I ask him a third time but he just shrugs his shoulders, so giving up I wind the window closed and urge Keith to get going. A few yards down the road and all three of us burst into spontaneous laughter, at how we seemingly managed to select one of the few deaf mute postal workers in Birmingham to ask directions.

With less than thirty minutes to kick-off, any hope of making the pub was long gone, and now we were looking at missing the start of the match too. Yet somehow, and more by luck than judgement, we managed to rejoin the Aston Expressway, only we were now heading out of the city. To make matters worse, either there is no exit for Aston, or we miss it again, and so we have no choice but to travel up the M6 motorway, turn around at the next junction and start back, making sure that we don't miss the exit this time.

We make it to the car park with about ten minutes to spare, and after a brief sprint through Aston Park, we make it to our seats just as the players are lining up for the kick-off.

Now, all we needed was for the players to put in a good performance in order to help us forget the chaotic events of the previous two hours, and seeing as we had already won the League encounter at Villa Park earlier in the season my hopes were high.

The funny thing about football is that your team can surprise you when you least expect it. They can beat the likes of Arsenal and Manchester United, and then the following week they'll lose an easy looking cup tie against some minnow like Shrewsbury or Hartlepool.

Don't get me wrong, I didn't expect this match at Villa to be easy, but having already won there this season, I did expect the scoreline to be a bit closer than it turned out.

We lost 4-0 and in truth, that scoreline flattered us, as we churned out one of the most abject displays I had seen since the dark days of Branfoot's reign.

Villa looked as though they were going to score with every attack, yet somehow, we were only one goal behind midway through the second half. That was when the floodgates opened as Villa hit us on the counter-attack as we poured men forward in a desperate search for an equaliser that we probably didn't deserve.

When your team is only one goal behind, there is always hope that they can snatch a goal, no matter how badly they have been playing up to that point, but our hopes of an equaliser were dashed by one of the most absurd defensive howlers I had ever seen from a Saints player up to this point.

French full-back Patrick Colleter had been signed the previous season, and the no-nonsense hard tackling defender had added much-needed bite to our tame defence, something that went some way to help us avoid relegation. He had a solid playing history, having played in France for the likes of Paris St. Germain and Marseille. However, this particular night, he decided that he would try a headed back-pass to goalkeeper Paul Jones from fully 30 yards out. Needless to say, the ball fell a smidgen short of the penalty area (about 10 yards short in fact), and Villa's lively forward Julian Joachim nipped in to round the advancing Jones and slot the ball into the empty net to double Villa's advantage.

That two-goal advantage soon became three, then four, and I was just grateful to hear the final whistle so I could get the hell out of there, but little did I know that this would just be the beginning as far as shameful League Cup away trips go. In the next few seasons, there would be other appalling and embarrassing cup displays, and I'm sad to say, I would be there for the majority of them.

In Hod We Trust

Bradford City 1 Saints 2   Premier League   8 April 2000

That shambolic night at Villa Park would be the third of five games in a row where the team failed to score. They lost all but one of them (a 0-0 draw at home to Coventry the only highlight, if you can call a 0-0 draw a highlight), and there was now growing discontent with the manager amongst certain sections of the fans.

We were now once again hovering around the relegation zone, something I hoped the club would avoid this season, but things were not running as smoothly as I'd anticipated, and the attitude amongst supporters was that Dave Jones' off-field problems were beginning to affect his ability to do the job properly.

Early in the season, we had been conceding many goals, but we had also been banging them in at the right end too. Now, that was starting to change, as our ability to score goals had waned, but our predilection for letting them in remained the same. The perfect example of this was a 5-0 thrashing at Newcastle that Sky broadcast live to the nation, and it seemed as though the patience of the supporters was beginning to wear thin, with some of them even calling for the return of Alan Ball as manager.

The board semi-agreed with the fans in as much as Dave Jones' court case was affecting him and his ability to do the job, and they gave him a twelve-month leave of absence so that he could devote all of his time to clearing his name.

The one thing the board didn't agree with the fans on was the person who would take the reins during Jones' sabbatical, and instead of Alan Ball, they opted for former England manager Glenn Hoddle.

Dave Jones described the decision to give him time off as "devastating," and it turned out that when Saints chairman Rupert

Lowe visited Jones at his home to deliver the news, the conversation became quite heated.

Lowe appeared at the press conference to announce the arrival of Hoddle sporting a black eye, and many people assumed that it was a result of his spat with Dave Jones. Despite claiming that it was an injury he picked up playing hockey, it later transpired that Dave Jones' wife had whacked Lowe, but whether it was a hard enough hit to give him a shiner only they will know.

For a club of our stature, the appointment of Glenn looked like a bit of a coup, and the consensus amongst the supporters was that Jones would not be returning if Glenn's tenure turned out to be a success.

Some people argued that appointing Hoddle could be a costly gamble, especially after the circumstances surrounding his dismissal from his previous job as England national team manager.

Problems arose for Glenn when he gave a newspaper interview in which he stated that he believed that disabled people were being punished for sins they had committed in a previous existence.

Glenn was (and still is) deeply religious, and he believed strongly in faith healing (he introduced faith healer Eileen Drury to the England set-up) and reincarnation and his contentious words caused a media storm and a public outcry at the time.

With the Sports Minister and even the then Prime Minister Tony Blair condemning Hoddle's statement, the pressure was mounting on the Football Association to terminate Hoddle's managerial reign.

Hoddle held firm for a while, stating, "My words were taken out of context by the media," and he point blankly refused to resign. In the end though, with pressure mounting from all sides, the FA had no choice but to terminate his contract. Now, after almost a year out, here was a chance to resurrect (no pun intended) his managerial career at Southampton.

Things got off to a good start for Glenn, as the Saints won their first two games under his stewardship (at home to West Ham and away to Sheffield Wednesday), before a run of three defeats in four (including a 7-2 mauling at his former club Tottenham) kept us in trouble at the wrong end of the table.

By the time I made the long trip north to Yorkshire for this match at Bradford, we were a healthy looking eight points clear of our opponents who occupied the last relegation place, so although a draw would do, we could not afford to lose and thus let them close the gap to five points.

Arriving at the city of Bradford itself wasn't exactly a welcoming experience, and having decided that the train journey was too expensive (partly due to the fact that my wife and I was expecting our first baby in the autumn) I decided to travel on one of the official travel club coaches.

The journey was uneventful until we reached the outskirts of Bradford, where a bunch of the surliest and most forthright police officers you could wish to meet greeted us. Our coach had been the first to arrive, but the police informed us that we could not travel any further until all the other coaches had caught up. An idea that seemed a bit over the top considering that we were not local rivals or enemies, but I guess it was just the normal hostile welcome that all southerners get when they arrive in Yorkshire.

For the next twenty minutes, our coach sat stationary on a bridge overlooking the M1 motorway whilst we waited for the other coaches to join us, just so we could have a police escort to the ground.

Bradford is a horrible place, full of deserted and abandoned buildings long since boarded up, and as our coach weaved its way through the maze of grey and grimy streets, I had the feeling that the police had somehow guided us into some post-apocalyptic wasteland.

We arrived at the stadium with no time to find a pub for a pre-match drink, so it was straight into the ground. The stadium is an odd one as sits on the side of a hill, something that allows for spectacular views over the distant Yorkshire Dales.

The away end itself is a curious two-tier affair, which is only a few rows deep and a number of roof supports make viewing the game difficult, although thankfully my seat in the lower tier afforded me a good view of the action.

Of course, for football fans of a certain age, Valley Parade will always be synonymous with the tragedy that struck the club in May 1985, when the main stand caught fire resulting in the deaths of 56 people. It was an awful tragedy at a time when football supporter safety was a minor concern to football clubs in general. The people who died that day paid the price for years of neglect and underfunding in supporter comfort and safety. The only positive thing to come out of the disaster was the sweeping away of years of neglect by football club owners who spent more money on players than they did making sure their supporters were safe and comfortable.

Allowing people to smoke in a wooden grandstand with a tar-covered roof seems almost absurd by today's stringent health and safety standards, but nobody seemed to care back then, but Bradford now has a ground that is much safer than it had on that fateful day in May 1985.

The first half of the match was a tame affair with neither side having the ingenuity to break the deadlock, but 11 minutes into the second half, we got a big slice of good fortune when Chris Marsden's low and wayward shot deflected off the unfortunate Bradford striker Dean Windass and into the net past the wrong-footed goalkeeper.

Then with 15 minutes remaining, Marian Pahars came off the bench and scored within 30 seconds of taking to the field, when he latched onto Kevin Davies' knock down and ran through to score from 20 yards.

Although City pulled one back a couple of minutes later, we held on for a deserved but hard fought three points, which all but confirmed our status as a Premier League club for next season.

The following week, we made sure that there wasn't to be another last day relegation battle when we beat Watford 2-0 at The Dell to make us mathematically secure, which was just as well as we only won one of our final four games.

With Dave Jones still on gardening leave, most fans looked forward to the new season, now that Glenn Hoddle had the chance to work with the squad during the off-season, and, I couldn't wait for the new season to start, although I had something else to look forward to, I was about to become a dad for the first time.

Bouncebackability

Saints 3 Liverpool 3   Premier League   26 August 2000

The first summer of the new millennium saw building work start on the new stadium at St. Marys to much interest and anticipation. Within weeks of the first stand beginning to rise out of the ground, numerous websites appeared containing still photo's of the construction efforts. After a few weeks, the club erected a viewing platform so fans could visit the site and satisfy their curiosity. After years of hoping and waiting, it almost seemed unreal that the club was finally going to get its own brand new home and a stadium that could potentially help the club to go on to greater things other than fighting relegation.

The upshot of this, of course, was that this would be The Dell's final season, and it staged one of the most remarkable comebacks in the clubs history in just the second game of the campaign.

An opening day draw at Derby (where we threw away a two goal lead) was followed by a disappointing reverse at home to Coventry, and then Liverpool came to town and what happened next has gone down in Saints folklore.

Goalkeeper Paul Jones had come in for some criticism from the fans of late, especially for Coventry's winner prior to this game against Liverpool, and Hoddle must have agreed with the supporters, as he dropped Jones in favour of his understudy, Neil Moss for this match.

I can't say that Paul Jones was one of my favourite players, and I never agreed with Dave Jones' decision to sign him from Stockport when he became our manager. We had a perfectly fine goalkeeper in Maik Taylor who was also a big Southampton fan, and it seemed a bit like a new manager surrounding himself with players he was already familiar with as following Paul Jones from Stockport was Lee Todd and he was bloody useless.

To his credit, Jones did win the fans player of the year award in 1998, but despite this, there were just too many occasions where he would drop an absolute clanger that would cost us points.

Neil Moss was an okay understudy, but in this match, he would find himself in the firing line from the early stages, and it wasn't long before he was picking the ball out of the back of the net, and with their fast flowing attacking football, it looked as though they would rack up a hefty score.

The second half started in the same vein, with Liverpool having the majority of the possession and the better scoring chances, whilst we used our pacy players to try to hit them on the counter-attack.

Liverpool eventually turned their possession into goals, as first Sammi Hyypia, and then Michael Owen scored to give them what looked to be a comfortable 3-0 lead going into the final fifteen minutes.

For some fans, the chances of Saints salvaging something from a three-goal deficit in the last quarter-of-an-hour against a team of Liverpool's calibre was slim to nil, and so it wasn't unusual to see some fans making their way towards the exits.

Despite the one-sided scoreline, I didn't want to leave the ground too early, as I know from bitter experience that a football match can be turned on its head in just a few minutes.

The year was 1997, and Saints were playing at home to Newcastle, a game I should have missed as I was suffering from a severe bout of flu, but being a season ticket holder I didn't wasn't to miss a match, so I dragged my aching body to The Dell on a bitterly cold January afternoon.

At this point I want to say that this was proper flu and not man-flu, I had the full-on fever with shivering and a head that felt like I had just gone 12 rounds in a boxing ring with Mike Tyson.

My decision to attend this match despite the fact that I felt like I was going to collapse at any minute, looked to have been a huge mistake as Newcastle stormed into the lead, which they increased to 2-0 with just seven minutes to go.

Feeling as though I was about to pass out, I made my way to the exit safe in the knowledge that the way we had been playing that we would never claw back a two-goal deficit against this Newcastle side.

As I walked through the narrow streets that led away from The Dell towards the city centre, a man walking in the opposite direction spotted my Saints scarf and stopped to ask me the score.

'We're losing 2-0.' I spluttered with a throat that felt like I was trying to swallow sandpaper.

'Oh really?' The man said as a huge smirk spread across his face. I put his reaction down to him being a Pompey fan, and I thought nothing of it until I got home.

Whilst waiting for the kettle to boil in order to make myself a much-needed hot drink, I switched on Teletext to check the scores in the other matches, and that was when my eyes fell upon the final score from The Dell.

Southampton 2-2 Newcastle

Either that's a typo or I'm sicker than I thought, I said to myself, but I checked the goal times, and sure enough, we had managed to score twice in the last few minutes to salvage a draw. It was so disappointed to have missed a great comeback, one that was on par with that 3-1 victory over the Geordies a few seasons back. It also explained the smug knowing smile that the man I met in the street gave me as I walked home. He must have been listening to the radio and had known the score before asking me. The thing is, I never even heard the Saints fans celebrating the goals so bunged up was my head, so I had no inkling. It certainly taught me a lesson, and I vowed that I would never leave a match that early ever again.

So, despite being 3-0 down with less than 20 minutes to go I was going nowhere, and everyone who stayed was rewarded for their loyalty with one of the best comebacks witnessed at The Dell in living memory.

The comeback started when in the 74th minute, Marian Pahars (our Latvian Michael Owen) nodded home at the far post from Jo Tessem's brilliant cross, and from that moment it seemed as though the Saints fans could sense something magical was going to happen.

I could see the Saints players visibly lifted by the roar of the crowd as they surged forward in search of more goals, whilst the Liverpool players, thinking the game won, sat deep.

Their defensive posture seemed to be working as they repelled a couple of Saints attacks before our pressure finally bore fruit when defender Tahar El Khalej stretched just enough to divert James Beattie's flick header past the keeper from 6-yards out.

The Liverpool players were stunned. From a winning position, they were now desperately clinging on for three points, as more and more Saints players joined the attacks on their goal.

Just as it looked as though they would hold out for the win, Matthew Le Tissier thumped a hopeful ball towards the edge of the Liverpool penalty area, where James Beattie and Liverpool's Traore jumped for the ball. It was Traore who jumped the highest, but for some reason, his header went back across the penalty area, where the grateful Pahars found himself unmarked in the six-yard box, and he coolly stroked the ball in from 5-yards out to delirious scenes of celebration around the ground.

As in life, football has a way of levelling things out, a few months later, a team would come back from 3-0 down with half-an-hour remaining against us, and this time the match would not end in a draw.

Misery

Tranmere 4 Saints 3   FA Cup 5th Round Replay   20 February 2001

Our League Cup campaign ended in round three when Coventry came to The Dell and beat us 1-0 with a goal in the last minute of extra-time, a match I only remember because my daughter Charlotte was born a few hours later.

Even though our League cup run had ended at the first hurdle, it looked as though a good FA Cup run seemed to be in the offing when the draws for rounds 3, 4 and 5 gave us home ties against lower league opposition.

In round three, we won a mundane affair against a Sheffield United side that had obviously come to defend in the hope of getting a replay back at Bramall Lane, and it took a penalty from Jason Dodd to see us through.

The fourth round draw paired us with United's cross-town rivals Sheffield Wednesday, in one of those quirks that the FA Cup often throws up, but unlike the game against the Blades, an early goal set us on our way, when Kevin Davies nodded in on 10 minutes.

Despite Wednesday getting an undeserved equaliser midway through the second half, another penalty award gave us the lead once more, when Wednesday's Andy Booth (who had scored their equalising goal) inexplicably handled in the penalty area. Jason Dodd duly dispatched the penalty, just as he had against United.

With the Wednesday players desperately searching for an equaliser, they were leaving plenty of gaps at the back, and in stoppage-time, James Beattie took full advantage to net our third goal and thus ensuring our passage into round five.

The draw for the fifth round paired us with First Division strugglers Tranmere Rovers at The Dell, and this match seemed to be nothing more than a stepping-stone into the quarter-finals.

All the same, those Saints fans who had done their homework on Tranmere would have been aware of the fact that in the 16 months prior to this fixture, Tranmere had actually claimed the scalps of six Premier League sides in various cup competitions.

We never looked like becoming their seventh victim during this match despite Tranmere's fast and furious start in the first five minutes, and it was not long before we started to take control of the match. Our first meaningful attack resulted in a corner which resulted in a goal from a Dean Richards header being ruled out because

Hassan Kachloul was deemed offside, a stupid decision which would not stand nowadays due to the changes in the offside rule regarding players being "active" or not. The match continued with us piling on the pressure whilst at the same time being aware of the threat that Tranmere posed on the counter-attack.

The second half pretty much followed in the same vein as the first, with Saints controlling the game but failing to find that killer final touch in front of goal. The Tranmere players seemed happy to just sit back and hold out for a chance to take us back to Prenton Park for a replay ten days later.

Unlike the games against both Sheffield clubs, Saints were unable to break down an unyielding Tranmere defence, helped as they were by a set of fussy and finicky officials who disallowed another Southampton goal in second half stoppage-time. Wayne Bridge's free kick just outside the penalty area flew straight in but the ref disallowed it due to an alleged foul by Uwe Rosler on the Tranmere goalkeeper. This meant that we had to do the whole thing again nine days later in a replay, but I was still optimistic that we could go to The Wirral and a get a result.

With the match chosen for live television coverage by Sky Sports (probably because they sensed an upset in the making), I opted to watch the match in my local pub rather than undertake the arduous midweek trip to Tranmere, and it turned out to be one of my better life decisions.

With 25 minutes on the clock, Saints were 2-0 to the good and any hope that Sky had of broadcasting an FA Cup upset looked to be fading fast, as we took total control of the game.

Our opener came after 11 minutes when Hassan Kachloul curled the ball into the net from just inside the penalty area, and Jo Tessem added a second on 25 minutes when he found himself completely unmarked in the Tranmere penalty area. On the stroke of half-time,

173

centre-back Dean Richards cemented our superiority when he bundled in a third from close range after some truly comical Tranmere defending.

With the Saints, three goals up and looking comfortable, my attention and that of my friend Mark turned towards acquiring tickets to the quarter-final tie at Liverpool in a couple of weeks time.

Despite the fact that Liverpool were riding high in the Premier League I fancied our chances of progressing to the semi-final, as we had been playing some excellent football, and in the FA Cup, anything can happen, as we were about to discover.

Our drink-fuelled chat turned to the possibility that this could be our year to make it all the way to the FA Cup final, which due to the building of a new Wembley Stadium, would now be played at the Millennium Stadium in Cardiff.

So immersed were we by our dreams of a cup final appearance, that we hardly noticed when Tranmere pulled a goal back just a couple of minutes shy of the hour mark. A familiar face to Saints fans, namely Paul Rideout, scored the goal, which was surely no more than a consolation. Paul had played for the club back in the late eighties, before being seen as surplus to requirements by the Beelzebub Branfoot, who shipped him out at the first opportunity, and boy was he up for revenge.

In a similar vein to our comeback against Liverpool when the fervent Dell crowd helped to inspire the team to salvage something from such a one-sided match, so the Tranmere fans upped the volume considerably as they sensed another giant killing in the offing.

The second goal duly arrived a few minutes later, as our defence gave Paul the freedom of Prenton Park from a corner, and he made no mistake with his header.

It was all Tranmere now, and with the Saints defence seemingly missing in action, Rideout completed a 21-minute hat-trick to level the scores. Not content on scoring three times against his former employers, Rideout completed a memorable night for himself and the Tranmere fans by setting up Barlow for the winner.

It was a humiliating collapse of epic proportions, and despite a late chance to force extra-time that fell to Dean Richards (his desperate lunge at the far post in injury-time did nothing more than raise the heart rates of the Tranmere supporters) the game was up, and we were out of the Cup in humiliating fashion.

Tainted love

Saints 0 Ipswich Town 3   Premier League   2 April 2001

To be fair to the players they did respond in a positive fashion after the Tranmere disaster, with wins at Middlesbrough and Manchester City, two grounds where we have traditionally struggled in the past. For the fans though, the pain from that cup capitulation would linger for a while longer, as when sixth round day came along, we found ourselves without a game.

To fill the void, the club arranged two friendly matches against the city's twin town, the northern French port of Le Havre, with one game at home and one away three days apart, we lost both.

There was one glimmer of hope though, as Matthew Le Tissier continued his rehabilitation from injury with two goals in the reserves 7-0 demolition of Tottenham, a match that Mark and I attended as it was one of the rare times that The Dell actually hosted a reserve team game.

Uwe Rosler and Stuart Ripley also grabbed a brace each and Kevin Davies got the other, in a match that saw Tottenham's goalkeeper Ian Walker totally humiliate himself.

Recently ousted from his position as Tottenham's first choice goalkeeper by Neil Sullivan, Walker had taken to mouthing off in the national press on the morning of the match about how he deserved to be Tottenham's number one goalkeeper. However, it doesn't take a football genius to work out that if you want to be your clubs number one stopper, then letting in seven goals in a reserve team game is not the way to go about making your case.

For Saints, though more trouble was lurking around the corner thanks to the Tottenham manager George Graham, who was coming under increasing pressure from the clubs new owners. He was never a popular choice with Tottenham fans due to the fact that he played and managed their hated rivals Arsenal, and after declaring publicly that he was disappointed with the transfer budget given to him by the clubs new board, he was subsequently dismissed after a fiery meeting.

It came as no surprise when I saw Glenn's name at the top of a list of prospective new Tottenham managers, and I felt it was just a matter of time before he left.

After struggling to beat Everton at home in our next home game, Tottenham announced that they had made a £10 million bid for our centre-back Dean Richards. It was a bid that was seen by many as a sign that Hoddle was going to jump ship and he wanted to take Richards with him.

The audacious bid failed, and Richards signed a two-year contract extension after the Everton game. More good news was to follow for Saints fans when Spurs announced that they would wait until the end of the season before appointing their new manager.

With another free weekend thanks to a round of World Cup qualifiers, Hoddle jets off on holiday, but on his return, news broke that in contradiction to their earlier statement about holding back on their managerial appointment, Hoddle is in fact in talks with Spurs' new owners ENIC.

Amazingly, after only a few hours of talks Hoddle agrees on terms and resigns as Southampton boss and the incriminations begin, with Saints chairman Rupert Lowe accusing Spurs and Hoddle of holding secret talks.

With the club now managerless once again, coaches Stuart Gray and Dennis Rolfe take over the managerial reins until the end of the season, and their first match in charge would be in front of the Sky Sports cameras against Ipswich at The Dell.

After going on a run of seven games without conceding a goal, a run that had stretched over three months, suddenly the roof caved in as Ipswich outplayed us in every department and could have won by a much bigger margin. Defeats against Chelsea, Leeds, and Sunderland at The Dell followed, all without Saints managing to find the back of the net, and a season that began with so much promise was quickly turning into a miserable myopic grind to the finish.

Hoddle left without having completed a single full season in charge, and it was a shocking way to treat a club that had given him a chance to regenerate his managerial career after his controversial departure as England boss. As for the Saints players, well they were quickly taking on the appearance of a team that just wanted the season to finish as soon as possible. Nevertheless, there were still some important games to come, as well as the small matter of saying goodbye to The Dell in only a few weeks time.

The Curtain Falls

Saints 3 Arsenal 2   Premier League   19 May 2001

To this day, I'm not sure how it happened, and I can't recall the exact moment I realised and the cold sweats began, but I had somehow

177

managed to book a family holiday to Cornwall that started on the day of the last ever league game at The Dell.

As oversights go, this was one of my biggest, and as my desperate pleas to delay our journey by a day fell on my wife's deaf ears, I quickly realised that I was going to miss one of the major events in the clubs recent history.

I swapped my precious ticket for this match with another Saints fan in return for a ticket for a home game against Sunderland a few weeks prior to this game. It was scant consolation.

That Sunderland match was a depressing defeat, but the next match at home, the penultimate league match, against Manchester United was a glorious victory, even if we did have a little help from a Wes Brown own goal in a 2-1 win.

There was no getting away from it, The Dell's days were numbered, and for all the excitement of moving into a big new stadium, there were plenty of sad thoughts in relation to the end of The Dell and its history.

So that is why, whilst Saints fans made their way to The Dell to see a competitive fixture for the final time, I was wending my way to a small Cornish village with my wife and daughter for the week. My absence from this match was having an effect on my mood as we travelled through Dorset and Devon, and my mood darkened further when I discovered that the match was not the live broadcast game on Radio Five Live that afternoon.

Out of the range of my local radio station, and this being an age before the mobile internet, I had to rely on the occasional reports from The Dell that Five Live drip-fed me throughout the ninety minutes.

As I assumed when I first discovered that I couldn't go, the match turned out to be a fitting end to over a century of football at one of

England's quaintest old stadiums, as the Saints ran out 3-2 winners courtesy of a stoppage-time winner from who else but Matt Le Tissier.

The fact that we won the match was no consolation for me, and neither was watching the highlights on that night's Match of the Day. I had cocked-up badly, and I hated myself for it, although I would get one more chance to attend a match at The Dell the following Saturday.

In order to allow as many fans as possible to say their own personal goodbyes to The Dell, the club had arranged for an end of season exhibition match against Brighton & Hove Albion, who were chosen because their predecessors Brighton United had been the very first visitors to the stadium when it opened in 1898.

I made sure we left Cornwall early on the Saturday of the Brighton game so as not to miss it, and I arrived in plenty of time to take my seat alongside Mark at the front of the Archer's Road end of the ground.

The match had nothing of the drama of the game against Arsenal the week before, and it took a solitary Uwe Rosler goal to separate the sides, but in truth, the result was only a secondary consideration.

At the final whistle thousands of fans, including myself, ran onto the pitch in celebration. Plenty of people were also on the hunt for souvenirs, and it quickly became a free-for-all, as fans tore up the turf and seats for keepsakes. Mark had managed to bring a small spanner along, and we wasted no time in dismantling our seats so we could take them with us (plenty of other people had the same idea).

It was a strange sight, witnessing grown men, women, and children carrying different parts of the ground home with them, as items including advertising hoardings, a Gents toilet sign, and lumps of turf all made their way out of the ground in the arms of fellow supporters.

For all the emotion on leaving The Dell for pastures new, there was no disguising the fact that the departure of Glenn Hoddle had had a negative impact on the end of the season, with a seven-game winless run only ended by those home wins against Manchester United and Arsenal.

I couldn't wait for the new season to start, as I desperately wanted to see the team run out onto the pitch of their brand new stadium, and also find out who the new manager would be, although rumours abounded that Stuart Gray would be given the job on a permanent basis.

A Friendly German

Bristol City 1 Saints 2   Pre-season friendly   4 August 2001

I and countless other fellow fans had been monitoring the building of the new stadium for the past eighteen months, and the wait to see it and experience it in all its glory was nearly upon us.

As for the new manager, well those rumours turned out to be true, as the club announced in the summer that Stuart Gray had been given the job on a permanent basis, with chairman Rupert Low spouting some nonsense about continuity.

Gray's appointment was not Earth shattering news, nor was it entirely unexpected, and his record as interim manager at the tail end of the previous season hardly inspired confidence.

To celebrate the opening of the new stadium, the club arranged an exhibition game, and I wondered what giants of European football the club had lined up. Would it be Barcelona, Real Madrid, Bayern Munich, or AC Milan? No, it would be Espanyol, who to be fair are from Barcelona, but to be honest not many Saints fans had even heard of them before.

With just the one pre-season home game, Mark and I decided to fill the football gap by attending a couple of our away pre-season friendlies, which is why we ended up at such alluring places as Farnborough and Bristol.

For the trip to Bristol, we decided that travelling by train was the best option, as this allowed both of us to down a few pints on the way, as well as have a pub lunch before making our way to the ground.

It was whilst we were stood on the platform at Southampton central train station waiting for our train to arrive that the day started to take an unusual turn. As the train pulled up, a rather lost looking gentleman wearing a Saints shirt sidled up to us and asked us in a heavy German accent whether this was the right train to Bristol.

We confirmed that it was and all three of us boarded the train and took our seats. Whilst Mark cracked open a couple of cans of lager, I noticed the German guy sitting a few seats further down the train, but I thought nothing more of it.

Upon reaching Bristol, we left the station as we looked around for a decent pub, our German pal latched onto us again. Not wanting to appear unfriendly, we invited him to join us, although we did have a bit of an ulterior motive for the invitation.

For anyone who has arrived for a game at Ashton Gate via the train station will know that it is quite a walk to the ground, so it is advisable to flag down a cab. With an extra person, we could now split the taxi fare three ways rather than two, saving us money and helping our new found German friend reach the stadium safely. It was a classic win-win situation.

Now I have to admit that I cannot remember his name, but I do remember that he told us that he lived in Dusseldorf and he had been following Saints for a number of seasons. He also told us that he always tried to come over to England to watch a couple of Saints games each season, and it's safe to say that this was certainly one trip that he wasn't going to forget in a hurry, and neither would I.

After a pleasant lunch and a few more pints, we decided we'd best make our way to the stadium, and as we had chosen a pub near to the station, it wasn't difficult to find a taxi to take us the two miles or so to Ashton Gate, City's home ground.

The match itself was a typical pre-season game, and goals by Marian Pahars and Dan Petrescu gave us a comfortable 2-1 win. Now, all we had to do was to find our way back to the train station, and that is where our day started to take a turn towards the comical.

Upon leaving the ground, we soon realised that we didn't have a clue how to get back to the train station, and neither Mark or I had made a note of the taxi firm's number, so phoning them up was out of the question.

Fans from both clubs seemed to be heading in all directions and we didn't know which ones to follow, but Mark decided that we should turn left and follow a group of Southampton fans that seemed to look like they knew where they were going.

I pride myself on having a good sense of direction, and I was certain that we were heading in the opposite direction from when we arrived. Unfortunately, my protestations fell on deaf ears, so we persisted in following this group of Saints fans for the next twenty minutes or so.

It was then that I noticed that the urban sprawl was gradually giving way to more rural type surroundings, with pavements becoming grass verges and buildings replaced with trees and shrubbery.

Now call me suspicious if you like, but when you see a road sign up ahead that reads Welcome to Somerset – then you should take that as an indication that you might just be heading in the wrong direction.

Eventually, I managed to convince Mark that we should turn back and start heading the way we came and after another twenty minutes, we ended up back at the now deserted football ground.

With our Teutonic sidekick still in tow (and probably wondering what these two idiot Englishmen were doing) we set about trying to

182

find our way back to the station in what I was certain was the right direction. Although by now we had another problem, time was against us. As in order to get the cheapest train tickets possible, I had ordered them online in advance, and in order to get the best deal, we had to get a specific train at a certain time. If we missed our train, we would have to get a later train and no doubt have to pay for a full price single fare.

With time fast running out panic was beginning to set in, and with no signs showing the way to the station the situation was looking bleak, but then Mark spotted a pub, and our evening was about to take another turn for the worse.

Mark's idea was to go into the pub and call a taxi from there, as they were bound to know a local minicab firm that could come and rescue us. I agreed that his plan seemed to be the best option, not that we had any other option but to wander aimlessly around the streets of Bristol for the rest of our lives.

Marching confidently into the pub we soon realised we had just made a huge mistake, as the pub was full of menacing looking and semi-inebriated Bristol City fans. Our arrival in their pub played out like a scene from an old western movie, where everyone turns around to face the strangers, whilst the background chatter and music stop for dramatic effect.

A chorus of boos broke the ominous silence, as those nearest to us spied our Saints shirts (wearing colours was a great idea), and although I felt the urge to say, "Come on guys it was only a friendly," I decided that this was one of those occasions when you just keep your mouth shut.

Mark quickly locates the card of a taxi firm on the wall by the pub's pay phone and dials the number on his mobile. It's at this point he realises that none of us had noted the name of the pub we are currently standing in, and so he pops outside to check, leaving me with our German friend.

With my heart pounding rapidly I'm desperately hoping that Mark comes back with some good news about a taxi, whilst realising that one word from my German friend could well spell disaster. It was bad enough being in enemy territory without the prospect of a pub full of disgruntled Bristol City fans realising that one of these three stupid looking interlopers was from Germany. The chances of the two of us leaving the pub through one of its windows were increasing by the second, but I like to think that if they were to set upon us that I wouldn't have shouted, "Oh my God lads, he's a German, get him," in order to save my own skin, but I couldn't guarantee it.

Thankfully, whilst thoughts of flying through the air like Superman to the sound of smashing glass raced through my mind, Mark re-enters the pub and tells us that a taxi is on its way in about ten minutes or so. Not wishing to hang around, I usher us all outside quickly and quietly to wait, and after what seemed like an age but was probably no more than a few minutes, the cab arrives and we make it back to the station with about ten minutes to spare.

Upon arriving back at Southampton, we say our farewells to our German friend and he goes off back to his hotel, whilst we recount our story to Mark's girlfriend who has kindly arranged to pick the pair of us up from the station. If only all trips to meaningless pre-season friendlies in far-flung places could be this interesting, but then again perhaps not.

Home Sick

Saints 0 Arsenal 2   Premier League   13 October 2001

Our first game of the new season was away to Leeds. The club had officially requested that they wanted the first fixture away from home, in order to give them an additional week to settle into the new stadium. They needed to settle too, as the game against Espanyol that officially opened the new stadium saw us 4-0 down by half-time. The Spaniards were obviously thinking job done as they took it easy in the second-half and we clawed three goals back to make the scoreline a bit more respectable, but that ropey first-half was a sign of things to come.

I travelled to Elland Road purely because I wanted to keep my own personal little run going of not having missed the opening game of the season since 1991, and I was travelling in hope more than expectation at anything other than a defeat.

Stuart Gray wasted no time dipping into the transfer market after taking over the Saints manager's job on a permanent basis, as he soon splashed out a club record fee of £4 million for Derby's Republic of Ireland midfielder Rory Delap.

Also joining the club during the summer was Swedish midfield playmaker Anders Svensson, who it was hoped would give our midfield the skill and guile missing since Matt Le Tissier stopped playing regularly.

The match itself was a dull one, with Leeds mounting attack after attack with us desperately defending deeper and deeper in a bid to keep them at bay. A tactic that didn't work, as Leeds broke through midway through the second-half, and then added another with less than 10 minutes to go. To compound our misery, centre-back Claus Lundekvam saw red in injury-time.

Chelsea would be the first Premier League visitors to the new stadium, and they wasted no time in showing us just how much of an advantage we had lost when we had said goodbye to The Dell.

The Dell may have been small, but it had a great advantage in that the fans were so close to the action. This gave the ground an intimidating and claustrophobic atmosphere for visiting players.

Now we had switched from the cosy confines of The Dell to the vast expanse of St. Marys, and for visiting players, this venue was much more to their liking, and the Chelsea players certainly seemed to be enjoying themselves when they strolled to a 2-0 win.

A week later and our season started to take on a depressing similarity as I travelled to White Hart Lane to witness our third 2-0 reverse in succession, with defeat to Tottenham. Although we created some chances, our profligacy in front of goal cost us again, causing manager Stuart Gray to start describing our problems as like having a "monkey on our backs."

Unperturbed by our poor start – as a Saints fan I was used to it – I travelled to Bolton the following week for our first visit to the Reebok Stadium. It was a game devoid of any redeeming features until Wayne Bridge's late run down the left set-up Marian Pahars to thrash the ball in from 10 yards out. That goal was enough to secure our first points of the season, and it made the long journey back all the more comfortable.

In true Saints fashion, we failed to capitalise on that hard-earned win at Bolton, by going down 3-1 to Aston Villa at St. Marys live on Sky on a Monday night.

We started the Villa game without our defensive lynchpin Dean Richards who finally completed his protracted on-off transfer to Tottenham for a then club record £8 million fee.

As disappointing as it was to lose a player of Dean's calibre, it was our form at home that was giving cause for concern, yet perversely, our form away from St. Marys was actually beginning to pick up, as a win at Middlesbrough followed on from that win at Bolton.

Yet again we undid all the hard work of winning away by losing at home in the next match as Arsenal came south and left with a 2-0 win, and the fans patience was once again starting to wear thin.

Gray responded to his critics by stating that he had spoken to the chairman about possible transfer targets, but when no new signings materialised, rumours started doing the rounds that the Saints board was holding the money back in order to give it to a new manager to spend.

Can't You Show Me Nothing But Surrender?

Saints 3 Ipswich Town 3   Premier League   24 October 2001

For once the assumptions about the manager's job security proved to be true, and the new managerial appointment wasn't long in coming, as after a 2-0 loss at West Ham (our fifth 2-0 loss in 8 games) Stuart Gray and his assistant Mick Wadsworth were sacked. It later transpired that people in the press had seen former Coventry City manager Gordon Strachan in the director's box at Upton Park alongside the Saints chairman Rupert Lowe. Again, the press boys were spot on, and within 24 hours of the West Ham defeat, Strachan replaced the departing Gray.

The appointment of Strachan wasn't welcomed by all sections of the Southampton fan base, with many questioning why we would appoint a man who had been sacked by Coventry just six weeks previously.

Strachan had been in charge of Coventry since 1996, and despite mixed results, they eventually lost their place in the top tier of English football in 2001, relegation ending a 34-year continuous stay among the elite.

Strachan's popularity with the Coventry fans plummeted in the wake of relegation, but the City board and chairman ignored the negativity and gave him the chance to return City to the top-flight at the first attempt. Unfortunately, early results suggested that a swift return to the Premier League was going to be a tough ask, and eventually, Strachan received his marching orders

This game against a free-scoring Ipswich side seemed to be going according to plan (new boss takes over results improve etc) and at 3-1 up with half-an-hour to go everything seemed rosy. However, the "curse of St. Marys" seemed to strike again, as Ipswich pulled one back on 62 minutes, before tying it up 10 minutes later, and in fairness, they probably should have won the match late on.

Our lack of form at home was perplexing. Surely, the players had had enough time to get used to their new surroundings by now, but whatever the problem was it needed sorting sooner rather than later if we were to avoid fighting another relegation battle.

The most popular theory doing the rounds was that restless Anglo-Saxon spirits had been disturbed during the stadium's construction, whilst a more outlandish theory was the one relating to the origin of the men who worked on the ground.

Construction of the new stadium had unearthed artefacts relating to the ancient Anglo-Saxon settlement of Hamwich, and it was this find that people played on when Saints couldn't win at home, with the explanation that the Anglo-Saxon Gods were angry at the disturbance.

Another more absurd theory was that one of the workers on the new site had buried a Portsmouth shirt somewhere under the stadium. There was no doubt that some of the men who worked on the construction of the stadium originated from Portsmouth, but the idea that one of them would have buried a shirt under the pitch is laughable, let alone the idea that it was somehow affecting results. If there is a Pompey shirt under St. Marys then it is in its rightful place, below Southampton.

Between this match and the following Saturday's trip to face Fulham at Craven Cottage, Strachan dipped into the transfer market, returning to former club Coventry to bolster his defensive options by signing centre-back Paul Williams and full-back Paul Telfer.

Strachan also inherited a deal that had begun prior to his appointment, and that was the signing of Ecuadorian striker Agustin Delgado from Mexican side Necaxa for £3.2 million. The deal seemed a strange one, as Delgado was carrying a knee injury that was severe enough for him to fail the medical that all footballers undertake before signing for a new club. However, he would return to South America for a World Cup qualifier with his home nation, before undergoing a knee operation in early November.

There was no doubt about his goal scoring talent though if the musical montage that was played on the giant screens before the kick-off of the Ipswich match was anything to go by. His goal scoring exploits with both club and country seemed to be just what we needed to bolster a shot shy attacking force, but it would be three months before we got the chance to see him in action.

The trip to Craven Cottage was another fruitless one, and in typical Saints style, after Beattie equalised an earlier Steed Malbranque strike, we allowed Fulham and that man Malbranque to restore their lead within seconds of the restart.

Fulham were far the better side, although we could have gained something from the game had Pahars not fluffed a good opportunity, and we had a good shout for a penalty turned down. To be fair, we did not really deserve anything from the match and I found myself joining in with a group of other fans in a chorus of "you're not fit to wear the shirt" at the end of the game, such was my anger at the players perceived lack of effort.

The fitness of the players was something that Strachan had promised to deal with and he wasted no time in putting the squad through their paces in training, and in direct opposition to the St. Marys ground staff, Strachan ordered some training to take place on the pitch rather than at the training ground.

The idea behind this change was to get the players used to playing at the new stadium, and whether it was this piece of Strachan psychology, or the white witch the club employed to lift the Anglo-Saxon curse, but we finally managed to win a home game.

Football is a very superstitious game, and fans and players alike have their own superstitions and rituals that they believe can affect the outcome of the match. Hokum I know, but we all do it, I myself have worn lucky pants, lucky socks and walked a certain route to the stadium all because we won a match or went on an unbeaten run previously.

It is with this in mind that it came as no great surprise when the club announced in the local press that they had decided to employ the services of a white witch. It seemed as though the club was taking at least one of the "curse" theories seriously (obviously not the Pompey shirt one) and the witch was hired to exorcise the Anglo-Saxon demons that were plaguing the club.

Whatever it was that she did, it seemed to work, as Charlton Athletic discovered when they made their first visit to St. Marys at the end of November. In front of a new record crowd of 31,198 who made a tremendous noise, a single Marian Pahars goal just before the hour mark was enough to register our first win in our new surroundings. Moreover, if we needed any further proof that the Anglo-Saxon gods had been appeased it came in the 89th minute when a Charlton shot hit the post and bounced to safety, much to the collective gasps of the home support, players, and manager.

Freed from our superstitious burdens we then went on to win our next two home games all without conceding a single goal, as both Sunderland and Spurs left empty handed, and with our away form staying strong, we shot up the table.

Happy New Year

Chelsea 2 Saints 4   Premier League   1 January 2002

Going into this match, Chelsea had only conceded seven goals in nine home games this season, and had just beaten second-placed Newcastle 2-1 at St. James Park, three days previously. Not to mention the fact that they had scored nine goals in their last two home games, a 5-1 win over Bolton, which followed a 4-0 undressing of Liverpool just days before. Therefore, it was looking like it was going to be a long afternoon, similar to my previous away day and a trip to Old Trafford where I witnessed a 6-1 humbling, however, this is Southampton, and we never normally take much notice of the form book.

I'm not sure if the Chelsea players had been on the beer on New Year's Eve but they were lacklustre early on and we took a shock lead on 7 minutes when James Beattie thundered in a 35-yard free-kick into the top corner.

That goal seemed to sting the Chelsea players into action, and for the next few minutes, there was constant pressure on our goal as Chelsea threw men forwards. Their reward for all this pressure was an equaliser midway through the half when Eidur Gudjohnsen was quickest to react when Paul Jones failed to hold onto Jimmy Floyd Hasselbaink's header.

In fact, Hasselbaink's pace and strength were causing us all kinds of problems, and he could have secured a first-half hat-trick if it wasn't for some wayward finishing. In the end, he had to settle for just a solitary goal, which came on the stroke of half-time when he slipped away from his marker Claus Lundekvam, to slot home from Gudjohnsen's neat pass.

As a Southampton fan, being a goal behind at half-time away from home usually means a certain defeat, and going into this match, we hadn't actually won away from home after being behind at the break for eight long years.

Today just happened to be the day when that long barren run ended, as at the start of the second half we took the game to Chelsea and it wasn't long before Marian Pahars levelled the scores. Marian latched onto Paul Williams' long low ball out of defence, before leaving John Terry in his wake and finishing neatly with his right foot.

"This won't last!" I said to Mark after we had finished celebrating, but my lack of faith proved to be wrong as we ended up scoring twice more to seal a memorable away win at star-studded Chelsea.

Chris Marsden was the man who put us in front after he ghosted unmarked into the Chelsea 6-yard box to nod home Telfer's corner after Frank Lampard had inadvertently flicked it on at the near post.

Now we had to weather another wave of Chelsea attacks, but with a pacy front line, we could hit them on the counter-attack, and it was from one of those attacks where James Beattie sealed a famous win with less than twenty minutes to go. It was a sensational volley from a Pahars cross, and it sparked pandemonium in the away section, as we all celebrated an unlikely three points against one of the top teams in the league.

There was no time to dwell on that famous win, as in just a few days, we faced a rather tricky looking FA Cup Third Round tie at lowly Rotherham United, and with the Tranmere disaster from the previous season still fresh in everybody's minds, we could take nothing for granted.

Now, Saints and Rotherham had little history, with matches between the sides rarer than an MP keeping their election promise. This would be the first meeting between the two clubs in the FA Cup, and the first since Rotherham knocked us out of the League Cup in 1983.

Sadly, they would knock us out here too, on a bitterly cold mid-January evening after the original tie had to be postponed due to a frozen pitch. I had a ticket for the original tie, due to be played on a Saturday afternoon, but unable (and partly unwilling) to secure time off work to go to the mid-week rescheduling I stayed home. My mate Mark was not so lucky and had the misfortune of travelling back from Yorkshire on a freezing cold night, whilst I went shopping with the wife and followed the game on the radio. It was bitterly disappointing to lose in the third round to a lower league side but I think, in fact, I know, that we would all have felt better if we knew what was coming in 12 months time.

Just Like Watching Brazil

Ipswich Town 1 Saints 3   Premier League   2 March 2002

Despite that loss to Rotherham, Saints manager Gordon Strachan secured the Manager-of-the-Month award for January, which was down in no small part to our fine league form that had seen us move away from the relegation places.

A 2-0 home win over Liverpool followed that mauling of Chelsea, which helped us up to twelfth in the table, and despite a 3-1 home loss to Manchester United, we went to Anfield and held Liverpool to a one-all draw.

We finished the month with a convincing 2-0 win over West Ham in front of another record crowd at St. Marys of 31,879 and then followed that up with a handy and unexpected point at Arsenal at the beginning of February.

We had been playing some really neat football of late, and no more so than on this trip to sunny Suffolk to face an Ipswich side that was in desperate need of the points in order to ease their own relegation fears.

We found ourselves six points clear of the relegation places going into this match, but just one point ahead of a very inconsistent Ipswich side that had just shipped six goals in their previous home game against Liverpool.

I travelled to Ipswich fearing that we may well be on the receiving end of a backlash to that 6-0 defeat, coupled with the fact that our record at Portman Road wasn't a good one, and to make things even more difficult, both James Beattie and Marian Pahars were absent through injury, as was skipper Jason Dodd.

This meant we took the field with a bit of a patched up side, although it meant that recent signing Brett Ormerod could stake a claim for a regular first-team place. Strachan had signed Brett from Blackpool for £1.5 million back in October, and now this was his chance to shine.

The first half of this match gave no indication of the drama that was to unfold in the second forty-five minutes, as this was a classic example of a game of two halves.

The scoring commenced in style when Rory Delap's low drive from just outside the penalty area flew into the net via a deflection, and it was 2-0 ten minutes later when Brett Ormerod raced on to Matt Oakley's well-weighted through ball to fire in his first Premier League goal.

The best goal was yet to come though, as Chris Marsden scored the goal for which he will always be remembered (in Southampton anyway), which helped to restore our two-goal lead after Finidi George had pulled a goal back for Ipswich.

With little over two minutes of the match remaining, Chris received the ball on the left wing just a few yards inside the Ipswich half. With no one around him, Chris set off on a run towards goal, and with no teammates to pass to; he just kept going and going. Confronted by two Ipswich defenders closing him down he dealt with them with a quick dip of the shoulder as he surged towards the edge of the Ipswich penalty area.

His Volant-like run inside the penalty area took him past two more Ipswich defenders before leaving him to face the onrushing Ipswich goalkeeper. In many one-on-one situations like this, a player often panics and either hits the ball at the keeper or else miles over the bar, even more so if they're not a striker. Not our Chris, as he jinked past the goalkeeper before sliding the ball almost nonchalantly into the empty net from 10-yards out. It was an amazing goal of pure quality and not unlike the goal John Barnes once scored for England against Brazil in the mid-80s, you will find both goals on YouTube and they are well worth searching for.

After that win at Ipswich, Saints would draw the next four games as they continued to look over their shoulders at the relegation scrap going on below. In fact, we would only win one more game before the visit of Newcastle in the final game (a 2-0 win over Derby at St. Marys at the start of April) however, thanks to the continued poor form of the teams already in the relegation zone, Saints were never really in serious danger of going down. In fact, we finished in mid-table, nine points clear of the relegation zone, despite only winning one of our last four matches.

There would be a sad and sentimental farewell at the season's end, as we said goodbye to club legend Matthew Le Tissier after he announced his retirement from professional football earlier in the season.

As a thank you for his years of loyal service, the club granted him a testimonial match, against an England select XI, where Matt would play 45 minutes for each team.

It was an emotional night for everyone concerned, as we said a collective farewell to a player who had served up some stunning goals and entertainment over the years, as well as almost saving us single-handedly from relegation on a number of occasions.

In an age where footballers leave clubs after only a few months, Matt never left Saints, even when he had the chance (offers from Chelsea, Tottenham and Liverpool were all rejected) as he said he'd rather be a big fish in a small pond than vice-versa.

Southampton had been lucky when it had come to player loyalty during the 90's and into the new millennium as both Francis Benali and Jason Dodd remained one-club men throughout their careers. How we can dream about that happening again, but sadly, I don't think it ever will.

The Beat Goes On

Saints 4 Fulham 2   Premier League   27 October 2002

During the summer of 2002, the FIFA World Cup takes place in Japan and South Korea, and the upshot of the tournament taking place in the Far East was the novelty of breakfast time kickoffs.

I remember how weird it felt watching England play Brazil at half-past six in the morning. It was certainly a novelty watching the England team falter at the quarter-final stage once again, whilst eating breakfast in bed, although the downside was cleaning up after I spewed half-chewed cornflakes across the bed sheets when a Michael Owen goal gave us the lead midway through the first half.

Just as it appeared as though England would make it to half time in the lead, Brazil equalised two minutes into stoppage-time thanks to a goal from Rivaldo.

Worse was to come in the second half, however, as Brazil took the lead in almost comical fashion. David Seaman was an accomplished goalkeeper, don't get me wrong, but he did seem to have a habit of letting in goals that were punted towards him from distance.

The first of these was when he was playing for Arsenal in the 1995 UEFA Cup Winners Cup final against Real Zaragoza. A hopeful last-ditch punt towards the goal by former Spurs player Nayim totally bamboozled David Seaman, and the ball flew in over his head despite his despairing lunge, and history was about to repeat itself in this match.

It began when the referee awarded Brazil a rather soft free kick about thirty-five yards from goal.

Ronaldinho struck the ball with some force, and at first, it looked as though the shot was going to go way over the bar. Then the ball began to dip, but even so, it still looked as though it was going to be a straightforward catch for Seaman. From then on, everything seemed to happen in slow motion, from Seaman's panicky backpedalling run to the ball arching towards the top of the net. With Seaman no more than a yard off his line the ball dipped into the net between the crossbar and Seaman's hand, giving Brazil a 2-1 lead they never looked like relinquishing, and England was out of another tournament.

Brazil's semi-final opponents would be Turkey, and most people agreed that England had blown their best chance of getting to a World Cup Final since their semi-final penalty loss to West Germany back in 1990.

Back at St. Marys, and Gordon Strachan obviously thought that he had his squad spot-on, with the only major signing of the summer being Swedish centre-back Michael Svensson. This obdurate Scandinavian defensive enforcer was lovingly nicknamed "killer" by the fans at his previous club Troyes of France, due to his uncompromising style. Saints fans would swiftly take up this nickname too.

This season would also see the introduction of the dreaded "transfer window", where clubs had only until the 31st August in which to sign contracted players, after that, only those players out of contract could be signed. The window would open for one month on the 1st January then that was your lot as far as signing contracted players was concerned. As is typical, the rule makers seemed to think that this would help to even up the playing field, but all it did was to jack-up the prices of even the most mediocre players, something that favoured the wealthier clubs.

On the pitch, and it was to be our customary slow start to the season, with a dull 0-0 home draw against Middlesbrough at St. Marys on the opening day. A 3-0 drubbing at Liverpool a week later followed this up, and it wasn't until our fifth match that we registered our first three points of the season, thanks to a controversial penalty by Marian Pahars in the home game against Everton, a match where the visitors missed a hatful of chances to win.

In one of those weird twists of fate that football sometimes throws up, Tranmere travelled south to play the first ever cup match at St. Marys. Tranmere, of course, were the last team to play a cup match at The Dell two seasons ago, where they drew 0-0 before recovering from a three-goal deficit in the replay to win 4-3.

There was to be no repeat of that fiasco this time, as the Saints dispatched the Rovers from the competition in spectacular fashion, with Chris Marsden's goal after only 16 seconds setting us on the way to a 6-1 victory. That Marsden goal from the kick-off was the fastest by a Saints player since 1954 when Tommy Mulgrew found the net after a mere 15 seconds, and it is still the fastest goal from the kick-off at St. Marys in a competitive match.

Striker Brett Ormerod would score a hat trick in that League Cup match, and he would score two in the next league match three days later. That 2-0 victory over Manchester City would be the first of three consecutive wins, culminating in this 4-2 win over Fulham. A 1-0 win at Aston Villa sandwiched in between.

Saints would make a disastrous start to this match, falling 2-0 behind inside 25 minutes in a match played in gale-force winds. Yet, Saints would pull themselves level by the break, thanks to a brace by James Beattie, the first from the penalty spot after a handball, then he leapt highest at the far post from Fabrice Fernandes' pinpoint cross.

At the start of the second half, Beattie carried on where he left off at the end of the first, scoring with another header, this time from an Anders Svensson free-kick in the 53rd minute. Brett Ormerod would round off the scoring on a remarkable afternoon with his sixth goal in four games. With Ormerod and Beattie forging a strong striking partnership in attack, and with the two Svensson's, Anders and Michael, controlling the midfield and defence respectively, the fans were starting to think that this squad had the makings of something special.

Just a Little Bit of History Repeating

Saints 1 Millwall 1   FA Cup 4th Round   25 January 2003

This would be the only cup tie that I would manage to get to this season, yet I was to miss its most pivotal moment, and it was quite possibly the most pivotal moment of the entire season because, without it, none of what happened afterwards would have been possible.

The Third Round of the FA Cup had given us a plum home tie against the hated Tottenham, which saw the return of Glenn Hoddle just three days after they had played at St. Marys in the Premier League (a match we won 1-0). That win propelled us to sixth place in the table, heady heights indeed, and now we were all up for ending Tottenham's FA Cup run too.

In the previous encounter, the two teams appeared evenly matched, but in this game broadcast live on BBC 1, it seemed as though there was an almighty chasm between the respective squads.

The dramatic changes in my life – I was now separated from my wife and I had recently been given sole custody of my daughter – meant that my chance of attending matches in person during the second half of the season, were looking slim, but at least I could watch this match from the comfort of my armchair.

Saints gained the upper hand from the kick-off, and just 14 minutes in Saints won a free on the edge of the Spurs penalty area for a foul on Wayne Bridge.

The kick was well within the range of James Beattie, and his fierce drive bounced in front of the Spurs keeper Kasey Keller, hitting his chin, and bouncing just far enough away to allow Michael Svensson to slide in and prod the ball home.

Any Saints fan fearing a Tottenham fight back at the commencement of the second-half were going to have those doubts quashed within ten minutes of the restart, as first Jo Tessem and then Anders Svensson added to the first-half Michael Svensson strike to end the game as a contest.

Saints were now playing with a swagger that matched their position of sixth place in the table, and they could have quite easily have added to their goal tally before James Beattie rounded off the scoring with the fourth twelve minutes from time. That goal was the signal for the Tottenham fans to leave in their droves, and they skulked towards the exits with chants of "It's just like watching Brazil..." from the Saints fans ringing in their ears. It was a glorious evening to be a Southampton fan, yet things would be very different three weeks later when Millwall came to St. Marys for a fourth round tie.

With my daughter spending the day with her mother, I had the luxury of making it to what appeared to be a routine fixture against lower league opposition, and I took my place in the Chapel Stand with my pal Mark and his girlfriend Amy for company.

After the thrashing of Tottenham in the previous round, the thought of facing a mid-table side from the division below did not seem to hold much fear, however, this is Southampton and they never do things the easy way if there's a chance to make a meal out of it.

The league fixtures that took place between the rout of Tottenham and this match were a mixed bag. A 2-2 draw at Middlesbrough had sent us to the dizzying heights of fifth in the table, but this masked the fact that we threw away a 2-0 lead with seventeen minutes to go.

Then a week later, Liverpool came to St. Marys and left with all three points in a 1-0 win, our first home defeat of the campaign, and certainly not ideal preparation for this cup-tie, and to make matters worse we were suffering something of an injury crisis too.

With our Ecuadorian striker Augustin Delgado now seemingly permanently injured, and without another long-term absentee in Marian Pahars, our strike force was looking a bit thin, whilst the defence didn't look in great shape either, with both Wayne Bridge and Claus Lundekvam unavailable for this match.

This meant a recall for old-stager, Francis Benali at left back, for what would be his first appearance at St. Mary's Stadium, whilst Paul Williams would also return to the starting line-up in place of the injured Lundekvam.

There were plenty of reasons for Saints fans to feel antipathy towards Millwall in this tie, as they had amongst their ranks, former Portsmouth player-manager Steve Claridge in their starting line-up, and he was to come in for plenty of stick this particular afternoon.

Despite some early pressure, Saints could not find the net, and they had several attempts on goal either blocked or saved as Millwall defended bravely.

It was shaping up to be one of those games where one side has all the chances, fails to score, then the opposition goes down the other end and scores with their first shot on target, and that's exactly what happened.

Of course, the Millwall goalscorer had to be the aforementioned Steve Claridge, who was given the freedom of our penalty area by the makeshift defence to slot home a somewhat scuffed shot past Niemi. Having been on the receiving end of plenty of abuse from the Southampton supporters Claridge took great delight in celebrating his goal in front of the Northam end by turning around and pointing to the name on the back of his shirt.

This performance was turning out to be the complete opposite of the Tottenham game only three weeks before, everything in that match we did well we were now doing wrong in this one.

To make matters worse, our main goal threat James Beattie had to go off injured, and he was replaced by the largely out of favour Kevin Davies. Kevin had hardly played for the Saints since Gordon Strachan's arrival, and it appeared that Strachan didn't rate the player (in fact Kevin had spent some time on loan at Millwall back in September) but here he was given the task of salvaging something from this match.

On a personal level, I could not see us salvaging a draw from this match, and as the clock showed that the ninety minutes were up, I made my way down to the concourse to make use of the toilet facilities.

What happened next would be the pivotal moment of this cup run and perhaps the season. As I stood at the urinal, doing what I needed to do after a few pints of lukewarm stadium lager, there was an almighty roar from those still sat in their seats within the stadium bowl. Leaving the toilet block, I met my friend Mark and his girlfriend Amy who confirmed that we had indeed equalised with only a few seconds of stoppage-time remaining.

This one moment would have older fans harking back to 1976 and a third-round tie at The Dell against Aston Villa, where, losing 1-0 in injury-time, Hugh Fisher had equalised, Saints won the tricky replay and went on to Wembley to lift the cup. This time Kevin Davies just happened to be in the right place at the right time to slam home the last-gasp equaliser, yet the replay at Millwall ten days later was certainly not going to be any easier.

Cup Fever

Saints 2 Wolverhampton 0   FA Cup Round 6   9 March 2003

The replay was a tough contest and went all the way to extra-time before Matthew Oakley scored his second goal of the night in the last couple of minutes of the first extra-time period to secure our passage through to round five.

For Oakley, it would be a great night, as he had already scored to put us ahead in the first half of normal time, only for Millwall to level things up before the break. That is the way the scoreline stayed, until Oakley's extra-time winner and although nothing like their third round performance against Spurs, Saints had proved that they had enough about them to be able to grind out a win in difficult circumstances.

Another side from the First Division (now The Championship) was to be Southampton's opponents in the fifth round. Norwich City would be the visitors to St. Marys as Saints received their third consecutive home draw in the competition.

Due to my personal situation, I had to make do with following the Norwich match on the radio, something I hate doing, but it was Hobson's choice, as I had neither the money nor the time to attend the match, and it wasn't a fixture deemed worthy of live television coverage.

It seemed from early on, that Norwich had come to defend, in the hope of earning a replay at home or maybe with the chance of nicking an unlikely goal on the counter-attack.

Their stifling tactics seemed to be working as the Saints players struggled to break down a resolute Norwich defence, and chances for both teams were limited to speculative long-range efforts.

The second-half started in the same vein, although it was Norwich who almost took the lead when McVeigh's shot came back off the post. This narrow escape seemed to stir the Saints players into action, and within a couple of minutes, we took the lead when Anders Svensson produced a neat finish after some excellent work down the left-hand side by the tireless Chris Marsden.

Before the cheers had the chance to fully subside, it was 2-0, when Jo Tessem scored with his first touch after coming on as a substitute for the tiring James Beattie. That knocked the stuffing out of Norwich after going down to ten men with just a few minutes to go, the game was over as a contest, and we could look forward to Monday's quarter-final draw.

That quarter-final draw paired us with Wolverhampton Wanderers, again at home, and it meant a return to Southampton for a certain former manager, Dave Jones for the first time since his unceremonious departure back in 2000.

The match was live on Sky and had a 4 o'clock kick-off time, so by the time the players took to the field, we already knew the results of the three other quarter-final fixtures.

This was the season when second-tier teams would excel in the competition and two of the four semi-finalists were First Division sides Watford and Sheffield United, whilst the other quarter-final tie between Chelsea and Arsenal needed a replay.

As with the previous two rounds, the visitors did their best to remain defensive whilst trying to hit us with a speedy counter-attack, and in a half of few chances, the better ones fell to Wolves. Thankfully, Anti Niemi in the Southampton goal was up to the task and when the half-time whistle blew, we were grateful to go in still goalless.

After what was probably a bit of a half-time talking to from Strachan, the Saints players came out for the second-half a bit more fired up, and within a few minutes of the restart, Beattie narrowly missed a chance to put us in front when he somehow contrived to head over from 2-yards out.

The opening goal was not long in coming, however, when a corner from the left from Tessem found an unmarked Chris Marsden in the penalty area. Unfortunately, Chris had his back to the goal, but somehow he managed to hook the ball back over his shoulder with his left foot and it found its way in past a flummoxed Wolves defence and goalkeeper. To say it was a spectacular bicycle-kick is probably being a bit kind, as Chris's body never actually left the ground, his right foot remaining on the turf, but either way, it was a much-needed breakthrough.

If the first goal had a hint of good fortune about it then the second was just pure luck, as Tessem whipped in a right-wing cross, Beattie got ahead of his marker and took a wild swing at the ball, missed it completely, and ball ricocheted in off the unfortunate Wolves captain Paul Butler and into the net.

The last ten minutes or so were comfortable, despite Wolves desperately pushing forward in the hope of salvaging something, but as the final whistle blew, we all knew that we could bask in the glow of having reached our first FA Cup semi-final since 1986.

Everybody Wants to Rule the World

Saints 2 Watford 1   FA Cup Semi-Final   13 April 2003

FA Cup semi-finals are in my opinion one of the worst days on the football calendar, because of the mixture of emotions that the fans of the four teams suffer from in the hours leading up to kick-off. If your team loses a semi-final, it can be worse than actually losing the final, as you have seen your team get this far but fail at the penultimate hurdle. People remember Cup final runners-up, but nobody remembers losing FA Cup semi-finalists. For me, the only way I was going to enjoy FA Cup semi-final day was when the final whistle blew and we had won the match. It was going to be a long nerve-shredding day.

When Southampton reached their previous FA Cup semi-final back in 1986 my passion for all thing Saints was not at its peak, and I kind of knew that we had little to no chance of beating that great Liverpool team of the time (so it proved as we lost 2-0, although we took them to extra-time).

However, I do remember being upset at losing the 1984 FA Cup semi-final to Everton, a match I listened to on the radio, but for some reason, the 1986 semi seemed to pass me by. There was no chance that I would miss the 2003 semi-final, although I wasn't able to get a ticket to the match, so I had to make do with purchasing a ticket that allowed me to watch the match in The Dell bar, the Saints fans social club. They were showing the match on a big screen, and although I could have watched it at home or down the pub, I thought that being able to watch the match at St. Marys Stadium was the next best thing to being at Villa Park in person.

Apart from the distance and the hassle that both sets of fans had of getting transport to Birmingham on a Sunday, older Saints fans wasted no time in denouncing Villa Park as a bit of a jinxed venue for the Saints. Apparently, Southampton had played two FA Cup games at Villa Park as the neutral venue(they had lost the 1963 semi-final there, and also a quarter-final second replay in 1923), so in order to reach the final, another cup jinx would need to be overcome.

Saints went into this game with yet another mini injury crisis on their hands, and without the injured Jason Dodd and goalkeeper Anti Niemi things were looking less comfortable for us by the minute. Niemi's absence was a particularly bad blow as he had been in outstanding form this season, and with Watford seemingly banging in the goals in the weeks prior to this match (they had won 7-4 at Burnley the week before I seem to recall) the match had a much more even feel to it all of a sudden.

The match didn't start well for the Saints, with Watford nearly scoring from a free-kick in the opening few minutes, and it took us awhile to get a foothold in the match. Semi-finals are rarely classics as there is too much at stake. In fact, Saints didn't have an attempt on target until three minutes before half-time, when good work down the right by Anders Svensson set up Chris Marsden to chip a lovely lofted ball into the box from the byline, his target being Brett Ormerod, and his neat header beat the keeper to give us the lead.

Right at the start of the second-half, it should have been 2-0 when Beattie's cross from a half-cleared corner was met by the head of the centre-back Michael Svensson, but he couldn't direct his free header anywhere other than straight at the keeper.

That let off seemed to inspire the Watford players and they surged forward in search of an equaliser. A few desperate tackles and clearances kept them at bay, although there was a heart-stopping moment when Paul Jones had to tip a Watford header onto the bar.

With 12 minutes to go we were holding on, and that was when Strachan decided to make a change, replacing Anders Svensson with Rory Delap, and Delap was straight into the action, as he helped to set up the second and decisive goal.

Delap's well-timed tackle sent the ball to Ormerod, whose run down the right took him clear of a couple of Watford defenders. Accompanying him on his run was James Beattie who had the foresight to scamper through the middle. Ormerod spotting his man wasted no time in delivering a hard low cross into the penalty area, and with two defenders marking him, it seemed as though his chances of receiving the ball were slim. However, somehow all three men and the ball ended up in the back of the net, with Beattie claiming the goal, although it would later go down as an own goal by one of the Watford defenders. No matter, it was 2-0 Saints with ten minutes to go, and jubilation in The Dell bar was unrestrained, as it was amongst the Saints fans at Villa Park.

Watford would set up a tense finale with a goal three minutes from time, but despite throwing players forward in a desperate bid to force the game into extra-time, the Saints makeshift defence held firm, and we were in the FA Cup Final.

The walk back to the bus stop from the stadium was a memorable one, as there seemed to be people everywhere celebrating, singing, and dancing. Passing motorists honked their horns in celebration at anyone they could see wearing Saints colours.

For me, the celebrations had a hint of regret, as being a season ticket holder at the start of the season meant that I would have been eligible for a final ticket, but having had to give it up due to my difficult home life, I knew that I would have to make do with watching the match at home.

You Can't Always Get What You Want

Saints 0 Arsenal 1   FA Cup Final   17 May 2003

So here we were, at our first FA Cup final since 1976. After a couple of semi-final defeats in the 80s, cup runs for Saints usually got no further than the quarter-finals, but now we had a chance of getting our hands on only our second ever piece of major silverware.

The opposition in Cardiff would be Arsenal, who had dispatched a plucky Sheffield United side in their semi-final. They also dispatched Saints 6-1 at Highbury in a league fixture just ten days before, which was a humiliating capitulation against our forthcoming cup final opponents, and it did nothing to boost the fans hopes of witnessing Saints lift the trophy.

In fact, our form after the semi-final win was poor. After a 3-2 win at home to Leeds the weekend immediately after the Villa Park semi, Saints could only muster a solitary point from the next four games (a dire 0-0 draw at home to Bolton), although in fairness, three of those four games were away from home.

As great as it was to be in our first FA Cup final in 27 years I couldn't help but feel slightly cheated that it wasn't going to be played at Wembley, and I'm sure many other Saints fans felt the same way.

Wembley needed rebuilding, that was much was certain, as it had become more of a national embarrassment rather than a national stadium. Old and antiquated the stadium suffered from terrible sight lines after its conversion to an all-seater stadium in the early 1990's.

The England national team said a rather meek goodbye by losing their last two competitive games under the shadows of the twin towers to Scotland and Germany respectively, both by a 1-0 scoreline.

With no national stadium, the England national team went on the road, playing their home games at various grounds across the country (including St. Marys Stadium), which was a refreshing change, and gave more people the chance to see the England team than usual, but cup finals had to be switched to The Millennium Stadium in Cardiff.

Not having the money to buy a ticket from a tout at a hugely inflated price, it was a few beers in front of the television for me, although being in charge of my young daughter meant keeping the drinking to a minimum.

There were two big talking points pre-match, with the biggest being the inclusion of 21-year-old right-back Chris Baird, not just in the squad, but actually in the starting line-up. Chris had only started one game for the first-team, and now here he was starting in the FA Cup Final.

The second talking point was the closure of the Millennium Stadiums retractable roof, due to the typical wet Welsh weather outside, which would make this final, the very first FA Cup Final played indoors.

The match itself nearly got off to the worst possible start when Thierry Henry ghosted past a static Saints defence in the opening thirty seconds. Saints centre-back Claus Lundekvam pulling Henry's shirt slowed his run into the box, and if the Frenchman had gone down in the penalty area, then surely the referee would have no option but to award a penalty and dismiss Lundekvam.

Thankfully, Henry didn't go down and instead, he used his strength to fend off the attentions of Lundekvam and get a low shot in on goal. A shot that Niemi deflected wide with his legs for an Arsenal corner, it was a fortunate escape.

Saints were struggling to contain a rampant Arsenal side; a side that contained two of the best-attacking players in Europe, the aforementioned Thierry Henry, and also the Dutch international striker Dennis Bergkamp. And it was Bergkamp who nearly gave Arsenal the lead in the seventh minute when his shot was cleared off the line by Baird. A few minutes later Henry hit a weak shot straight at Niemi when it looked easier to score. Could the Saints hold out against this attacking onslaught?

Yes they could, and it wasn't long before the Saints players began to gain a foothold in the match, and they even carved out a number of chances, with the best one being a Chris Baird long range effort that swerved and curled, forcing the Arsenal goalkeeper David Seaman to make a full-length diving save.

From then on, the game began to turn into something of a midfield battle, with neither side really creating many clear-cut chances. There have been many classic FA Cup finals in the past, but this wasn't shaping up to be one of them.

Strachan had decided to go defensive with his tactics (probably because of that 6-1 mauling at Highbury ten days before) and although it worked in nullifying the Arsenal attack, the downside was that it stifled our midfield creativity and attacking options.

Our dogged defending seemed to be working, and it looked as though we would make it to half time at 0-0, but just as we were looking comfortable, Arsenal got the breakthrough their attacking play deserved.

Henry received a pass from Ray Parlour, before setting Bergkamp free down the right with an exquisite pass. Bergkamp, in turn, fed the ball to Ljungberg, whose shot was blocked. Unfortunately for us, the ball rebounded to Pirès (who had scored a hat-trick in that 6-1 league encounter), who took one touch to set himself, and another to fire the ball in at the near post despite Niemi's best efforts to keep it out.

That goal seemed to rock the Southampton defence, and I watched opened mouthed as the Arsenal forwards poured forwards once more, and it took yet another last-ditch clearance off the line to prevent Bergkamp from extending Arsenal's lead.

The second half was only a few minutes old when Arsenal squandered another gilt-edged chance to extend their lead when Freddie Ljungberg hit his shot into the side netting when it looked easier to score.

If luck was keeping the score down to a solitary goal, then luck deserted us a few minutes later when goalkeeper Anti Niemi collapsed in agony after taking a goal kick. It was a game ending calf injury, and he hobbled off and replaced by substitute goalkeeper Paul Jones.

The rest of the match saw Saints desperately trying to find an unlikely equaliser, with Arsenal content to hit us on the counter-attack. Brett Ormerod had a shot from a tight angle saved with just a few minutes left on the clock, and with that, Arsenal seemed to shut-up shop, their players' content to keep the ball in the corner at the Saints end of the stadium.

There would be one last opportunity for a Saints equaliser when they managed to break free and force a corner with the game now deep into stoppage-time.

Matt Oakley's corner found an almost unmarked James Beattie in the Arsenal penalty area and as he leapt highest, time seemed to stand still. Almost in slow motion and with me literally on the edge of my seat, Beattie's head met the ball perfectly and it sailed towards the far corner of the goal. For a split second, I readied to launch myself off the sofa and into a euphoric celebration of a famous last-gasp equaliser, an equaliser that would give us an extra 30 minutes, and the possibility of a penalty shootout. However, the ball didn't ripple the back of the net; there were no loud and raucous celebrations, just groans of despair as the ball was cleared off the line by Ashley Cole.

That chance turned out to be the last action of the match, and as the final whistle confirmed our runners-up status, I slumped back into my chair feeling mixed emotions of misery tinged with the relief that it was finally all over.

The only consolation to this loss was our qualification for the UEFA Cup, as Arsenal had already qualified for the Champions League, which meant we took their UEFA Cup spot as runners-up, our first foray into European competition for almost twenty years.

Revenge is a Dish Best Served Cold

Tottenham 1 Saints 3   Premier League   20 September 2003

The summer had seen little in the way of transfer activity, with only two transactions of note. The first of these saw Saints bolster their attacking options with the signing of striker Kevin Phillips from newly relegated Sunderland.

The only other transfer to make the headlines was Chelsea's capture of left-back Wayne Bridge. The fee was £7 million and the Saints received Chelsea's veteran left-back Graeme Le Saux in part exchange.

Kevin Phillips wasted no time in opening his account with a brace in the opening day draw at Leicester City after the foxes had taken an early 2-0 lead, thanks in part to one of the most outrageous penalty awards I have ever seen.

It all started with a hopeful punt forward from Leicester's Ben Thatcher from his own penalty area. The ball dropped a couple of yards outside of our box and bounced about 25-feet into the air before dropping inside the area, where Leicester striker Les Ferdinand leapt for the ball alongside our own Michael Svensson. Ferdinand leapt higher, missed the ball and as he came down he nudged the static Svensson before falling in a crumpled heap on the turf. To everyone's surprise (including Leicester fans), referee Mike Reed blew his whistle and amazingly pointed to the spot for a Leicester penalty. It was a shocking decision, and one I'm sure the referee was rightly embarrassed about when he watched it back on that night's television highlights.

Paul Dickov netted from the spot, and five minutes later Ferdinand made it 2-0 when Scowcroft was allowed to get to a loose ball near the goal line and his hit-and-hope cross was meant by a thundering Ferdinand header.

From our seats in the away end, Mark and I were starting to get the feeling that the Saints may very well be on the end of another humiliating thrashing. Thankfully, the score stayed at 2-0 until deep into the second-half when Strachan decided to throw new signing Phillips into the fray, and what an inspired substitution it turned out to be.

Phillips had only been on the field for a few seconds when he received the ball with his back to the goal about 35-yards out. As the Leicester players backed-off expecting him to loft the ball over the top for James Beattie, Kev turned took a couple of steps forward and launched an absolute screamer into the top corner of the net from fully 30-yards out.

Four minutes later and it was 2-2 when Beattie and the two defenders marking him missed Dodd's long ball forward and the ball fell kindly for Phillips who swivelled and shot almost in one movement. Unfortunately, for Kev, the ball hit the post but Beattie was the quickest to react and he had the simple task of scoring from the rebound.

Cue mass pandemonium in the away end, as the home fans just sat there with glum expressions on their faces. Our tails were up now, and with ten minutes left, it looked as though the Saints could actually win it, but in the end, a draw was probably a fair result, despite that awful penalty award.

It was a terrific start to his Saints career for Kevin Phillips, but that goal at Leicester would actually be his last in the League until January.

For James Beattie however, things were going to get a lot better as he hit the form of his life in the first few weeks of the season.

After scoring a late winner against Manchester United, and a brace the following week against Wolves (both at St. Marys) it was time to face an old foe on his home turf.

Despite having beaten Tottenham twice at St. Marys in a matter of days the previous season, Saints had lost at White Hart Lane 2-1 the previous August, and now we had a beleaguered Glenn Hoddle in our sights once again.

Hoddle's return to his spiritual home had not gone smoothly and Glenn was now under increasing pressure to deliver results.

The previous season, Glenn had failed to deliver Champions League qualification, and they had even finished tenth, two places below the Saints, who of course also ended their FA Cup participation at the Third Round stage.

Now under severe pressure, and with reports of player unrest in the Tottenham camp, Glenn took on a Saints side brimming with confidence.

Early results for Tottenham had been poor despite the amount of money spent on the playing squad in the summer, and before this match, they had already lost at Birmingham (2-1), as well as suffering a humiliating 3-0 home loss to Fulham.

It was a warm sunny Saturday afternoon in North London, real t-shirt and shorts type weather, although within two minutes of the start a small dark cloud seemed to form above Hoddle's head.

We opened the scoring when a leaping James Beattie met Matt Oakley's perfect corner on the left on the edge of the 6-yard box, and his flick header sailed in despite the keeper and a defender standing on the line.

The score stayed that way until two minutes before the break when Beattie grabbed his second in spectacular style.

215

The Saints won a free kick about 30-yards from goal, and it looked too far out for any of our players to consider having a crack at it. A few years ago, and this opportunity would be perfect Matthew Le Tissier range, but this time it was James Beattie who lined up to take it.

"He'll never score from there!" said the man sat next to me. However, Beattie stepped up and hammered the ball straight into the top corner and beyond the desperate dive of the Tottenham goalkeeper. It was a phenomenal strike that Le Tissier himself would have been proud of, and the boos that rang around White Hart Lane from the Spurs fans at half time did nothing more than to emphasise the fact that the next 45 minutes could make or break for Hoddle.

I was worried that the Spurs players would come out for the second half all fired up and desperate to salvage something from the match, but their lacklustre performances seemed to add weight to those pre-match rumours of player dissatisfaction with the manager.

The goal that really clinched the three points came on the hour mark when Le Saux's cross was bundled into his own net by Spurs defender Anthony Gardener whilst under pressure from Phillips.

Spurs did pull one back a couple of minutes later, but there was only going to be one winner, and that win pushed us to fourth in the table, whilst Spurs languished fourth from bottom.

The following day and the victory at Tottenham was all the sweeter when it was announced that the Spurs board had dismissed Hoddle, and it was a set of smug Saints fans who could now turn their attention to the UEFA Cup.

Well That Was Over Quickly

Saints 1 Steaua Bucharest 1   UEFA Cup 1st Round 1st Leg
24 September 2003

The draw for the UEFA Cup was a long and complicated one (as it is with its scion, the Europa League), and it would take a book in itself to explain the vagaries of the coefficient system employed by those in charge of European football.

In Britain, we are used to cup draws being random and anyone can be drawn against anyone else so long as they're in that velvet bag. However, in Europe, things are quite different, and for this particular draw, teams were placed into individual groups of 16 teams (eight seeded teams and eight unseeded), with teams from all four corners of the continent.

Due to our absence from Europe for the best part of 20 years, we were in the unseeded pot, although at this stage there was only one seeded team we needed to avoid, Steaua Bucharest.

"Southampton will play...Steaua Bucharest." Damn! The one team we wanted to avoid was the one team we got, which meant that progression to the next round of the competition was going to be a lot harder than anticipated.

St. Marys would host the first leg, with the return in Bucharest two weeks later, and that didn't make things any easier either, as I would have much preferred to have had the away leg first.

The first leg would turn out to be a bitter disappointment, and after Steaua took the lead it looked as though the first European match played at St. Marys was going to end in defeat.

For some reason, our attacks lacked any kind of urgency, and we were thankful when a defensive lapse allowed Kevin Phillips time and space to net the equaliser.

The game finished 1-1, and it was now 'advantage Steaua' as they had the luxury of that all-important away goal, which meant we had to score at least once in the return leg in Bucharest if we were to progress to the second round of European competition, something we hadn't achieved since 1981.

The Saints were semi-regular qualifiers for European competition through much of the late 60's and early 70's and again in the first half of the 1980's, but they'd rarely put in a decent run in any of the competitions. Their best showing was reaching the quarter-final stage of the 1976/77 European Cup Winners Cup, a competition that was only open to the teams that had won their countries knockout cup competition. This limited the tournament to just 32 teams and having beaten Olympic Marseille in the first round, and Northern Ireland's Carrick Rangers in the second, they then faced defending champions Anderlecht of Belgium for a place in the semi-final.

With the first leg in Belgium, it was important for Saints to grab an away goal, especially when they found themselves 2-0 down with time running out. Those who witnessed it have always seen what happened next as "dodgy." Saints thought they had a crucial away goal when Mick Channon netted late on, but as the Saints players celebrated, the ref had already blown for offside. Journalists, Saints players, and staff alike described the decision as "very dubious," but their protests fell on deaf ears, and so it was now down to the Saints players to right the wrong at The Dell a fortnight later.

They nearly did it too, storming into their own two-goal lead to tie the aggregate score at 2-2 with just 11 minutes left. Then a body blow, as a defensive slip by the usually reliable Jim Steele let in Anderlecht's tricky right-winger François Van der Elst to score in the 83rd minute, which inevitably would be the winner.

Saints were out; whilst Anderlecht went on to lose the final to Hamburg, before winning the trophy the following year in their third consecutive Cup Winners Cup final.

That was where the story should end, but in the late 1990's it emerged that the former Anderlecht chairman Constant Vanden Stock had bribed the referee before the second leg of their UEFA Cup semi-final against Nottingham Forest in 1984. Vanden Stock had "loaned" the referee a sum of $30,000, and Forest crashed out of the competition in controversial circumstances. Forest held a 2-0 lead from the home leg but lost 3-0 in Belgium, and they had had a perfectly good goal ruled out for offside, whilst Anderlecht were given a very soft penalty. Sound familiar? Although there was no doubting the validity of Anderlecht's two goals they scored against Saints in Belgium in 1976, the disallowed goal by Channon seems to suggest that maybe the Saints had also fallen victim to Vanden Stock's penchant for "loaning" large sums of money to referees.

I couldn't go to the away match in Romania as my second child was due to be born on the date of the second-leg, and with the game not considered worthy of television coverage, I had to be content with the good old-fashioned radio to inform me of what was going on in Bucharest.

The match was played in torrential rain, and I really felt for the Saints fans that were located in a stand that was open to the elements, although I was still annoyed that I wasn't there to share the suffering.

With the onus on Southampton to attack, that's exactly what they did, and I was surprised by just how many good goalscoring chances we created. Unfortunately, either wayward finishing or brilliant goalkeeping kept us at bay.

With just eight minutes to go, Steaua hit us on the counter-attack and scored what would turn out to be the match-winning goal. It was a damp and disappointing end to what could and should have been a decent run in Europe. Steaua were good, but they weren't that good, they just had more experience of what it takes to play in European competition, and they used that experience to good effect.

Derby Days

Saints 3 Portsmouth 0   Premier League   21 December 2003

You wait for ages for a South Coast Derby match, and then two of them come along at once. We hadn't played our local rivals in a competitive fixture since that 3-0 FA Cup win back in 1996, and the two sides hadn't met in the league since way back in 1988. Now, with Pompey's promotion to the Premier League the previous season, hostilities were to be renewed.

The first meeting should have been this league match just four days prior to Christmas, but the God's of football fate had other ideas when the two teams drew each other in the League Cup fourth round.

St. Marys was also the venue for the cup match, a match that would be played on 2 December, which meant two home games against our hated rivals in just a few weeks, and fans of both clubs couldn't wait.

In the past, I'd never really hated Portsmouth or their fans; there wasn't really any need to as we had hardly played each other in my lifetime. Yes, they had beaten us at The Dell in 1988, but we had erased that memory with that 3-0 FA Cup win in 1996. I didn't like them as they are our local rivals, and disliking your local rivals is just something most fans get caught up in, but I didn't hate them with the kind of vitriol that some of our more aggressive fans did. Besides, most of the hatred seemed to flow from their end of the M27 motorway.

Years in the wilderness whilst watching your local rivals climb the league and be moderately successful must have been galling for the blue lot down the road. A team that had once been haughty and proud had declined dramatically, dropping from the old First Division to the Fourth between the mid-60's to the early 80's. In that time, they had to watch as Saints gained promotion to the First Division, took part in several European campaigns, had played at Wembley three times, and won the FA Cup.

Then in the early 80's with Pompey struggling to leave the bottom division, Saints shocked the football world with the signing of England captain and European Footballer of the Year Kevin Keegan. Other internationals and flair players would follow, with players such as Mick Mills, Frank Worthington, Joe Jordan and Peter Shilton all signing for the club during the first half of the 80s.

In addition, to which, a shrewd scouting, and youth set-up meant that we could produce our own talent too, with the likes of Danny Wallace, Steve Moran, Mark Wright and Andy Townsend coming through the ranks.

Our rise just happened to coincide with the rise of football on television, and it seemed as though Saints were the only team on the south coast, something that must have irked Pompey fans even further. If highlights of our matches weren't on the telly, then our manager or players were often to be seen in the studio conveying their wisdom (and in Mick Channon's case an inability to pronounce the name of Gary Lineker).

Even when they did manage to recover enough to claw their way back to the Second Division they were still not quite good enough to make that final leap back to the top table, whilst we challenged for the title. Then in 1984, there came a chance for them to put us in our place, to knock us off our lofty perch as the kings of the south coast, namely the fourth round of the FA Cup.

They had home advantage too, and a team that was more than capable of matching us on the day, yet they still couldn't beat us, and our injury-time winner must have felt like a punch to the guts.

In spite of that solitary win for them in 1988, the chip on their collective shoulders grew and grew until it exploded in a fit of fury during an end of season testimonial at Fratton Park in the mid-1990s.

Despite the fact that the game between the two sides was a celebration and a chance for their fans to say "thank you" to their long-serving goalkeeper Alan Knight, the 5-1 score in favour of the Saints caused their fans to riot after the game, with many homes and cars suffering damage in the roads surrounding the stadium.

Now, after a revival under Harry Redknapp, they would face us once more on a level playing field, but we had home advantage for the first two games of the trilogy, and boy would we make it count.

In the run-up to the first of these matches, the League Cup encounter at the beginning of December, news emerged that our former player, manager, director, club president, and legend Ted Bates had passed away. Ted was (and is) seen by many as the creator of the modern Southampton, as under his managerial reign the club escaped from the depths of Division Three (South) to becoming a force in the First Division.

After Ted retired from management, he stayed at the club and his loyalty earned him the sobriquet "Mr Southampton."

It was unfortunate that the first match after his death should be at St. Marys against Portsmouth, and although hindsight is a wonderful thing, someone should have raised concerns about choosing this particular match to honour Ted.

As I made my way to St. Marys for the match, I hoped that the minute silence would pass off peacefully and wouldn't be ruined by lots of crass whistling and booing from the Pompey supporters, but that was just wishful thinking on my part.

Within seconds of the referee's whistle signalling the commencement of the minute's silent reflection, the response from the away section of St. Marys was worse than even the most cynical of Southampton fan could have envisaged.

The booing and whistling that had begun after just one or two seconds were soon joined by chants of "scum" from those in blue and

222

after 30 seconds the noise was so loud that the referee had to option but to abandon the minute's silence.

After the match, some Pompey fans tried to play down their fans lack of respect during the minute's silence, stating, "It was only a handful of supporters who had made a noise," when it was blatantly obvious to anyone there that night, that it was actually the majority. If their disrespectful and childish chanting had been to turn our dislike of them into hatred then it succeeded, as many other Saints fans attitude to Pompey fans changed that night.

The disrespect shown by the Portsmouth supporters also succeeded in riling up both the Saints fans and the players, and I don't think I have ever heard the home support so loud at St. Marys than it was that night. Urged on by a home crowd baying for blood, the Saints players tore into the opposition, and although Portsmouth had a couple of chances to open the scoring themselves, the Pompey goalkeeper was definitely the busier of the two.

Just past the half-hour mark, Saints got the breakthrough that their swashbuckling start deserved when James Beattie opened the scoring in style.

Pompey defender Zivkovic lost possession in a dangerous area to Brett Ormerod, and he slipped a neat pass behind the Pompey defence for Chris Marsden to drive across the face of goal. Beattie made one of his timely runs to the near post before slotting home from close range.

For all their efforts in the second half, Pompey never really created any clear-cut scoring chances, and with a nervy stoppage-time period looming, another Portsmouth defensive mistake sealed our progress to the next round of the competition.

De Zeeuw fouled Beattie, whose whippet-like run into the penalty area sent him clear, and referee Graham Poll had no hesitation in awarding the penalty and a red card to De Zeeuw. Beattie made no mistake from the spot, and a match that had begun with jeering, booing and whistling from the away support, finished with a collective sigh of relief from the home supporters.

The minute's silence for Ted Bates was rearranged for the following Sunday's home Premier League encounter with Charlton, and was observed impeccably by both home and away fans.

Now, all we had to do was to wait for round two in the south coast trilogy and the more important Premier League match in two weeks time.

If nothing else, the actions of the Portsmouth support that night certainly gave their return to St. Marys for the league match an extra edge, not that the fire needed much stoking. Nevertheless, only a comprehensive win would be enough to satisfy our lust for justice. As good as the cup win had been, it was the bread and butter of the Premier League that mattered the most.

Even before Jason Dodd swung a vicious curling corner that found its way in at the far post via the head of a defender, Saints should have been in front, as we were outplaying our opponents all over the pitch, but this time we didn't have to wait until the 90th minute for our second.

Marian Pahars had been in and out of the team for quite some time due to recurring injury problems, but he was fit enough to start this match, and in the 67th minute, he made his mark with a sublime goal.

Chris Marsden found Pahars with a neat pass through a throng of players and the little Latvian striker did the rest, darting between Foxe and De Zeeuw before curling a breathtaking right-foot shot beyond the reach of goalkeeper Harald Wapenaar.

There would be another goal in second half stoppage-time and again from Beattie, but this time it was from open play. Making one of his customary darting runs into the box, he found himself unmarked, which gave him plenty of time to head home Jason Dodd' pinpoint cross.

So, two derby games, two victories and a 5-0 aggregate scoreline to boot, but if things on the pitch had the Saints fans smiling, events off the pitch would soon give more cause for concern.

Strach-gone!

Saints 3 Everton 3   Premier League   21 February 2004

Something was wrong. Despite our improvement under Gordon Strachan's stewardship and the fans and players seemingly happy, Gordon was holding out on signing a new contract. With his current deal due to expire at the end of the season, fans were left in the dark with regards to the delay. As is typical in these situations, rumours began to fly around, and there were those who figured that he had fallen out with Chairman Rupert Lowe. Others suggested that he might have a more prestigious job lined up, maybe at one of the big Glasgow clubs, Rangers or Celtic, or even the Scotland national job.

Whatever the reason, there was no doubt that the longer his refusal to sign a new contract went on, the more intense the speculation about his future became, especially in the press. The fans weren't happy with the situation either. The uncertainty had begun to show itself in the performances of the players on the pitch as results and the overall style of play suffered.

After the 3-0 win over Portsmouth, the club won only one out of nine games, which included a dire 3-0 home FA Cup defeat to Newcastle. Goals were also seemingly in short supply with Saints firing blanks in six of those nine games.

Most fans agreed that something had to be done, and so did the board of directors and chairman. With pressure mounting from the press and the fans, it was inevitable that something had to give, and after a 2-0 defeat at Arsenal, Strachan decided to walk.

In his autobiography, Strachan denied that there had been any falling out with Rupert Lowe, and he admitted that Lowe was the only one on the Saints board who had wanted to give Gordon the job in the first place.

Strachan's reason for leaving was that he had been playing, coaching, and managing for decades and he felt that he needed a break, as well as needing to undergo an operation on his hip.

With Gordon gone, it was up to youth team coach Steve Wigley to steady the ship and prepare the players for this home game against Everton, whilst the board began the process of searching for another new manager.

One name that cropped up was that of Glenn Hoddle, who was still without a job in football management after his dismissal from Spurs. Rupert Lowe made no secret of the fact that he wanted Hoddle to return as manager, but the rest of the board and the majority of the supporters were less enthused at the prospect of Glenn's return.

No sooner had the press mentioned Hoddle's name as a possible successor to Strachan than fans began to make their feelings known, with some threatening not to renew their season ticket. Another smaller but more vocal group of Saints fans formed a rather cringeworthy protest group called ABH (Anyone but Hoddle), even going as far as wearing T-shirts bearing that slogan to the next few home games.

For me, the appointment of Hoddle would have been interesting, and although I wasn't one hundred percent behind the idea, sometimes it's a case of "better the devil you know than the devil you don't."

Despite the apathy towards the appointment of Hoddle, only around 2,000 or so actually stood up and made their protest loud and clear at this match, although, that atmosphere may have affected the players somewhat.

To say that our start to this match was sluggish would be a huge understatement, as Everton's attacking play caused us no end of problems. In fact, their strike force of old hand Duncan Ferguson, and newcomer Wayne Rooney had a field day and perhaps should have had more than the two goals they scored in the first 45 minutes.

It was the seventh minute when Rooney opened the scoring, but he had already missed an easy chance from 12 yards in just the first minute.

After that, chance after chance went begging for Everton, but they finally extended their lead on 33 minutes thanks to a Duncan Ferguson header.

At the other end, Southampton didn't trouble the Everton goalkeeper until the 37th minute, and when the whistle blew for half time, the 2-0 score certainly flattered us.

During the break, Wigley decided to shake things up a bit with the introduction of James Beattie and Fabrice Fernandes, and our attacking play drew a reward when just before the hour mark we pulled a goal back thanks to Kevin Phillips.

As is typical of Saints, just when it looks as though they are back in the match, they go and concede another soft goal, and with just twelve minutes to go Rooney scores to restore the Toffees 2 goal lead.

Not to be outdone, the Saints pour forward and create numerous chances that are repelled by the Everton defence, that is until on one foray forward David Prutton goes down just inside the Everton penalty area, and James Beattie slams home the resultant penalty to reduce the deficit to one.

It looks as though all our attacking efforts are in vain as the fourth official lifts his board to signal the amount of time added on for stoppages, but then a flash of brilliance from Fabrice Fernandes salvages a point, as he curls a majestic left-foot shot from the right wing that flies into the top corner for 3-3.

It was a cracking end to a match that we really weren't entitled to get anything from, and for a few minutes, all of the protests about the return of Hoddle were seemingly forgotten.

However, they wouldn't be for long.

A Town Called Malice

Portsmouth 1 Saints 0   Premier League   21 March 2004

A couple of days after that breathtaking draw against Everton, Glenn Hoddle officially rules out a return to Southampton as manager. He cited the lack of support from the board of directors as his main reason for not taking up Rupert Lowe's offer, saying that a manager needs to have the board of directors 100 percent behind them in order to succeed in the job. He also explained that the protests by certain sections of the supporters had no influence on his decision, and that rebellious fans are often easier to placate than dissenting directors are.

With Hoddle out of the running, the Saints board need to look elsewhere, and the man who would eventually take over the managerial reigns would be a man who yet again had no previous experience of managing in the Premier League.

Paul Sturrock was plying his trade in League One with Plymouth Argyle when Saints came calling, a team he had taken from the depths of League Two to being 12 games away from promotion to the Championship.

The move up was a surprising one, both for the fans and as it would later transpire, the Saints players themselves.

228

The overriding feeling amongst the supporters was that this was another huge gamble by chairman Rupert Lowe, in appointing a man who had no experience in managing at the highest level.

Sturrock didn't exactly look the part either and was often seen as being rather scruffy and unkempt, but he did hit the ground running results-wise winning his first game in charge 2-0 against Liverpool at St. Marys. However, his first away game was going to be a bit of a baptism of fire, the local derby at Portsmouth's Fratton Park.

Such is the animosity amongst both sets of fans towards the other, there was going to be a heavy police presence at this game, as there had been for the two games at St. Marys earlier in the season. Due to the prospect of serious trouble, I was in two minds about going, but if nothing else it was going to be an experience, and I certainly wasn't wrong on that score.

As for travelling to the match, there were only two realistic options, travel by train or travel club coach. I plumped for the travel club coaches, as it seemed the slighter safer option than travelling by train and then making the walk to the stadium.

Unusually, our police escort started from the moment we left the car park at St. Marys, and travelling like this was a surreal experience, as we made our way eastwards through Southampton surrounded by police motorcycle riders and police cars, with passersby stopping to look. Those who knew what was going on smiled and waved to us as we passed, whilst others stopped and stared.

No one was under any illusions that the reception we were going to receive upon entering Portsmouth was going to be anything other than hostile, as this was our first competitive game at Fratton Park since August 1987. In fact, our record at Fratton Park was actually quite good, and Portsmouth hadn't beaten us on their home turf since September 1963, a run of six games in league and cup. Add to the mix our two wins earlier in the season at St. Marys, and you had a recipe

229

for a very fervent and hostile home support, which bordered on the rabid.

Thankfully, we made it through the city to the ground without any major incidents, although, the wanker hand signs, V-signs and other gestures increased the closer we got to their decrepit old ground.

After leaving the coach, the police herded us down some dingy graffiti-covered back alleyways to the away section of the ground, and after a thorough frisking by more police officers, they allowed us through the turnstiles.

Back then, the away end at Fratton Park consisted of seats bolted onto the old terracing and was without any kind of cover whatsoever. The toilet facilities consisted of about four portaloos, with refreshments served from a rather small and unpleasant looking snack bar that seemed to be serving lukewarm tea and something resembling food.

Some people say that Fratton Park is one of those old traditional football grounds. Grounds that are fading into the mellow mists of yesterday thanks to brand new identikit modern stadia taking their place, but in truth, Fratton Park is an anachronism and a cramped low capacity anachronism at that. The away end has now improved, with the addition of a roof, so at least away fans will now only get wet from the spittle that the home fans send their way.

Unfortunately, for us, there was no protection from the elements and the pre-match hailstorm that seemed to fall from a clear blue sky did rather dampen our spirits somewhat, as well as causing great merriment amongst the home support.

The match itself was a rather scrappy one, as local derbies tend to be, and with Portsmouth battling against relegation, and with our players playing into the teeth of force 6 gale, it was no surprise that it was the home team that carved out the best chances early on.

In fact, Pompey should have been ahead and out of sight by half-time, but poor finishing kept the scores level at the break, and now it would be our turn to benefit from playing with the wind at our backs.

As we managed to get a foothold into the game, it looked as though we had ridden out all of that early pressure, and could actually secure our third win of the season against our hated rivals.

Both Kevin Phillips and James Beattie squandered chances to put us in front, and those wasted opportunities came back to haunt us when Portsmouth took the lead on 68 minutes when Yakubu slotted home from four yards. It was a poor goal to concede, although to be fair they probably deserved it on possession and the number of chances they had wasted.

The goal seemed to stir our players into action, and it wasn't long before we started to pepper their goal with shots, but alas, the closest we came was in the final minute, when a Kevin Phillips shot beat the goalkeeper only to rebound off the inside of the post and away to safety.

Shaka Hislop in the Pompey goal had made a number of important saves and blocks in the final quarter of the match, and now it seemed he also had luck on his side as well. He would have the last word though, as he somehow managed to claw a Claus Lundekvam header off the line in injury-time.

When the final whistle went, three-quarters of the stadium erupted in celebration, whilst we had plenty of time to ponder our missed opportunities as the police decided to keep us locked in the ground whilst they cleared the surrounding streets of marauding Pompey fans. So we waited, and waited and waited some more. 20 minutes became 30 minutes, which became 40 minutes, and people were starting to get restless, although there was no trouble, just plenty of friendly banter between the fans and the police and stewards.

Finally, after a delay of 45 minutes, the police deemed the surrounding streets to be safe enough to allow us to leave, and we all filled mournfully out of the ground. I wanted to get away from this place as quickly as possible and return to the safety of my home city. I don't think I have ever been so pleased to see the bright lights of Southampton appear in the distance as I did that evening, and it wasn't until later that evening when we were all safely back in Southampton that the reason for the long delay in us leaving the ground became apparent.

Instead of celebrating their victory as any normal group of supporters would, a large group of Portsmouth fans decided to wait for us to leave the ground in the hope of ambushing us. However, the police had other ideas, and as they attempted to move the horde on, they became the subject of the hatred and anger (I often wonder just how bad their reaction would have been if *we* had won the match). Fuelled by rage, the Pompey posse grabbed hold of anything they could to use as missiles against the police, including stones, scaffolding, and bricks. Eventually, the riot police managed to clear a path big enough to allow us to leave the ground, although, those making their way to the train station would still have one final gauntlet to run.

To chants of "You'll never make the station," those Saints fans making their way to the station had to dodge stones and other missiles raining down on them before reaching the safety of their train.

In all, 95 people were arrested for their part in the riots, with 85 given custodial sentences; all were given football banning orders of up to three years, including a 10-year-old boy, and a 14-year-old girl who became the youngest female to receive such a banning order.

To be fair, the players bounced back well after their first taste of an away derby match, and we won three out of our next four games, including two convincing away wins (4-1 at struggling Wolves, and a

3-1 win at Manchester City's new Etihad Stadium), as well as another home win versus Spurs (1-0).

It seemed as though Sturrock might be the right man for the job after all, and Rupert Lowe's gamble was starting to bear fruit. Alas, nothing stays the same in football for long, and we failed to win any of our last five games, finishing in 12th place and mid-table obscurity.

There were rumours of player unrest during this barren end to the season, and these rumours would gain momentum during the summer.

We're Not in Your League

Watford 5 Southampton 2 League Cup 4th Round 9 November 2004

Not only had the club failed to get the player unrest sorted during the close season, but by the time the 2004-05 season started it was a full on revolt. With tensions rising within the club, it was imperative that results on the pitch didn't suffer, and despite losing the opening game at Aston Villa 2-0, Saints bounced back in their next game by beating Blackburn Rovers 3-2 in front of the Sky TV cameras. Although, they did make hard work of it, and had to rely on a 90th minute James Beattie penalty to secure what would be our only 3 points in our opening 12 matches, a horrendous total.

Just hours after that Blackburn victory, the club announced that manager Paul Sturrock had vacated his position by "mutual consent," which is a diplomatic language for sacked but with a huge payoff. It seemed as though player power had won the day, and in a surprise move, Chairman Rupert Lowe announced that first team coach Steve Wigley would take charge.

Now Steve had taken over on a caretaker basis the previous season when Gordon Strachan had resigned, and most Saints fans thought that this would be the same deal. Steve would take charge for a couple of matches before a more experienced man would be appointed (again as in March, Glenn Hoddle's name was being touted as a possible replacement), but to our horror, Lowe confirmed that Wigley had been given the job on a permanent basis.

So now, we had a team that was obviously involved in yet another relegation battle, led by a man who made no secret of the fact that he really didn't fancy the job on a permanent basis, but obviously, something had changed.

After the Stuart Gray debacle a few seasons back, you would think that Rupert Lowe would have learned his lesson about promoting coaches to the manager's chair, but it appeared not.

Wigley didn't last long, and it is no exaggeration to say that his fourteen match stint in charge was an unmitigated disaster, the only high spot being a 2-1 home win over Portsmouth in mid-November. The lowlight was very definitely this 5-2 humiliation at the hands of Championship also-rans Watford on a chilly November night at Vicarage Road.

Saints fans of a certain age will still break out in cold sweats when remembering the last time we played a League Cup tie at Watford due to the extraordinary turnaround in the two-legged tie.

September 1980 and the draw for the two-legged second round paired us with Second Division Watford, with the home leg at The Dell up first. It was a match we won 4-0, a scoreline that seemed to make the second leg at Vicarage Road a couple of weeks later purely academic. However, this was a Watford side on the up, with Graham Taylor in the manager's seat, music legend Elton John as chairman, and a team filled with promising youngsters and shrewd old heads.

The return match was nothing short of a disaster for the Saints, with Watford's long ball tactics causing mayhem at the back, where even the usually rock solid Chris Nicholl was having problems containing

234

the aerial assault. By half-time, Watford had halved the aggregate score with two first half goals, but even a Saints side without the injured Kevin Keegan should have been able to wrap up the tie, but no.

The second-half continued in the same vein as the first, and Watford squared up the aggregate score at 4-4 before Saints finally got on the scoresheet courtesy of an own-goal, putting us ahead on aggregate once more.

Watford were not to be denied a famous comeback win though, and they made it 5-1 on the night and 5-5 on aggregate to force extra-time, where a shell-shocked Saints side conceded twice more, losing the tie 7-1 on the night and 7-5 on aggregate.

If that night was a shocking capitulation, then this was right up there with it, as instead of putting their poor league form behind them to progress in the cup, they put in a performance of such abject ineptitude that it only seemed to magnify the trouble we were in.

Our cause wasn't helped by the fact that first choice goalkeeper Antti Niemi was a long-term injury absentee, and his understudy Paul Smith was also out injured, and so for this match young reserve goalkeeper Alan Blayney filled in between the posts. It was a night that the young goalkeeper would probably not want to dwell on, as the defence often seemed to go AWOL whenever Watford attacked, leaving the helpless Blayney high and dry.

Ironically, it was Saints who had the best chance to take the lead early on, but the gilt-edged chance that fell to Mikael Nilsson went begging when he miss-kicked in front of goal when any sort of half decent connection would have diverted Paul Telfer's cross into the net.

It was one of only two decent chances we managed to contrive during the first half (the other being a Kevin Phillips shot that was well saved by the keeper), but Watford stormed forwards at every opportunity. Their forwards – and in particular the live wire Bruce Dyer – could sense an upset in the offing, and we were fortunate to only go in one goal behind at half time.

The second half though was a complete and unmitigated fiasco, of the like I hadn't witnessed for many seasons, as Watford doubled their lead in the 52nd minute, before adding two more in the next 14 minutes.

To show what a rotten performance this was when we did manage to get on the scoresheet in the 84th minute through Dexter Blackstock, Watford scored their fifth of the night within seconds of the restart. Brett Ormerod pulled another goal back with two minutes to spare, but it was met with the most muted of cheers from the Southampton faithful.

I trudged out of Vicarage Road that night with the rest of the travelling Saints fans, shell-shocked and numb at the ignominy we had just witnessed. Losing 5-2 to a team in 9th place in the Championship is bad enough, but to be honest, if it had ended 9-2 or even 10-2, then we would have deserved it.

When the draw was made later that night, Watford were drawn at home to Portsmouth in the quarter-finals, so at least we avoided another South Coast Derby match, but of course, our next match in four days time was to be the visit of Portsmouth to St. Marys.

Harry's Game

Saints 2 Portsmouth 1   FA Cup 4th Round   29 January 2005

The only highlight of Steve Wigley's time in charge of the Saints first team was the 2-1 win over Portsmouth in the Premier League a few days after that humiliation at Watford, but it wasn't enough to save his job. Another run of games without a win forced the club to act, and now the club was looking for its fourth manager in little over eight months, but what the club did next sent shockwaves along the south coast.

Harry Redknapp surrounded by photographers at St. Marys whilst holding aloft a Southampton scarf was something I never thought I would ever witness, but there he was large as life, doing just that.

Harry had been the man who had taken Portsmouth from The Championship to the Premier League and was a hero amongst Pompey fans. However, in the weeks leading up to his appointment as Southampton boss, things had changed at Fratton Park, and Harry had fallen out with his chairman Milan Mandaric, and the final straw seemed to come with the controversial appointment of Velimir Zajec as Director of Football, and Harry Walked.

Two weeks later and he was replacing Steve Wigley as manager of Southampton, and now the Pompey fans were apoplectic, whilst Saints fans strangely jubilant (and I include myself) to be getting a manager from "down the road". After all, he had worked wonders in not only getting Portsmouth promoted to the Premier League but also keeping them there too and there was no reason why he couldn't help us to secure our Premier League status for another season.

He also didn't have to worry about facing his old club until April in the league for the return match at Fratton Park, however, it seems as though footballing fate had other plans for the two South Coast rivals.

Both Saints and Pompey had negotiated their way into the fourth round of the FA Cup after dispatching lower league opposition, and the draw for the next round would take place on the following Monday afternoon.

I was in the cinema when my phone's vibration alerted me to a text message from my friend Mark, "Pompey in the cup!" it read and it was a heart stopping moment. After seemingly never coming up against each other, we would be playing our fifth match against them in less than two seasons, with the away league match at Fratton to come.

I never usually use my mobile phone in a cinema, and I hate those people who do, but I had one question to ask, and it needed answering straight away, where was the game being held? Mark's one-word reply of "Home" a few seconds later caused me to leap up out of my seat and mutter "Yes!" whilst giving a fist pump, much to the consternation of the half-a-dozen or so of my fellow cinema patrons.

As always with these types of occasions, the start to the match was tight and tense, and Portsmouth seemed to look the most threatening, with some last ditch Southampton defending keeping Diomansy Kamara off the scoresheet. That is not to say that it was all one-way traffic, as both Paul Telfer and Callum Davenport tested Pompey's debutant Greek goalkeeper Kosta Chalkias.

It had been an entertaining first half, but the second forty-five minutes would not only be entertaining but also highly controversial, thanks to two highly dubious penalty decisions.

The first of these came just three minutes after a Matthew Oakley long-range screamer had put Saints into a 1-0 lead. With the sound of the home fans celebrations beginning to die down, Pompey's tricky winger Kamara jinked his way into the Saints penalty area, whereupon he ran headlong into Saints defender Claus Lundekvam. The contact was minimal, and there was certainly no diving tackle by Claus, but this did not stop Kamara from falling to the ground like an old man on an icy pavement. To everyone's incredulity, the referee pointed to the penalty spot, and Yakubu had no problem in levelling the score at 1-1.

There was to be justice, however, and karma for Kamara in particular, after he needlessly handled the ball in the middle of the park, and already being on a yellow, he received his marching orders from referee Steve Bennett.

238

Now it was a case of Pompey trying to hold out for a draw and a replay back at Fratton Park, where they would obviously be favourites to go through, but once again, the footballing Gods had other plans.

With Pompey looking as though they had done enough to earn a replay (they could and perhaps should have won it when Ricardo Fuller blazed over from 7-yards out in the 89th minute) the game entered stoppage-time, and it was then that Saints were given a golden chance to win the match.

An innocuous looking cross into the Pompey penalty area was halted by the body of Matthew Taylor, but it was with which part of his body the ball had collided with that was to be the bone of contention. As a few half-hearted cries of "handball" rang around the stadium, the referee seemed content to play on, but after a couple of seconds, the whistle was in his mouth, and his right-hand was pointing towards the penalty spot. It transpired that the assistant referee on that side had had a clear view of the incident and had deemed it intentional handball by Taylor.

It must have taken about two minutes for the protesting Portsmouth players to vacate the penalty area, in order for ex-Portsmouth striker Peter Crouch to take the spot-kick. If ever there was a pressure penalty then this was it, but as cool as you like, Crouch dispatched the ball into the corner to send three-quarters of St. Marys Stadium into raptures.

It had been a cracking second half, and thankfully one with the right result for us. Now if only we could take this newfound belief and energy into our league programme, we might be able to beat the drop after all.

The Crying Game

Saints 1 Manchester United 2   Premier League   5 May 2005

It seemed as though that cup win had fired the players up as we embarked on a five match unbeaten run immediately after that win over Portsmouth, but we couldn't maintain our form, and results worsened.

The FA Cup run ended at the quarter-final stage with a depressing 4-0 home loss to Manchester United at St. Marys. It was another abject performance of defensive ineptitude, where the score could easily have been much higher. To make matters worse, Manchester United would be visiting St. Mary's for the final game of the season, so it was imperative that we were mathematically safe from relegation before that fixture.

Unfortunately, being safe from relegation before the last game of the season was beginning to look unlikely as our form never picked up.

As was the norm for this season though, any good solid win was undone in the following fixtures as we proceeded to lose the next three. A 3-1 mauling at home to Chelsea followed a decent 3-1 win at Middlesbrough, and two more extremely depressing results followed, firstly a 3-0 loss at Blackburn, then a 3-2 reverse against Aston Villa at St. Marys that saw us throw away a 2-0 half time lead.

If losing a 2-0 lead at home is bad enough, next up was two away games at Bolton and then Portsmouth. An away local derby at this stage of the season when you're fighting for your Premier League life is not something that fills the average fan full of hope, and I was certainly not looking forward to it.

I decided not to go, after my experience the previous season I just couldn't be bothered with all the hassle, after all, they rioted when they won last time, what would happen if we won this time?

As it transpired, that question was academic, as we went down to a 4-1 defeat. I watched the horror unfold with friends in a pub, and I was thankful that I decided not to go, as the alcohol helped to numb the pain, just a little bit.

Time was running out for us to save ourselves from relegation, and we had three games left with two of them against fellow strugglers Norwich and Crystal Palace.

The match against the Canaries was a classic seven-goal thriller, with The Saints edging it by a 4-3 scoreline thanks to Henri Camara's 88th-minute thunderbolt strike from 18-yards that fizzed in low past the keeper.

It was an immense goal in a crucial game and thanks to results elsewhere, it meant that we were now out of the bottom three. Now it seemed that our fate was back in our own hands. Two games to go, win them both, and we pull off another great escape. However, if we didn't win them both, then we would be relying on other results to see us safe.

A week after Camara's late winner against Norwich, another late goal at Crystal Palace salvaged a point and meant that our survival hopes went down the final game of the season.

I watched the Palace match in the King George pub in Southampton (sadly gone), a pub that had one of those illegal satellite dishes that could pick up the 3 o'clock matches that just happen to be broadcast all around the world but not in Britain.

Word of this illegal satellite hookup had obviously spread as even though we arrived a good 45 minutes prior to the kick-off the place seemed packed to the rafters, and it was a challenge just to get to the bar to order drinks.

The importance of this match meant that the game was full of incidents and niggly fouls, but Palace broke the deadlock on 34 minutes through ex-Saint Fitz Hall, although their lead lasted all of two minutes before Popovic handled in the area from Camara's flick, and Crouch dispatched the resultant penalty with ease. All square at half-time and the result was still in the balance.

As the second half went on the players began to get even edgier, and this underlying bad mood spilt over when Crouch and Palace's Sorondo clashed on the touchline, which led to several players and officials from both sides squaring up to each other.

When everyone had calmed down the referee dismissed both Crouch and Sorondo for their part in the fracas, which for us meant that Crouch's season was over.

To make matters worse, Palace retook the lead with little over 17 minutes remaining thanks to some more shambolic Southampton defending.

At 2-1 down and the match entering stoppage-time (of which there was plenty due to the melee earlier) it looked as though the game was up, but with the Palace fans whistling and baying for the ref to blow for time, Danny Higginbotham sneaked in at the far post to slam the ball home from close range for the equaliser. Cue delirium amongst the players on the pitch, the Saints fans in the stands at Selhurst Park, as well as those of us watching the drama unfold in the pub.

It looked as though footballing fate wanted us to pull off another miracle escape from relegation, but that meant beating a Manchester United side we had already lost to a combined score of 7-0 in two games already this season. The only plus point was that they had nothing to play for and we had everything to play for, surely that would be enough?

The final round of fixtures would see Norwich travel to Fulham, Crystal Palace travel the short distance to Charlton, whilst the other team in the mix West Bromwich would host Portsmouth.

In the days leading up to the final Sunday of the season, Pompey fans took great delight in telling us how their players would "take it easy" against West Brom in order to seal our relegation.

Most Saints fans knew that if the boot was on the other foot, we would be saying the same things, but we had to hope that the Portsmouth players would be professional enough to do their job properly.

For now, we just had to worry about our own result and hope that results elsewhere went our way.

We started the match well, and duly took the lead on 10 minutes when United's John O'Shea diverted a corner into his own net. It was a perfect start, and with Norwich already losing at Fulham, things were looking good.

I had my trusty radio with me for this match, as did many other people around me, and our situation looked to be even better when news filtered through of Charlton taking the lead against Crystal Palace. At the Hawthorns, West Brom and Pompey were still deadlocked at 0-0. If the scores stayed like this, we would be safe.

Of course, with so much football to be played, hoping that the scores after a quarter of an hour would stay the same is nothing more than wishful thinking.

The first thing that went wrong was United's 19th-minute equaliser when Darren Fletcher headed in from close range, and despite Norwich seemingly conceding goals for fun at Craven Cottage, both Crystal Palace and West Brom had taken the lead in their matches.

There was no doubt that we were struggling to create enough scoring chances, and those we did create we wasted.

We paid for our profligacy in front of goal when United took the lead on 63 minutes. That goal was a body blow, and the mood at St. Marys visibly changed, as we now had to score twice in little over 27 minutes to save ourselves.

United's steely defence held firm, and when the final whistle blew, it brought to an end our twenty-seven-year tenure in the top-flight of English football.

243

It was a heartbreaking moment, and although I managed to keep my emotions in check, plenty of others around me let the tears flow.

Even though it was academic to us, Norwich lost 6-0 at Fulham, a horrendous result when you consider how important the match was for them, and Palace joined us in the Championship, courtesy of a late Charlton equaliser. West Brom were the lucky survivors, as they became the first team to avoid relegation after being bottom of the table at Christmas since the Premier League began. Bottom of the table was our final resting place, but now wasn't the time to dwell on the final league placing, now was the time to get totally and utterly drunk.

That was where Mark and I encountered a bit of a problem. The problem wasn't finding a pub; the problem was dodging the groups of angry looking Manchester United fans who seemed to be up for causing the maximum amount of trouble.

After walking from the stadium to the centre of town in order to procure some cash for our forthcoming beer binge, I noticed a rather boisterous group of men (around twenty in number) heading in our direction. I knew they were not home fans because nearly every Saints fan this day was sporting club colours, and these guys looked riled up, rather than looking despondent as most Saints fans were that afternoon.

"I don't like the look of this," I said to Mark as we checked the bus times (for getting home later that evening) on a bus shelter, and nodding in the direction of the approaching mob. Deciding that discretion really is the better part of valour, we made haste to the nearest Saints fans pub we could get to, The Eagle.

We hadn't run but had walked bloody quickly, and no sooner had we entered the pub than the landlord locked the doors behind us. As we turned around, we noticed to our horror just how close we had come to being on the receiving end of a good kicking. That mob of twenty or so Manchester United fans were now outside the pub kicking the doors, thumping their fists on the windows, and generally trying to find a way to break in.

Thankfully, the doors and windows held firm, and the police soon arrived in great enough numbers to move the mob on.

It wasn't until much later on that we realised how much of a close run thing it had actually been, as we heard the news that pre-match, a Manchester United fan had been beaten into a coma. His attackers were Saints fans from the local working man's club who piled out to dish out instant justice to a small group of United fans who had been unfortunate enough to be singing United songs as they passed.

Once word of this serious assault permeated through to the rest of the United faithful, some of their more irate fans decided that revenge would be the order of the day, and so they went hunting in packs for anyone in a Saints shirt.

It later transpired that several Saints fans had come in for a beating after the match, and sporadic episodes of violence had broken out across the town centre, especially outside pubs packed with Saints fans.

Overall, it had been a wretched day on and off the pitch, but I was just glad that I survived the day physically intact, although the mental scars of relegation would take a lot longer to heal.

If I Ever Lose My Faith in You

Saints 1 Watford 3   The Championship   20 March 2006

It was going to take a while to adjust to life outside of the top flight of English football for the first time in 27 years for both the fans and the club itself.

For me, the reality didn't kick-in until the fixture list was published in June. Gone were Manchester United, Arsenal, Liverpool et al, to be replaced by Luton, Crewe, and Plymouth. They don't call it "the drop" for nothing!

Despite plenty of press speculation that he might leave during the close season, manager Harry Redknapp decided to stay on, but we lost our main strike force when both Peter Crouch and Kevin Phillips left for pastures new. Crouch departed for Liverpool in a £7 million transfer, whilst Phillips left to join Aston Villa for £1 million. Coming in was Ricardo Fuller who came from Portsmouth in a £90,000 deal, and youngster Kenwyne Jones was given his chance to shine with the first team.

Other youngsters who would begin to make a mark this season included Gareth Bale, Andrew Surman, Nathan Dyer, and Theo Walcott. The precocious 16-year-old winger Walcott would become the youngest ever Southampton first-team player when he made his debut in the opening day goalless draw against Wolves. In fact, he was so impressive during the season that by the end of January Arsenal shelled out £5 million for the youngster, a fee that could rise to £12 million with add-ons.

Even though home attendances were a few thousand down on the previous season, signalling a supporter apathy towards the Football League Championship, my enthusiasm for the team didn't falter. With new grounds to visit and a possible promotion push in the offing, I was slightly more enthusiastic about the coming season than I had been for the past few seasons.

This newfound fervour didn't last long though, as the season turned out to be anything other than a straightforward march towards promotion back to the Premier League.

By early November we were handily placed in sixth, and if we could improve our form just a little bit (we were drawing far too many

246

games) we should be well in the promotion hunt come April. Then three things happened that entirely changed the direction of our season.

The first of these events concerned the appointment of Sir Clive Woodward as Performance Director (whatever that is) and then as Director of Football. Now, Sir Clive was famous for being a rugby union coach, and an excellent one at that. After all, he had led the England national team to glory in the rugby world cup, but he had no experience in association football. Unfortunately, what he did have was a solid friendship with our former public schoolboy and current club chairman Rupert Lowe.

The appointment bewildered the fans and infuriated Redknapp, who had reportedly left his managerial role at Portsmouth due to the club appointing a Director of Football above him. Redknapp was an old school manager, he wanted carte blanche when it came to running a football team, and he saw the appointment of someone above him (and in this case someone with no technical knowledge of football) as an affront to his ability.

The second incident that seemed to have a negative effect on our season was a home game against Leeds United in early November.

Remember that capitulation against Tranmere in the FA Cup a few seasons back, well here comes the sequel.

As per the Tranmere game, we had rushed into what looked like an unassailable 3-0 lead by half-time, thanks to goals from the fit again Marian Pahars, and two from midfielder Nigel Quashie. We held the lead for most of the second-half, and even though Leeds pulled a goal back on 71 minutes, it looked like a mere consolation goal. However, a collapse that the England cricket team would be proud of followed as just six minutes later it was 3-2. Game on!

Leeds poured forward with energy and passion, something that appeared to be sorely lacking from our players, and they duly equalised with an 84th-minute penalty after a handball by Danny Higginbotham. Now there were just six minutes for someone to find a winning goal, but in truth, there was only going to be one victor, and it wasn't us. With four minutes to go, Leeds duly scored again to lead 4-3 and they saw out the rest of the match quite comfortably. A result that seemed to knock the stuffing out of our players, and we won just three games out of the next twenty-three in the league.

Our freefall down the table hurtled us towards the relegation zone, and instead of pushing for promotion, we were now staring down the barrel of a second successive relegation.

During this poor run of form, Harry Redknapp finally left his position as manager, something that had seemingly been on the cards for weeks. What we didn't know was that he would rejoin Portsmouth in the Premier League just days later.

In a move that stunned both sets of fans, Portsmouth's chairman Milan Mandaric announced that Redknapp would be making the return journey along the M27 to become Portsmouth boss once more.

The Portsmouth fans, still angry with him for leaving to join us in the first place, wasted no time in venting their fury at his reappointment, whilst he had now become public enemy number one in the red half of Hampshire too.

As Saints lurched from one poor result to another, the press began speculating that Rupert Lowe was lining up Sir Clive Woodward as the next manager. It was news that most Saints fans didn't want to hear. How could a man with no history within the game, and without the required Football Association coaching badges become the next manager of Southampton Football Club?

Mercifully, it seemed as though an outbreak of common sense took hold of the board of directors and they instead appointed former Ipswich Town and Heart of Midlothian manager George Burley.

If his appointment was supposed to steady the ship, it didn't, our form was still abysmal, and our slide towards the relegation zone continued unchecked.

A 3-0 humbling at Sheffield United, a result that left us in 20th position, just two places above the drop zone, quickly followed this 3-1 home defeat to Watford on my birthday, and with just six games left, our survival in The Championship came down to how many points we could acquire during April.

Just as we needed a hero, one appeared on the horizon beyond the silhouette of the gas works, and his name was Ricardo Fuller.

Ricardo Fuller had had a torrid time since his arrival from Portsmouth in the summer. Despite making a solid start, the goals soon dried up, and his languid displays often made him a target for abuse from certain sections of our support. Part of the problem was his connection to Portsmouth, and as the catcalls grew, so his confidence seemed to diminish, and it wasn't long before he was shipped out on loan to Ipswich.

Fuller returned from Suffolk a different man, in the final six games of the season he bagged six goals, and those goals helped us to avert a second successive relegation.

It was a strange end to the season, but in the summer of 2006, the soap opera that was Southampton Football Club was going to take an even more dramatic twist.

All or Nothing

Saints 4 Southend United 1   The Championship   6 May 2007

No sooner had the previous season ended than the mumblings of discontent among the support grew to an almighty crescendo. How long could Rupert Lowe go on mismanaging the club at all levels?

The only good thing about being the club being a plc was that things could change in very quick time, and that is exactly what happened during the summer of 2006, as those shareholders who had the influence and the money to change things, attempted to do just that.

Whilst the rest of the country followed the England national team's performance at the 2006 FIFA World Cup in Germany, things were beginning to happen behind the scenes at St. Marys.

Certain shareholders were starting to lose patience with Rupert Lowe's leadership, and plans were afoot to oust him and his board of directors before the club stagnated in The Championship.

The biggest voice of discontent came from two local executives, Michael Wilde and Leon Crouch, and with Crouch's blessing, Wilde began buying up enough shares to challenge Lowe's leadership.

Just 72 hours prior to an extraordinary general meeting of shareholders, where it looked in all likelihood that Rupert Lowe would be defeated in a vote on his removal, Lowe decided to fall on his sword and resign.

With Lowe out of the way, the rest of the board followed his lead and left too, so it was goodbye and good riddance to Andrew Cowan, Guy Askham, Michael Richards and David Windsor-Clive. The only person left from Lowe's regime was Sir Clive Woodward, but he wouldn't last much longer either, and he was gone by the end of August.

On the pitch, this would be Gareth Bale's breakthrough season, as he announced himself in style in the opening match of the season, scoring a sensational 25-yard free kick as Saints drew 2-2 at Derby.

The new board wasted no time in giving manager George Burley the funds to finance a full-on push for promotion, and as well as Gregorz Rasiak making his loan move from Tottenham a permanent deal, we also signed midfield wizard Rudi Skacel from Hearts.

The club announced the signing of Skacel as the final piece in the jigsaw that would allow the club to make a realistic promotion bid, as Rudi had played for George Burley at Hearts, where he had often set the Scottish Premier Division alight with his playmaking ability.

Other new signings during the summer included goalkeeper Kelvin Davis, midfielder Inigo Idiakez, Bradley Wright-Phillips and Jermaine Wright to name just four, but overall the squad had a much different look to it when compared to the previous campaign.

Maybe it was too many players trying to settle in all at once, but early results were not great, and it seemed as though consistency was going to be a major hindrance to securing one of the two automatic promotion places.

Good results against fellow promotion favourites Wolves, Birmingham City, and Sheffield Wednesday were overshadowed by defeats at Colchester, Southend and Cardiff. It was that kind of season.

By the time this final day game against Southend United came around, we were in the last playoff place (sixth) but with both Stoke City and Preston North End clinging on to our proverbial coattails. Anything other than a win could open the door for one of them to overtake us and grab a chance to get to a Wembley play-off final and possible promotion to the Premier League.

Southend had nothing to play for, but that didn't stop them from taking the lead, but they never looked likely to keep us off the scoresheet, and by the final whistle, two goals each for Leon Best and Kenwyne Jones sealed an easy win.

That final day win confirmed our sixth place finish, and set up a playoff semi-final against Derby County, with the first leg at St. Marys, and it would be an interesting clash of styles with our neat short passing game going up against Derby's physical and direct approach.

Their fans came down in their thousands for a game of such importance, but a large majority of them seemed to be intent on causing trouble, and there were sporadic incidents of disorder around the stadium and surrounding areas. I found myself threatened with physical violence when a minibus full of Derby morons pulled up alongside me as I walked to the stadium.

The aura of menace emitted from certain sections of the Derby following seemed to carry over to the players as well, as their team proceeded to kick any Saints player they could.

In an ill-tempered first first-half, the referee produced 6 yellow cards, four of which were awarded to Derby players, and they would pick up a further two during the second-half, although in my opinion there should have been a couple of red cards in there too.

Despite the fact that our players were having lumps kicked out of them at any given opportunity, it was Saints that took the lead, thanks to a 20-yard screamer from Andrew Surman, but it was to prove the only highlight of the afternoon.

After having what looked like a cast-iron penalty claim waved away by the referee (who was always on the verge of losing control of the game) we proceeded to twice hit the woodwork, and Derby took full advantage by levelling the scores on 36 minutes.

The second half pretty much followed the same pattern, with our neat passing football contrasting sharply with Derby's hoof ball tactics. As the game went on it looked as though one goal would probably settle the tie, and it duly did when Derby were awarded a rather dubious penalty on 58 minutes. A penalty they converted to give them a slender advantage going into the return leg at Pride Park to be played the following Wednesday.

As Derby fans rampaged through the city centre after the match, most Saints fans were trying to console themselves with the fact that our away record this season was almost as good as our home form.

Turning the tie around wasn't impossible, but it was going to require gargantuan effort and a huge slice of good luck.

The gargantuan effort wasn't a problem, as the Saints players gave their all and then some in the return match, but lady luck seemed to desert us once again.

The match got off to the worst possible start as Derby bombarded our defence straight from the kick-off with a succession of high balls into the box, and they broke the deadlock inside four minutes.

Now leading 3-1 on aggregate we needed to waste no time in scoring ourselves, and with the Derby fans still celebrating the goal they thought would be enough to take them to Wembley, we did just that.

Jhon Viafara scored on the volley from fully 30-yards after a mix-up in the Derby defence. An under-hit back pass caused the Derby goalkeeper to head the ball clear outside of his own penalty area, and the ball fell kindly to Viafara to smash home an almost instant equaliser.

After this frenetic start, the match quietened down into the edgy midfield battle most people had expected, and it wasn't until the second-half when the blue touch paper was lit once more.

On 54 minutes, Saints took the lead on the night and levelled the tie on aggregate at 3-3 when Jhon Viafara grabbed his second of the night with another ferocious shot.

Now it was anybody's match, but our joy at clawing our way back into the tie was short-lived when Leon Best somehow contrived to shin a Derby corner into his own net on 66 minutes. 4-3 on aggregate to Derby, and that's the way it stayed until the 89th minute when former Derby striker Gregorz Rasiak lashed home an equaliser after being put through by Best's brilliant run.

That made the score 3-2 to Saints on the night, and 4-4 on aggregate, and now there was going to be another 30 minutes of extra-time and the possibility of a penalty shootout, but to our chagrin, the away goals rule was not used in the playoffs, because if it was, we would have gone through to the final.

The extra 30 minutes produced chances at both ends, but neither side could find that little bit of good fortune to win the tie, and so it all came down to a penalty shootout.

Leon Best had had a mixed night, firstly conceding that own goal, but also bagging two assists for our second and third goals, but now his night was to end in misery as he missed our first spot-kick. Despite our next three penalties all being successful, Derby had managed to convert all four of theirs, so when ex-Derby midfielder Inigo Idiakez stepped up to take our fifth, he knew he had to score to put the pressure on Derby's final penalty taker.

Idiakez blazed his penalty so far over the bar that it probably landed back in Southampton, and that was our promotion dream over for another year. It was a cruel way for our season to end, and now we had to regroup and go again in the hope of gaining automatic promotion next season. As it turned out, things were going to get worse, as the club lurched to another off-field crisis.

On a Life Support Machine

Saints 3 Sheffield United 2   The Championship   4 May 2008

Not gaining promotion the previous season would have dire consequences for the club, as now with two seasons in the Championship behind them, the parachute payments from the Premier League would now stop.

With such a gulf in prize money and television money between the Premier League and The Championship, the financial implications of relegation were huge, and several relegated clubs fell on hard times, that was when it was decided to help ease the financial burden, and parachute payments were born.

For Southampton, things would be no different, after throwing millions of pounds at gaining promotion during the 2006-07 season and falling short, and with the parachute payments stopped (these payments were for two years originally, but even this wasn't enough, and it is now four years) there wasn't a lot of money available.

Having gambled large sums of money on promotion the previous season, the failure to gain a place at football's top table meant severe financial implications for the club. As a result, there were no new signings of note, and the club had no choice but to accept a £5 million bid from Tottenham for our promising young left-back Gareth Bale.

If that wasn't bad enough, certain players who thought themselves too good for Championship football started to push for transfers away from the club, and the most notable of these was striker Kenwyne Jones.

After the club rejected a bid from Derby, Jones downed tools and refused to play for the club again. It was a startling case of a player throwing a tantrum in order to engineer a move. The problem was that the club was in no position to have an unhappy player rotting in the reserves, so when another bid came in from Sunderland, the club allowed him to go, with striker Stern John coming in as part of the deal.

You can often tell if you are going to be in for a good season, an indifferent season, or a bloody hopeless one by the result of the opening match of the season, and I took my seat for the opener against Crystal Palace hopeful that we could get off to a good start.

We lost the match 4-1 with one of the most inept defensive performances I had witnessed from a Saints side (and there have been many over the years) in recent years, on par with that 5-2 loss at Watford during our relegation season.

Our defence was as leaky as I had ever seen it and we let in five goals on three separate occasions with defeats at Preston (5-1), Sheffield Wednesday (5-0) and Hull (5-0).

By January, a large majority of fans had had enough of George Burley's managing of the club, although to be fair, he had lost two influential players in Bale and Jones, but the results and the performances were not exactly inspiring.

Even though results and performances were nothing short of poor, the Scottish FA approached Saints in order to talk to Burley about their vacant national team manager position, a situation that seemed to suit everyone.

Burley left on the 23 January, and taking over the managerial responsibilities were former club captain Jason Dodd and John Gorman who had been assistant manager during Glenn Hoddle's tenure.

I suspect that the board was hoping that results would improve enough to keep Dodd and Gorman in the job until the end of the season, but it's no exaggeration to say that the results during their time in charge were nothing short of disastrous.

Four defeats in five in the league and an embarrassing FA Cup Fifth Round defeat at League One Bristol Rovers, a match broadcast live to the nation on the BBC, meant that Gorman and Dodd lasted a mere four weeks in the job before the board decided to act.

Nigel Pearson came in to try and steady the ship, but the expected improvement in results didn't materialise, and although we only lost three games under Pearson, too many draws meant that our survival would go down to the final game of the season.

Just as in 2005, our survival hopes rested on us getting a win whilst hoping that the results in other matches went our way, and another tense 90 minutes awaited us.

At the start of play, we occupied 22nd place (the last of the three relegation places) with 51 points, with four teams above us all separated by two points, so it certainly made from a nervous and dramatic last round of fixtures.

Sheffield United came to St. Marys with a slim chance of making the playoffs, so with so much riding on the match, it was no surprise that the game drew our biggest crowd since our Premier League days.

The opening exchanges were full of tension and nerves for players and fans alike, but the Blades started the brighter. They had already come close to opening the scoring on two occasions before they managed it at the third attempt when Stephen Quinn headed home unmarked on 23 minutes.

In spite of the early setback, the home fans roared their team on in a way that I hadn't heard since all of those relegation battles in the early to mid-90s, and it seemed to have the desired effect, as we started to gain a foothold in the match.

Even so, for all of our possession, we just couldn't convert our chances, with Polish striker Marek Saganowski one of the most wasteful in front of goal. In fact, we were extremely fortunate not to go 2-0 down, when keeper Richard Wright stopped a bullet close-range header from Matt Kilgallon on the line.

Just seconds after that escape we managed to level the scores, when Jason Euell's right wing cross, looped off a defender, wrong-footed Paddy Kenny in the United goal, and the ball fell invitingly for Saganowski to head in from a yard out.

When the half-time scores were announced over the tannoy, neither Coventry or Leicester were winning, so there was still a chance that we could drag ourselves out of this mess.

Things looked hopeful at the start of the second period, when we took the lead for the first time thanks to a thunderous Stern John shot after great work from Saganowski set him up. With Leicester still held to 0-0 at Stoke, that goal pulled us out of the relegation zone, a scenario that could change if we conceded or Leicester took the lead.

As was to be expected United did find an equaliser, when more awful defending allowed John Stead to nip in at the near post to convert Quinn's cross from 6-yards out, and the 2-2 scoreline sent us back into the relegation zone on goal difference.

It was to be our day though, when Stern John scored his second of the match on 69 minutes, and although he would receive his marching orders (for two yellow card offences) with five minutes to go, we held on.

When news filtered through that Coventry had lost 4-1 and Leicester had only managed a goalless draw at Stoke, the fans invaded the pitch in celebration of another miraculous escape from relegation.

As I joined the thousands of fellow Saints fans running onto the pitch in order to laud the players for their effort in keeping us in The Championship, I remember thinking to myself that we couldn't possibly this bad next season. How wrong could I be?

The Return of Rupert

Saints 1 Birmingham City 2   The Championship   16 August 2008

The boardroom shenanigans that had plagued the club for the past eighteen months or so continued to cause concerns amongst the supporters during the close season, as more uncertainty loomed. Wilde had stepped down as chairman, with Leon Crouch taking over, but now with the club in a perilous state financially, Wilde shocked everyone by announcing his intention to team up with Rupert Lowe.

Wilde called another EGM in order to oust his former ally Crouch from his position as chairman of the football club, but as Lowe did,

Crouch resigned from his position before the date for the EGM, along with three of his fellow board members.

With Crouch gone, Michael Wilde returned as Chairman of the club, with Rupert Lowe returning as Chairman of the parent company Southampton Leisure Holdings plc. However, it soon became apparent that Wilde was really just a puppet, with Rupert Lowe pulling the strings from behind the scenes.

This scenario became apparent when manager Nigel Pearson did not have his contract renewed during the summer, and instead, Lowe and Wilde decided to appoint two men in his place.

Lowe announced Dutchman Jan Poortvliet as the new man in charge of the first team, with another Dutchman Mark Wotte coming in as his assistant.

Apparently, the reason for this managerial change was money, with Pearson's contract apparently too high to maintain, but it was apparent to most Saints fans that the only real reason why Pearson had been cast aside was that he was a Leon Crouch appointment.

If Saints were a mess off the pitch, then on it was a total shambles, as the squad struggled to find a win. The releasing of several pivotal players from the previous season, the most prominent of these being Stern John who had bagged 19 goals the previous campaign didn't help the overall strength of the squad.

Morgan Schneiderlin had been signed for £1 million (but apparently there was no money to keep Pearson), but the rest of our signings during the close season were nothing short of pathetic. Anthony Pulis, son of football manager Tony Pulis, joined on a free transfer from Stoke but would never play in the first team, then followed the signing of goalkeeper Tommy Forecast, a man so inept that he would struggle to stop a balloon let alone a football.

Lee Molyneux came in on a free from Everton – he made four appearances before leaving – and Ryan Smith came in from Millwall,

259

again on a free, and like Pulis left without having ever made an appearance for the first team.

This opening day defeat to Birmingham City set the tone for what would be a season to forget for Saints fans everywhere, as the team lurched from one humiliating defeat to another as we spent the first half of the season in and out of the relegation zone.

The odd highlight of wins at Derby County, Reading, Preston and Ipswich were overshadowed by shameful losses at home to Blackpool, Doncaster, Bristol City and fellow strugglers Charlton, a match that was a massive relegation 6-pointer.

Two days prior to that Charlton game, just when fans thought that things couldn't possibly get any worse, they got a lot worse.

On the 2 April 2009, the stock market announced that Southampton Football Club's parent company, Southampton Leisure Holdings plc had gone into administration. A seismic body blow to anyone who held the club in their hearts and minds, and it meant that the Football League could impose a 10-point penalty.

In the recent past, so many clubs had used administration as a way of wiping out either all or large parts of their debts that the Football League decided that any such application to enter administration would incur a 10-point deduction. For Southampton though, this would prove to be a big cause of disagreement.

On Borrowed Time

Saints 2 Burnley 2   The Championship   25 April 2009

The main point of dispute came from the fact the parent company had filed for administration, not the football club. The rule makers at the Football League argued that the club and its parent company were inexorably linked, something that the club and its administrator Mark Fry vehemently denied.

Another problem was the fact that there was a cut-off point for the 10-point deduction, which we had missed by a matter of days. If a club were to enter administration before March 31, the 10-point deduction takes effect there and then, after that date, ten points would be deducted at the start of the following season.

For now, most Southampton fans were more worried about events off the pitch than on it, but that didn't stop me and 27,000 other Saints fans turning up for a must-win home game against Charlton Athletic.

Charlton were the only team below us in the table, and they were certain to be relegated to League One, but that didn't stop them coming to St. Marys and leaving with all three points though, as the Saints players put in a performance that certainly suggested that we would be accompanying Charlton down a division come the season's end.

It's no exaggeration to say that the return of Rupert Lowe had divided the fans, with supporters split into two groups, those who wanted him gone, and those who thought that he was the best man to save the club from financial oblivion.

The atmosphere at home games was abysmal, despite the best efforts of the fans to urge the players on; it was obvious that the majority of fans had had enough. Those who didn't vote with their feet and came every week sat in near silence, whilst during one game in particular (the visit of Doncaster Rovers) Saints fans in the Northam end of the ground were seen fighting amongst each other. It was a club divided on all levels.

Burnley arrived for our last home game of the season, and anything other than a win would send us down, although in truth, most fans knew deep down that relegation was inevitable. We had had a lucky escape the previous season, but with a better and more experienced squad, whereas this squad contained inexperienced youngsters and a few older heads.

Manager Jan Portvliet had gone in January, his resignation opening the door for his assistant Mark Wotte to take over for the remainder of the campaign. The managerial change didn't halt the slide and if anything results and performances were actually worse under Wotte than Portvliet.

To be fair to the players, they actually gave it their all in this match, and should have won quite convincingly, however, as it had been all season, their effort wasn't quite enough, and when Burnley equalised with a few minutes to go, it was all over.

The pitch invasion at the final whistle was a surreal experience. Whereas the previous season there had been joyous scenes celebrating our survival, this felt more like a wake.

I remember standing in the middle of the pitch wondering what I was doing there and what to do next. Some fans made for the section where a couple of hundred of Burnley fans were seated, and a few kicks and punches were exchanged before the police and stewards took control.

Unlike the relegation from the Premier League, there didn't seem to be any tears shed this time, at least I couldn't see any, and the overriding mood amongst the fans was anger and frustration, tinged with worry.

Saints went down with one game to spare, a meaningless dead rubber of a match at Nottingham Forest (we lost 3-1), but for every Saints fan, it was now a case of waiting to see if the administrators could find a buyer for the club.

There were plenty of rumours linking certain individuals or consortiums to the club in the weeks following the final game of the season, and one of these consortiums would feature a club legend and a shady character called Michael Fialka.

Here's Our Starter For Minus Ten

Saints 1 Millwall 1   League One   8 August 2009

The first potential purchasers of the club to throw their hat into the ring were a group called Pinnacle, whose representative was a man called Michael Fialka, and he had persuaded club legend Matthew Le Tissier to back their takeover bid. Pinnacle was not the only interested party, however, with the administrator Mark Fry stating that he was talking to two other potential buyers.

With the club losing money hand over fist, and with no income during the close season things were getting so bad for the club financially, that staff and players worked free as a gesture of goodwill. Leon Crouch also used some of his own money to keep the club afloat during this time, a selfless act by a man who loved the club as much as the fans.

Ultimately, in order to save the club from going into liquidation, Mark Fry demanded that any potential buyer would have to pay £500,000 up front in order to secure a twenty-one day period of exclusivity. This would allow the bidder to deal with the administrator without other interested parties nipping in with a better offer, and the Matthew Le Tissier-backed Pinnacle bid got in first.

Pinnacle's spokesperson Michael Fialka stated that the group was not prepared to accept the 10-point deduction imposed by the Football League, but the more sceptical Saints fans suggested that they were struggling to raise enough money to buy the club.

What made matters worse was that Sky Sports News seemed to be adamant that Michael Fialka was to be the saviour of the Saints,

263

despite the fact that once newspaper journalists began to look into Fialka's background it was evident that the numbers didn't add up.

They discovered that despite coming across as some kind of great executive with the financial backing to buy the club, Fialka was actually no more than a letting agent and a director of two companies that had a combined turnover of a little over £100,000.

No sooner had the exclusivity period ended then the Pinnacle bid collapsed; causing them to officially withdrew their bid on 30th June. The collapse of the Pinnacle bid was both good news and bad. The good news was that someone with the wherewithal to buy the club now had the chance to make their bid. The bad news was that with the new season about to start, the club was on the verge of being wound up.

The Football League were putting pressure on the club to confirm that it could complete its fixtures in League One for the 2009-10 season and to be honest, as June became July, that was looking increasingly unlikely.

With just two days before the liquidation process was to begin, Mark Fry announced Swiss billionaire Markus Liebherr had finalised the purchase of the club, thus securing its long-term future.

I'm not afraid to admit that I shed a few tears when I heard the news, and no doubt a lot of other Southampton fans did the same. This time they were tears of relief and happiness, rather than sorrow and despair, and now we could look forward to taking our place in League One for the forthcoming season.

Within days of the takeover, Markus Liebherr wasted no time in bringing in a friend and executive Nicola Cortese in to run the club, and he, in turn, wasted no time in sacking manager Mark Wotte.

Wotte's replacement was Alan Pardew, and his task was simple, get the club promoted at the first time of asking, even with the handicap of the ten-point penalty.

Even without the points deduction promotion was going to be a big ask, as the playing squad needed a major revamp to get it anywhere near the top of the table, let alone challenging for promotion. However, Liebherr wasted no time in splashing the cash, allowing Pardew to make several signings during the transfer window.

The biggest outlay was the £1 million fee for Rickie Lambert from Bristol Rovers. The club was severely short on striking talent after several players left the club during the summer, most notably, Bradley Wright-Phillips and David McGoldrick, and the arrival of Ricky was a major boost.

It was strange that only a few weeks previously the club was on the verge of going out of business, but now here we were splashing out seven-figure sums on a new striker. Fans of other clubs moaned about the injustice of it all, but we were now debt free so why shouldn't we take advantage of having a wealthy owner?

Even though things off the pitch were now settled, with such a traumatic close season, it was no surprise that our poor on the pitch form carried over to the new campaign, and it wasn't until our eighth league game of the season before we notched our first win in the league.

By the time we played Exeter City at St. Marys in front of a 30,000 people on Boxing Day, results had improved so much that we were now at the lofty heights of 15th in the table, a mere 9-points from the play-off places.

We weren't doing too badly in the cup competitions either, reaching the fifth round of the FA Cup and the Southern area final of the Johnstone's Paint Trophy, a competition exclusively for teams in League's One and Two.

After everything the fans and the club had been through over the past few months, it seemed as though footballing fate was going to

give us a day out at Wembley, just so long as we successfully
negotiated the two-legs of the Southern Area Final against MK Dons.

Phoenix from the Flames

Saints 4 Carlisle 1   Johnstone's Paint Trophy Final   28 March 2010

Our route to Wembley Stadium started back in October in a second
round tie versus League Two Torquay United in front of a paltry
crowd of a little over 9,300. For some reason the match kicked-off at
7 pm rather than the standard 7:45, and this may have had something
to do with the low turnout, not that this competition was used to big
crowds turning up to watch its matches.

To be fair to the Torquay players, they gave it a real go, and it looked
as though we were heading for an early exit from the competition
when they stormed into a 2-0 lead by half time.

Pardew made a couple of changes during the break and they made all
the difference when our Senegalese winger Papa Waigo, (who was on
loan for the season from Italian club Fiorentina) scored two goals in
ten minutes midway through the second half.

With no extra-time, the game went straight to penalties, where Waigo
scored one of our five successful spot-kicks, which was enough to see
us through to the third round after Torquay failed with one of theirs.

The Third Round was a more straightforward 2-1 victory over fellow
League One side Charlton, also at St.Marys, which set up a Southern
Area Semi-Final tie at home to Norwich City.

This game would be the closest we came to being knocked out of the
competition when Norwich took a 2-1 lead in to the final minute.
However, that man Papa Waigo again came to the team's rescue,
scoring in the final minute to send the match to penalties. Waigo had
also scored the opening goal of the game in the first half and had

266

become a bit of a cult figure amongst the fans. This emerging cult status was not just due to the fact that he seemed to be scoring crucial goals at crucial times in this competition, but also for his pace, which often saw him flagged offside countless times during a match.

"PapaWaigo, he's always offside!" was the chant that echoed around St. Marys whenever the assistant referee's flag curtailed one of his Speedy Gonzales style runs.

Saints would go on to win a tense and nervy penalty competition despite being the first side to fail to convert one of their five spot-kicks, but Norwich missed two of theirs, and that set up an area-final against MK Dons.

Milton Keynes Dons are probably most football fans least favourite team, due to how they came into existence from the carcass of the old Wimbledon FC. Nicknamed "Franchise FC" by many fans around the country, a lot of people boycott going to their clubs away games at their ground, and it was an attitude I embraced.

We won the first-leg 1-0 and the second leg a fortnight later drew a bumper crowd of almost 30,000 to St. Marys, and I was there after boycotting the first-leg on the principle that the MK Dons would never get any of my money.

Despite my pre-match nerves, the second-leg turned out to be nothing other than a straightforward 3-1 win for the Saints, and after everything the fans had been through in the past few months, getting to Wembley was the least that we deserved.

As Southern Area winners, we would face the Northern section winners, which turned out to be fellow League One side Carlisle United.

There is nothing like a Wembley final (no matter how insignificant the competition) to get fans interested in their club again. Even though I expected that interest in tickets would be high, I didn't expect (and neither did the club) that the interest would reach fever pitch. Nevertheless, I did manage to get a ticket and so did a couple of friends. We had arranged for one friend to drive us to the outskirts of London where we would park, get the tube into central London have a couple of drinks (well several actually) before heading off to watch the final, before doing the journey in reverse. That was the plan. Unfortunately, it was a plan that changed at short notice, as our friend who was driving suddenly announced on the night before the game that he could no longer go. This was annoying, as the two of us who could go now had to take our chances in trying to get on trains that were already going to be chock full of London bound Saints fans.

After queuing for nearly 45 minutes, we finally boarded a train, and we were on our way to London, a capital city that was about to be invaded by tens of thousands of red and white clad Southampton fans, as a little bit of London became Hampshire for the day.

Officially, over 44,000 Saints fans made the trip to Wembley; however, I think that there were much more than that in the 73,476 attendance, as the Carlisle end of the stadium appeared sparsely populated in comparison to the sea of red and white at our end.

If any Saints fans were expecting this match to be a tight game they were wrong as we tore into Carlisle from the kick-off, and by halftime we had already established a 2-0 lead thanks to Rickie Lambert's penalty, and an Adam Lallana strike.

Papa Waigo added a third five minutes into the second half, a goal I missed due to still consuming a half-time pint, but I was back in my seat in time to witness our fourth goal on the hour mark from Michail Antonio.

Although Carlisle managed to get on the scoresheet with six minutes to go, it was nothing more than a consolation goal, and the scenes of joy at the final whistle were unconfined.

When captains Dean Hammond and Kelvin Davis lifted the trophy aloft, I didn't see a piece of silverware, I saw a phoenix rising from the ashes of its demise, a symbol of how a football club so close to death could come back to glory.

If we could get a promotion too, that would really round off a perfect season.

Frustration

Yeovil 0 Saints 1   League One   17 April 2010

With the trophy safely locked away, attention once again turned towards the league campaign and that elusive League One playoff spot.

The problem with that was although we were winning the majority of our matches, the teams we were chasing were also doing the same, and games were running out. We had five games to play, and we had to win them all and hope that the two teams above us (Huddersfield and Colchester) slipped up. At least we had the advantage that three of those five games were at St. Marys. Huddersfield, who occupied the last playoff spot, only had three games to play but had an eleven-point advantage over us, so it was going to be tight but not impossible so long as we kept winning. Colchester were directly above us in seventh had four games left in their schedule and a five-point advantage.

Yeovil were mid-table and it seemed as though this should be a straightforward 3-points, and so I made the trip to Somerset hopeful that we could maintain our playoff push in some style.

I decided to forgo the easy option of getting one of the official travel club coaches to the match and instead make my own way there on the train, it would be a decision I would later come to regret.

The day started well enough, although, it was an unusually hot day for mid-April, and I would come to regret not taking a hat with me or slapping some sunscreen onto my exposed head and arms.

269

If you have ever travelled to Yeovil for a football match by train you will know just how far the station is from the stadium. For those of you who have not, then let me assure you, it is miles – five miles in fact. Fortunately, when I alighted the train, as well as being greeted by a whole constabulary's worth of police (they must have got us confused with Millwall fans, or worse, Portsmouth) there was also a rather dilapidated coach, which I was informed by the police, would transport us all to the ground.

The police, in particular, were keen on Saints fans using this coach rather than making our own way to the ground, and it was whilst I was queuing to board the coach that I realised that this service wasn't free.

Asking for a return I was told by the irascible old git in the driver's seat that he couldn't change the £20 note I was holding in my hand, therefore I used my remaining loose change to buy a single. I'll just have to buy a single on the way back I thought. If not wearing a hat on this hot sunny day was my first mistake of the day, not being able to secure a return ticket on this charabanc would be my second, but more on that later.

I've never been on a rollercoaster, and I never will either as it's not my thing, although the coach journey to the ground was probably the closest I will ever come to going on one. The roads leading from the station towards the stadium seemed to consist of narrow single carriageway roads. These roads and their tight blind corners were taken at speeds that Lewis Hamilton would have been proud of, as those of us who had made the mistake of boarding this conveyance of the damned were flung about like rag dolls in all directions. I just hoped that we would make it to the ground unscathed, as hairpin bends were taken on two wheels, give way signs ignored and the speed limit flouted as we thundered through the Somerset countryside.

We made it to the ground in one piece, although more by luck than anything else, but the speed of our journey meant that there were less than three hours until the kick-off. A couple of pubs that welcomed away fans were situated a few minutes' walk away, so I just followed everyone in a Saints shirt who seemed to be heading away from the ground until they led me to one. It was packed, even at half-12 and after fighting my way to the bar and waiting for another 10 to 15 minutes to be served I made my way back outside in order to enjoy my pint of overpriced ale. If there is one thing that publicans know how to do it's to charge the maximum they can to visiting supporters, especially when competition for watering holes is scarce.

By now, it was near 1 o'clock and I was already feeling myself burning in the afternoon sun as I supped my rapidly warming pint. Not wishing to fight my way through the throng for a second I headed back towards the stadium. With little under an hour to kill before the turnstiles even opened, I bought a programme and proceeded to sit on one of the shallow grass banks that seem to surround the ground.

Eventually, the turnstiles opened but with an hour to go until the kick-off and with a ticket for the open terrace, my burning skin was telling me that this was not going to be a pleasant afternoon.

The match itself was a dull affair and it looked to be petering out to a goalless draw until Lee Barnard popped up with a stoppage-time winner to keep our slim playoff hopes alive for another week.

As I made my way out of the ground, greeting me was the rusty sight of that fans coach that would take me back to Yeovil Junction train station, and feeling ever so slightly hot and dehydrated, I decided to take my life into my own hands once more.

Cash in hand, I boarded the coach and asked the same kamikaze driver for a single to the station.

"I'm only taking return tickets." He huffed matter-of-factly and with a little bit of amusement.

"You didn't tell me that when I bought my single," I replied, I was feeling hot and annoyed and I could feel my temper rising. However, he just shrugged his shoulders in a "couldn't give a fuck" way that was beginning to wind me up. I was just another anonymous face to him in a town full of them.

I trudged off the bus and considered my options, which were limited to be fair. It was too far to walk, but there had to be a local bus that ran to the town centre. At least from there, I could get a bus or a taxi to the train station, so my only option was to follow some Yeovil fans who would lead me to the nearest bus stop, I hoped.

I was seriously hot, dehydrated, and sweaty by the time I managed to find my way to a bus stop, but with no timetable and no idea of when the next bus was due, or even for that matter if it would take me in the right direction, my hope of ending this nightmare anytime soon was receding.

After spending the best part of five hours in the late spring sunshine, I must have looked redder than a boiled lobster, and I certainly felt like one by the time a bus eventually arrived. Well, I call it a bus but it was more like a sardine tin. It was a minibus and I was fortunate enough to be able to get on it let alone get a seat. Eventually, we made our way through the heavy traffic and into the town centre, where I now had to get to the train station, which was still about two to three miles away.

I managed to find the bus stop I needed for the bus that would take me to the station, but after checking the timetable against that of the train service, I was stuck in Yeovil town centre for the best part of an hour and a half. There was one train left back towards Salisbury (where I would need to change to get back to Southampton) and if I missed that, it meant spending the night in this God forsaken place.

In the meantime, I had no option but to hunker down in a pub for over an hour and consume a couple of pints and a much-needed meal.

Mercifully, and despite my fears, the bus arrived and I made it to the station with about 10 minutes to spare, and I've never been so happy to see a train in all my life, that was until I got on and realised that the train was packed. Taking a seat in first-class, I hoped to bluff my way through the journey by avoiding having my standard ticket inspected. Not having my ticket scrutinised was the least of my problems though when the train pulled into a station about 10 minutes into our journey. Boarding at this stop was a group of the rowdiest most obnoxious Saints fans I have ever had the misfortune to share a train carriage with. They must have got an earlier train and then got off to get bladdered at a nearby pub, before getting on this last train home. They also had the same idea as me as they stumbled into first-class beer cans in hand shouting and singing.

During the remainder of the journey, they proceeded to sing anti-IRA songs and pro-Glasgow Rangers songs (despite obviously being Southampton fans – strange bunch), and their behaviour included climbing into the overhead luggage racks, jumping up and down, spilling beer, and arguing with each other. They didn't even tone it down when the guard passed, and he did nothing to stop them, but I didn't blame him for that, I wouldn't want to confront them either.

During this journey of the damned, I made a mental note to put as much distance between them and me when we changed trains at Salisbury, but my luck changed, as when the time came to change trains, the rowdy group boarded a train to Romsey instead.

By the time I got home, I was suffering from mild heat stroke, dehydration and my skin colour had gone from lobster to beetroot, but at least Saints still had a chance of making the playoffs, especially as Huddersfield had lost and their lead was now down to eight points.

Unfortunately, we failed to close that gap to five points with three games to play when we could only manage a 0-0 draw against Oldham at St. Marys the following Tuesday, thus blowing our game in hand. Now the gap was seven points, and both clubs now had three games left, which meant we had to win all three and hope that both Huddersfield and Colchester faltered.

We couldn't do our bit, and despite beating Carlisle at home on the following Saturday Huddersfield also won, making the seven-point gap insurmountable with two to play. It was a disappointing way to end the season, and that 10-point handicap coupled with our slow start to the campaign was just too much to overcome.

Next season, however, we would be starting on level playing field, and if we could get off to a flying start, there was no reason why we shouldn't walk away with promotion, and hopefully, the League One championship trophy in what would be the clubs 125th anniversary season.

Farewell Our Saviour

Saints 0 Plymouth 1   League One   7 August 2010

We didn't get the start to the season we had hoped for during the summer, and this game seemed to hammer home the realisation that perhaps this wasn't going to be a cakewalk to the title after all.

The comings and goings during the summer had been unspectacular, the only signings of note being bald-headed Richard Chaplow from Preston, Danny Butterfield from Crystal Palace, and Brazilian striker Guly Du Prado who signed on loan from Italian side Cesena.

No players left for a transfer fee during the summer, but plenty found themselves loaned out or released, and those packing their bags for pastures new included Graeme Murty, Paul Wooton, Chris Perry, and Lee Molyneux.

Just days after this depressing opening day defeat to Plymouth came the news that the club's owner Markus Liebherr had passed away suddenly from a heart attack at the age of 62. It was devastating news and rocked the club and the fans to their core. As a mark of respect, the Football Association agreed to postpone the game at MK Dons scheduled for the following Saturday, thus allowing everyone connected to the club to grieve.

When the club finally played their next fixture, it turned out to be a rather disappointing 1-1 draw at home to Leyton Orient, as our stuttering start to the season showed no signs of improving.

As a Saints fan, you know that the word "turmoil" is never far away from being used, and just hours after a thumping 4-0 away win at Bristol Rovers it was in use once more, as manager Alan Pardew was sacked. It was another shock to the system of every Saints fan and one that seemed to come completely out of the blue.

In the days after Pardew's dismissal, rumours began circulating as to the reason behind his sudden departure, with some saying that player morale was low, or that he had fallen out with chairman Nicola Cortese. There were also more scurrilous rumours about his private life, which I won't go into here as they could be libellous, but most Saints fans will know what I am referring to.

Stepping into the breach as caretaker manager was Dean Wilkins who had been Pardew's assistant, and his first job was to see Southampton safely through to the next round of the Johnstone's Paint Trophy. We faced Swindon Town at home in the first round and as holders, we had hoped to become the first club to retain the trophy, but that dream came to an abrupt end when we lost 3-0 thanks to an insipid display.

Any Saints fans looking for a positive aspect to this early exit would tell you that this meant that we could now concentrate on the league and securing promotion back to The Championship, but I won't deny that missing out on another trip to Wembley was disappointing.

I wouldn't have minded so much if the league form had begun to improve, but if anything it was getting worse. I was in a crowd of just over 18,000 who witnessed an appalling 2-0 home loss to Rochdale (they would complete a humiliating double over us later in the season), and this was quickly followed by a 1-0 loss at Swindon.

A day after the Swindon loss, it was confirmed that Scunthorpe boss Nigel Adkins would become the next permanent Southampton manager. Adkins had worked wonders at Scunthorpe taking them out of League One and into the second tier after an absence of 40 years. Even though their stay was short-lived, he managed to secure instant promotion back to The Championship at the first attempt via the play-offs. It was obvious that he had the credentials to get a team out of the third tier, and with a better squad and a bigger budget, there was no reason why he couldn't do the same here.

Early results under Adkins didn't inspire much confidence that he could get us promoted, to be honest, and his first game in charge was the re-arranged away game at MK Dons, a match we lost 2-0. A tame 0-0 at home followed against Colchester, a result that left us in the relegation zone with one win in our first seven league games, hardly promotion form.

The rot stopped with a hard fought 1-0 win at Sheffield Wednesday where goalkeeper Kelvin Davis pulled off a string of fine saves in order to secure three valuable points. More wins followed, most notably at home to Bournemouth and Tranmere (both 2-0 wins), Notts County away (3-1) and Dagenham & Redbridge at home (4-0).

By the time we thrashed fellow promotion contenders Huddersfield Town 4-1 at St. Marys just after Boxing Day, we had clawed our way up to fifth, just five points behind leaders Brighton.

The New Year brought mixed results as we won 6-0 away at Oldham, only to draw 0-0 at home to Notts County a few days later. February also included an incredible 4-4 draw at Peterborough, where we conspired to throw away a two-goal lead twice. Not content on letting a Peterborough come back from 2-0 down, we let them come back from 4-2 down after we had worked so hard in re-establishing our two-goal advantage. To make matters worse, Peterborough's second equaliser came in the third minute of stoppage-time.

That double capitulation did not derail our ongoing promotion push, and throughout March and into April we won seven out of eight in the League, a run that took us up to second place in the table, but a whopping thirteen points behind runaway leaders Brighton.

Rochdale ended that unbeaten run when they completed their unlikely double over us at Spotland (another 2-0 reverse), and with Huddersfield pushing us all the way for the last promotion place, nothing was assured.

As we had experienced a few seasons ago, the playoffs can be a bit of a lottery, you can go into them with the best form in the division, and lose it all in one two-legged tie or worse, in the final at Wembley.

From desperately wanting us to make the playoffs the previous season, I, and every other Saints fan were desperately hoping to avoid them this time.

Happy Mondays

Saints 3 Walsall 1   League One   17 May 2011

The run-in to the end of the season was about as nerve-wracking as it gets as every time we won a match our nearest challengers Huddersfield won also, and they certainly lived up to their 'Terriers' nickname as we just couldn't shake them off.

After the loss at Rochdale, we sneaked past Bristol Rovers at St. Marys thanks to a solitary Guly Du Prado goal just eight minutes before the end of the match. Of course, Huddersfield won their game, and once again, we were clinging on to second place only by virtue of having a superior goal difference.

With automatic promotion hanging in the balance, the last fixture we needed was a trip to runaway leaders Brighton, a team that had just clinched the title the previous week.

There had been some bad blood between the two clubs back when they played out a goalless draw at St. Marys in November, a match where Brighton set up ultra defensively in order to gain a point. Ironically, they should have won the match, when in one of their rare forays into our penalty area, they won a very soft spot-kick, which Kelvin Davies saved.

After the match, a reporter asked Nigel Adkins whether Saints or Brighton would win the title, and his reply of "only if they can keep with us." I'm sure the statement was said tongue-in-cheek but it did seem to have the effect of riling up the Brighton management and players, with some even mentioning that those words from Adkins that had inspired them to go on and win the title.

Now it was time for the rematch at the ramshackle Withdean Stadium, and more controversy and verbal sparring in the days before and after the match.

278

As is typical for a team that has just secured the championship, it is traditional for the opposition players to form a guard of honour as the champions elect enter the field of play. However, there was no such line-up from the Southampton players, and the Brighton players and management perceived this as a lack of respect. It was certainly going to spice up a match that was already shaping up to be a red-hot battle royal.

Huddersfield had already played the previous day and had come away from MK Dons with a convincing 3-1 win, a result that placed them back in second with a three-point cushion, a result that heaped more pressure on us.

A win at Brighton was going to be a tough ask, as they had not been defeated at home in the league all season, and a victory looked even more improbable when centre-back Radhi Jaidi under hit a back pass in first half stoppage-time, which set up Brighton striker Ashley Barnes to put the Seagulls ahead at the break.

That was the way the score stayed until six minutes from time until a long ball into the penalty area created panic amongst the Brighton defenders, and diminutive striker David Connelly found enough time and space, to swivel and shoot the ball home.

I think most Saints fans would have taken a point before the game, but things were to get even better as deep into stoppage-time, another long ball into the box found centre-back Jose Fonte unmarked at the far post, and his lofty header across the six-yard box looped over everyone and into the net for the winner.

Cue scenes of delirium amongst the Saints travelling army as Fonte jumped over the advertising boards behind the goal and onto the running track. Ripping off his shirt, he disappeared under a sea of teammates and Saints fans that had spilt out from their home in the temporary stand that served as the away supporters section.

It was a massive three points, and once again put us back in control of our own destiny, as well as putting us back into second place in the league. After the match, furious Brighton manager, Uruguayan Gus Poyet, described our tactics as long ball, comparing us to strugglers Dagenham & Redbridge. His remarks were said with no hint of irony whatsoever, and it seemed as though his memory was a short one considering how he set his team up to play at St. Marys back in November.

Poyet would remain a target of disdain for Saints fans during the remainder of his time at Brighton, and oh, how we all laughed when he received the news of his sacking by Brighton in 2013 live on television. He was working as a pundit for the BBC's coverage of the FIFA Confederations Cup match between Spain and Nigeria when host Gary Lineker was handed a piece of paper from the production crew and read out the statement that Poyet had been sacked. His face was a picture, and whomever on the BBC crew decided that it was the right time to inform him of the news, I would just like to say a big thank you on behalf of all Southampton supporters.

Two days after that win at Brighton, it was back to St. Marys for a home match against mid-table Hartlepool, which would turn out to be another game where we struggled to break down a team that had come to defend deep in the hope of securing a point. In fact, it wasn't until the second half that we took the lead, thanks to a Lambert penalty just before the hour mark, then Fonte popped up again with another crucial goal to secure the points eight minutes from the end.

Yet again Huddersfield won, this time 2-1 at Dagenham & Redbridge to keep them within touching distance of us. How the roles had reversed on the previous campaign when we were chasing Huddersfield for that last playoff place, and now here they were trying to hunt us down for the last automatic promotion spot.

The next fixtures were tough looking propositions for both clubs, as we had to travel to Brentford, whilst Town had to play at Brighton, although not many Saints fans believed that Brighton wouldn't take it easy in a bid to scupper our promotion bid.

Our match was actually a straightforward 3-0 win, but just as though it looked like Huddersfield had slipped up they scored a last-minute winner to secure a 3-2 victory at The Withdean.

Now, we had to play away at Plymouth on Bank Holiday Monday, which was our game in hand. Win this, and promotion was all but assured, but anything less meant that promotion would come down to the last game of the season.

With Plymouth battling against relegation, I was expecting a tight game of few chances, but in the end, we dominated the match and won comfortably 3-1 a result that all but sealed our promotion to The Championship.

Only a defeat in our last game at home to Walsall, a win for Huddersfield over Brentford, and a seventeen-goal swing in the goal difference would prevent us from going up. It was never going to happen, and when Guly Du Prado put us in front on 26 minutes, it was the catalyst for another comfortable 3-1 win. The scenes of celebration at the final whistle were euphoric, and whereas the pitch invasion at the end of 2009 carried with it hints of sadness, confusion and elements of menace, this one was just the start of our promotion party.

After all, we had been through, the years of decline, the near bankruptcy of our club, the mismanagement at board level and on the sidelines, we were back in the second-tier, and the new owner's five-year plan to get us back to the Premier League was still on.

Launch Pad

Saints 3 Leeds United 1   The Championship   6 August 2011

The general consensus amongst Southampton fans was that we would be looking forward to a year of stability in The Championship, with the club gearing up for a promotion push the following season. I wasn't under any illusions that playing in The Championship would be a lot tougher than playing in League One, and I was just hoping the team could win enough matches to avoid a relegation battle.

This season also saw renewed hostilities with Portsmouth, with derby matches scheduled for Fratton Park in December, and St. Marys in April. Pompey had fallen on hard times since their fairytale rise had morphed into a nightmare. Heavily in debt, due to paying money they didn't have on players they couldn't afford, they had entered administration in April 2010, and as a result of this, they were deducted nine points by the Premier League. That points deduction resulted in their relegation from the Premier League as they were already struggling after selling several key players and high earners. Now back in The Championship, they continued to struggle both on and off the pitch, and they were lucky to avoid relegation at the end of the 2010-11 season.

The last time the two sides met, they had the advantage of being two divisions above us, but now not only were we back on an even footing, but also our squad looked much better on paper than theirs did.

As any Saints fan will tell you, our opening day record is abysmal, and it has been since the late 1980s, I think I'm correct in saying that you can count the number of opening day victories by Saints since 1988 on the fingers of one hand. Therefore, when the fixture list gave us an opening day fixture against Leeds at St. Marys for our first

282

match back in The Championship, I wasn't hopeful that we could secure all three points.

This was one occasion where I was delighted to be proved wrong, as we stormed into a two-goal lead inside the first half-an-hour, thanks to goals by Dean Hammond and Adam Lallana. We were in total control of the match from start to finish, and as I watched the players knock the ball around with aplomb in the warm August sunshine, I had the feeling that maybe this wasn't going to be a season of consolidation after all.

David Connelly wrapped up the points when he prodded home our third goal just seven minutes into the second half, and despite Leeds pulling a goal back to spark memories of that time they overturned a three-goal deficit to win, there was no such pain this time, and we saw the game out with ease.

This result was no flash in the pan either, as we won our next three games, which included an impressive 5-2 thrashing of Ipswich at Portman Road. In fact, we won six out of our first seven games (the only loss a 3-2 reverse at Leicester), as we made one of our best starts to a season since we joined the Football League in 1920. The most impressive performance during our winning start was a 4-1 win over Birmingham City at St. Marys. Birmingham found themselves back in The Championship after relegation from the Premier League as well as being the current holders of the League Cup. Not only that, but they were also most bookmakers favourites to make an instant return to the top-flight. However, when they left St. Marys, it looked as though only one team would be challenging for promotion out of the two this season, and it wasn't the blues.

After a defeat at Cardiff at the end of September, the Saints embarked on another long unbeaten run in the league. In the eight fixtures played between 1st October and 19th November, Saints won six and drew two. That run included a hard-fought but deserved victory over fellow promotion rivals West Ham, as well as a comprehensive 3-0 shellacking of Brighton at St.Marys, a match in which my new girlfriend Vicky and my son attended with me.

My personal life had changed so much over the summer, my marriage had ended, and I had met a new partner, on top of this one of my two sons moved in with me after he fell out with his mother and her new partner. Happily, the Saints and Vicky helped to get me through the tough emotional problems stemming from divorce proceedings and child custody battles. It felt as though the Saints winning start to the season was just for my benefit.

After that 3-0 win against Brighton, we hit a bit of a slump in league form. Such was our lead at the top of the table we had suddenly become the team everyone wanted to beat. They wanted to knock these upstarts from League One off their perch, and as a consequence, we only picked up three wins in twelve matches, although that included a 1-1 draw at Fratton Park in December. It was a match we should have won but a one-goal lead is always dodgy, no more so when playing your local rivals away from home. We only had six minutes to hold out before they managed to scramble home an equaliser, which was a bitter blow, but at least it was a better performance and result than our last trip there in the Premier League.

That poor run of results had been enough to allow West Ham to overtake us in the table as we slipped out of first place for the first time since early September, and now we had Birmingham and Cardiff breathing down our necks.

What we need was to put another long unbeaten run together to keep our automatic promotion hopes alive.

Back On Top

Saints 4 Derby County 0   Championship   18 February 2012

As a football fan of many years, I always get great pleasure in introducing new people to my obsession. I cajole new girlfriends into accompanying me after a few weeks of knowing me and I've introduced many friends both male and female into the delights of going to a football match, although it does tend to be the men who stick with it for a lot longer than the ladies.

One day at work a colleague of mine, Damien, showed an interest in coming along to see a Saints match, and so it was that I introduced him to a world of high ticket prices, dodgy food and the chance to sit in the pouring rain watching goalless draws.

Now, when introducing a new friend or partner to football, you have to be careful about which fixture you choose to take them to, as taking them to a match that ends 0-0 or in a heavy defeat for the home team, can quickly douse the flames of their interest.

Damien's first match was a League Cup first round match at home to Yeovil in 2006. I chose this match for a number of reasons. The first being that there would be plenty of tickets, secondly, that the ticket prices will be lower, and thirdly, there should be a goal or two.

We ran out 5-2 winners, a victory that meant Damien showed interest in wanting to make more visits to St. Marys. In fact, Damien became something of a lucky omen for the club, and his attendance always produced either a victory or at least a draw.

This particular February afternoon Damien attended the match with me and it was a match we needed to win in order to get back to the top of the table.

We had drawn three out of four games prior to this match; although considering they were draws against three of our promotion rivals

(Cardiff, Birmingham, and West Ham) I was more than pleased with the results. What we needed to do now was to start winning again, and winning consistently.

Commentators and pundits will often say, "These are the type of matches you should be winning if you want promotion," and they're right, and with Derby mooching about in mid-table, this was definitely one of those games.

A solitary Jos Hooiveld goal gave us a slender lead at the break, but it was during the second half that we really started to put on a show. The second forty-five minutes was probably one of the best displays by a Southampton side I had watched in a long time, as we stroked the ball around as if the Derby players weren't there. Goals from Aaron Martin, Adam Lallana and Japanese striker Tadanari Lee sealed three of the easiest points we would get all season, and in truth, we should have won by an even greater margin.

That victory over The Rams was the catalyst for another run of victories throughout February and March and included an Alamo-like performance at Leeds United, a match where goalkeeper Kelvin Davis almost single-handedly won us the match.

After Rickie Lambert had given us the lead on 16 minutes, it soon became apparent to those Southampton fans in the stadium and those – like me – who were watching it on the television that this was not going to be an easy lead to keep.

Inspired by the fact that this was new manager Neil Warnock's first home game in charge, Leeds had already shown their attacking intent in the minutes before we scored, and now, stung by our goal they laid siege to our penalty area for most of the next 74 minutes. We survived until half-time with our slender lead intact, only for the barrage to continue in the second-half.

If that performance against Derby was one of the best 45 minutes of team football I had seen from the Saints for a long time, then this was easily the best 45 minutes of goalkeeping I think I had ever seen by a Southampton goalie. Kelvin Davies stopped everything that night but also had luck on his side as Leeds hit the woodwork twice and had a couple of penalty appeals turned down.

Leeds United had twenty-two shots at goal during the match, twelve of which were on target, compared to our seven shots and four on target. Kelvin stopped the entire dozen, and even looking back at the footage now, I still find it hard to believe some of the saves he made that night.

If you want to show someone a master class in goalkeeping then search for the video of the match on the internet, it's well worth it.

That nail-biter at Leeds meant that we stretched our lead to four points over West Ham but we had played two more games than they had, and Reading who had stormed up the table after a slow start to the season were five points back in third place.

Four more wins in the next five games kept us on course for not only promotion, but also the title, and by the time we beat Doncaster 2-0 at St. Marys towards the end of March, we were five points clear of Reading in second, and six points ahead of third-place West Ham. If we could avoid another slump, then promotion would be certain.

Then we hit a slump.

Let's Get This Party Started

Saints 4 Coventry City 0   Championship   28 April 2012

The slump in form started at the end of March when we travelled to playoff chasing Blackpool. It wasn't going to be an easy match that much was certain, but there was to be no fun beside the seaside as we produced one of our worst displays of the season. When West Ham also lost, we knew that we had gotten away with producing such a poor performance at such a crucial stage of the season, although Reading's victory in their match had cut the gap to second to two points, and we still had to play them at home.

Next up for us was the derby match against Portsmouth at St. Marys. Derby games are by their very nature always fiercely contested, and it wasn't a match we needed at this stage of the season.

The resulting 2-2 draw is still a cause for celebration in Portsmouth to this day, although most Saints fans are at a loss to explain why a match that helped us win promotion and gave them a massive push towards relegation should be lauded so. Yes, they scored an equaliser in the fourth minute of stoppage-time, and the two points we dropped that day allowed Reading to draw level on points at the top, but for some reason, they think that the result prevented us from winning the title. Nothing could be further from the truth. Our failure to win the title was down to the 3-1 home loss to Reading a week after the Portsmouth game, nothing more nothing less, but Pompey fans love clutching at straws, and any myth will do to fit their tainted view of matches between them and us.

That loss to Reading was a real sickener, as I thought that we had a better squad and with home advantage, we should have taken at least a point if not all three. A win at Crystal Palace after the Pompey draw meant that going into the match against Reading only goal difference separated the two clubs, but by the end of the match, the lead had swung Reading's way. To make matters worse, that loss had allowed West Ham in third to narrow the gap to three points, and now from looking like winning the title, we were suddenly trying to cling on to the last automatic promotion place. With three games to go, it was a straight fight between West Ham and Saints to see who could avoid the lottery of the playoffs.

Our next match was at Peterborough, scene of that manic 4-4 draw the previous season. The Posh had followed us up via the playoffs, and now they were hoping to gain the three points that would secure another season in The Championship. West Ham also had a tricky away fixture at a Bristol City side that were also fighting to preserve their Championship status.

It was imperative to get a good start to the match, and that's exactly what we got with goals from Hooiveld and Billy Sharp giving us a 2-0 lead in the opening 10 minutes. Of course, we had thrown away two two-goal leads in the same fixture the previous season, so we couldn't exactly relax.

This time there was to be no such capitulation, as a Billy Sharp goal midway through the second half sealed the win, and better news was to follow when news of West Ham's 1-1 draw at Bristol City filtered through.

With the gap now five points with two games to play, we knew what we needed to do to secure promotion back to the land of milk and honey that is the English Premier League. A win in our penultimate match away to Middlesbrough would be enough, anything less and depending on how West Ham fared in their match, it could all rest on the final game of the season.

I didn't travel to the North-East for what was a crucial match as I didn't think we would win, and the match was also being televised live on the BBC. I didn't feel we could win simply because our recent performances suggested to me that the players were letting the pressure of securing promotion to get to them. Part of me also wanted it to go down to the final match so more Saints fans could celebrate at the final home game of the season against Coventry.

I got my wish, and despite the fact that Billy Sharp gave us the lead in the first minute of the match, Middlesbrough overturned the deficit to win 2-1.

Now we had to wait 48 hours before West Ham played their penultimate match of the season away at Leicester, where anything other than a win for The Hammers would seal our promotion.

In the end, they won a hard-fought match 2-1 after going behind midway through the first half, and that meant that the gap was two points with one game left in the season, and now it was win or bust in our final match against Coventry at St. Marys.

It felt like déjà vu as I walked through the turnstiles at St. Marys on a very pleasant late April afternoon. I thought I had left it too late to secure a ticket for the match but thankfully, Coventry couldn't sell their allocation of tickets due to their relegation to League One having already been confirmed. The tickets they returned were put to good use and the Saints ticket office opened up that block of seats for home fans, meaning I was fortunate enough to get a seat just a couple of rows from the front and almost behind the goal.

I was definitely more nervous for this match than I had been a year ago simply because we had to win this time, whereas a year previously, we could have lost and still have earned promotion such was the gulf in goal difference between Huddersfield and us.

This time the goal difference was just a couple in our favour, and a draw for us coupled with a big win for West Ham in their match at home to Hull meant that they could pip us by the cruellest of margins.

The crowd was tense, I could feel it all around the ground, and with the BBC cameras once again in attendance, we needed to get off to another strong start.

Rather than appearing nervous at the task ahead of them, the Saints players actually looked fired up and ready to battle their way to promotion, and it wasn't long before our high-tempo passing play paid off.

Just 16 minutes into the match, Billy Sharp scored to give us a lead we never looked likely to relinquish against a demoted and demoralised Coventry side.

Three minutes later, it was 2-0 when Jose Fonte stooped low to head home from a corner-kick.

Now the party was in full flow and with Coventry offering only minimal resistance, further goals from Hooiveld and Lallana in a 4-minute spell during the second half sealed a comfortable 4-0 win. At the final whistle, I ran onto the pitch with thousands of other jubilant Saints fans in order to laud the players on a magnificent and unexpected promotion to the Premier League. It was going to be one hell of a party.

The Return of the Saints

Saints 0 Wigan Athletic 2   Premier League   25 August 2012

The summer had been a glorious one, and the anticipation of the new season's fixture list was higher than normal. When the fixtures did come out it was somewhat underwhelming that our first home game back in the big time would be against Wigan Athletic, but first, we had to negotiate a tricky opening day away match at defending champions Manchester City.

There was no doubt in my mind that the squad would need heavy strengthening during the close season if we held out any hope of retaining our newly acquired Premier League status, a sentiment shared by the board as the club smashed its transfer record twice in a matter of weeks.

Striker Jay Rodriguez was the first to arrive, his £7.5 million move from Burnley smashing our previous record fee paid to Derby for Rory Delap (£4 million) over eleven years previously. A couple of

291

weeks later and that outlay was dwarfed by the £12 million spent on the signature of Uruguayan midfield playmaker Gaston Ramirez from Italian side Bologna.

Other additions during the summer included midfielder Steven Davis from Glasgow Rangers, right-back Nathaniel Clyne from Crystal Palace, centre-back Maya Yoshida and free agent goalkeeper Arthur Boruc.

We had to wait for our first game back in the big time when Sky Sports moved the match to a Sunday for live coverage, and it would be a match that was anything but the one-sided affair most fans had predicted.

Prior to the kick-off, manager Nigel Adkins stunned the majority of Saints fans by leaving Rickie Lambert on the bench. It was a bold move by the manager to leave out our top scorer for the past three seasons. For Rickie it must have felt so frustrating to be on the cusp of fulfilling his lifelong dream of playing in the Premier League, only to find himself named amongst the substitutes.

Rickie would eventually come on and score as Saints let slip a 2-1 lead to lose 3-2, but despite the loss, it was a good performance against the defending champions, although rumours surrounding Nigel Adkins job security continued to persist.

The rumours of discontent between Nigel and Nicola Cortese had first surfaced at the tail end of the previous season, and these grew in intensity during the summer, but Adkins started the season in the manager's chair, but for how long?

Following the plucky 3-2 loss at Champions Manchester City, the team experienced a taste of how harsh life can be at the top table when perennial relegation strugglers Wigan rode into town and left a few hours later with all three points.

The match itself didn't have the tension or the flowing football of the defeat at Manchester City, but if we had taken our chances the result would have been different. Adam Lallana hit the crossbar with a shot in the first half, and as both teams showed their profligacy in front of goal it always looked as though one goal would be enough to win it.

In the end, Wigan scored twice, and although the second arrived in stoppage-time by then we looked like a beaten side. Despite the money spent on strengthening the squad during the summer, it seemed as though this season would be one long battle against relegation.

Things would get much worse before they got better too, and in our next home match, another valiant effort against Manchester United yielded no points when United's Robin Van Persie completed an impressive hat trick in stoppage time, a goal that gave them a 3-2 win.

Our next away game saw us lose 6-1 at Arsenal, and it was becoming apparent to most Saints fans that wins this season would be harder to find than beauty contest entrants from Portsmouth.

One win in our first eleven games anchored us in the relegation zone, one point and one place above Harry Redknapp's QPR side, the team we would face next in West London.

There was added needle to this match as it would be the first time the club had come up against former manager Harry Redknapp since our relegation from the Premier League seven years ago. If not already a "must win" game, it was surely a "must not lose" game, and pre-match I just hoped that we would avoid the defeat that would send us to the bottom of the table. In fact, we went one better, and after Jason Puncheon added to Rickie Lambert's earlier strike, we took a comfortable looking 2-0 lead into the break.

It was a lead we held onto despite QPR pulling a goal back midway through the second half, and an Anton Ferdinand own goal put the lid on a 3-1 win and a vital three points.

A week later and it was time to square up against another of our former managers. This time it was the return of Alan Pardew to St. Marys for the first time since his surprise sacking two years previously.

It is an understatement to say that Alan Pardew was not a popular choice of manager amongst the Geordie faithful, and in fact, after the dismissal of their previous boss Chris Houghton, a poll compiled by Sky Sports showed that Pardew only received five percent of the vote to be their next boss.

Pardew wasn't particularly liked when he managed Southampton either, although I never had a problem with his appointment, unlike some other fans. One memory that springs to mind was an away game at Swindon in League One. It was only our third match of the season, and with all of the turmoil that took place in the summer, not to mention the new players having to bed in, it was obvious that we were going to start the season slowly. We had already drawn at home to Millwall on the opening day and had followed that up with a 3-1 loss at Huddersfield, and now we had to face Swindon at The County Ground.

I remember standing in the away end watching a rather heavy-set man with more tattoo's than brain cells shouting and screaming at Pardew for most of the match. As the match went on and it became obvious that we were facing another defeat, the guy seemed to get angrier and his face redder with each vitriolic tirade against the manager. I remember thinking it was a shocking way to treat a man who was less than three matches into his career as Southampton boss. I guess some fans take an instant dislike to a manager, and no matter what he does, that attitude will never change.

As with the previous match against Harry Redknapp's QPR side, Pardew didn't get the result he would have been craving for, and we ran out fairly comfortable 2-0 winners, thanks to goals in either half by Lallana and Ramirez.

294

Consecutive league wins for the first time since our return, gave us a glimmer of hope that we could beat the drop and retain our Premier League status, but that hope lasted for as long as it took us to string another winless run together. With the club still sitting in the relegation zone, it seemed as though time was starting to run out for Nigel Adkins.

All Good Things

Reading 0 Saints 2   Premier League   6 April 2013

Despite climbing out of the relegation zone, wins were still hard to come by, and we drew far too many games, and many from winning positions, which included an embarrassing collapse late on at Stoke, where we threw away a 3-1 lead to draw 3-3.

Our results in the cup competitions were not much better either, and our League Cup campaign ended in the fourth round and a 3-0 humbling at Leeds United. Worse was to come in the FA Cup when a rampant Chelsea side thrashed us 5-1 at St. Marys in round three.

Nigel Adkins final game in charge would also come against Chelsea, this time in the Premier League at Stamford Bridge, despite a much-improved performance that gained us a vital point in a 2-2 draw.

The sword of Damocles that had been hanging above Nigel's head for months finally fell two days after the Chelsea match and he was relieved of his duties. It was a sad end to a ride that had started near the bottom of League One and had led to the promised land of the Premier League, but I guess Nicola Cortese had his reasons.

The speculation about who was going to take over the job of preserving our top-flight status didn't last long, and despite Newcastle fans hoping that we would take Alan Pardew back, it was an Argentinean who would take the manager's chair.

The club wasted no time in announcing Mauricio Pochettino as the new boss just hours after the news of Nigel Adkins sacking had hit the headlines. Pochettino came from Spanish side Espanyol with a reputation as one of the best up and coming managers in the game. His preference for a 4-2-3-1 formation, coupled with a high-energy high pressing game, meant that his teams were hard to beat.

His first game in charge was a 0-0 at home to Everton, but it didn't take long for him to turn the club's fortunes around, starting with a 3-1 win over defending champions Manchester City at St. Marys. Other impressive results soon followed as both Liverpool and Chelsea came to St. Marys and left thoroughly beaten (3-1, and 2-1 respectively).

Our recent run of good form had seen us climb to the heady heights of twelfth in the league, and a win in the next match at Reading would see us win three Premier League games in a row for the first time since December 2003.

Despite finishing above us the previous season, Reading had failed to strengthen their squad sufficiently in the summer. Going into this match, they found themselves anchored to the foot of the table, seven points adrift of safety and they had turned to Nigel Adkins to turn their fortunes around.

With their need greater than ours, Reading started the better, and Adam Le Fondre missed a gilt-edged chance to put the Royals in front early on. After that fortunate escape, the Southampton players grew in confidence and it wasn't long until we took the lead thanks to Jay Rodriguez's third goal in as many games.

The second half saw the teams evenly matched, and it wasn't until the 72nd minute before the points were all but secured thanks to an Adam Lallana strike.

Nigel failed in his attempt to keep Reading in the Premier League, and they went down despite still having three games left to play.

We finished a respectable 14th in the final table after another run of games without a win where we drew far too many, but overall it was a solid first season back in the big time, and now with one of the world's highest rated new coaches, we had the chance to make a real impact the following season.

All Change

Saints 1 West Bromwich Albion 0   Premier League 11 January 2014

In spite of the fact that the club was on an upward trajectory, this would be the only match I would attend this season. Maybe it had something to do with the hideous plain red kit we were wearing this season, although, I suspect that the real reason was a lack of money.

With three children to provide for and a girlfriend who lived miles away, if I had any money left over I invariably didn't have enough free time to spend watching Saints. This was a shame as Pochettino had the team playing some excellent football, and even more impressively, he had managed to shore up our ever-leaky defence.

It's one thing to have a tight defence, but when you're not scoring many goals at the other end, then wins can be hard to come by, and this was especially true in the first three months of the season. We wouldn't score more than two goals in a league match until we beat Hull City 4-1 on the 9th November.

Some would say that we didn't need to score more than two goals a game as we either conceded one or none, which is a valid point, but football fans go to matches to be entertained, and that means goals. It's rare but occasionally you can get to witness a thrilling 0-0 draw, however, there has never been a boring 3-2 or 4-3 victory.

One of the main reasons why we had stopped shipping goals was partly down to the signing of Croatian centre-back Dejan Lovren from French side Lyon. Lovren would have an outstanding first season in English football, but he would go from a fan favourite to public enemy number one by the end of the season.

Partnered at the back by the ever-reliable Jose Fonte, and with defensive midfielder Victor Wanyama, a £12.5 million signing from Celtic in front of them, all of a sudden Southampton had become a difficult team to beat.

Saints certainly splashed the cash again during the close season, and with over £20 million spent on Lovren and Wanyama, and another whopping fee of £15 million pounds paid to Italian giants AS Roma for their striker Dani Osvaldo.

Osvaldo came to English football with a reputation for being something of a loose cannon and a hothead. Even so, Pochettino had managed the player at Espanyol so we hoped that his calming influence could bring the best out of Osvaldo, as well as keep him on the straight and narrow.

When your club signs a player who has been suspended in the past for striking a teammate during a match for no other reason than he didn't pass to him, you have to wonder why the club would take such a risk and spend so much money on a player who could disrupt the harmony in the dressing room.

It was a risk that would come to haunt the club on a financial level, as it didn't take long for Osvaldo's lack of anger management to raise its ugly head. The first incident took place during a match at Newcastle in January, where a minor touchline scuffle turned into a full-on bout of fisticuffs. Osvaldo wasn't even on the pitch during this incident (he was one of the substitutes), and he was later banned for three games and fined £40,000 by the Football Association for violent conduct for his part in the melee.

Not satisfied with this, three weeks later the club announced that Osvaldo had been suspended after a training ground fight with club captain Jose Fonte that Osvaldo had instigated, which resulted in Fonte sporting a black-eye for the following few days.

The suspension was for two weeks, but in truth, there was no real way in which Osvaldo could seriously expect to come back to the squad.

The club terminated his contract at the end of the season, losing a significant amount of money on a player who had great skills, but also the wrong kind of temperament for playing in England.

After his stint at Saints, he would drift from team to team, popping up back in Italy, then Argentina and Portugal before finally ending his trail of destruction when he announced his retirement, so he could concentrate on his music career. Good luck with that Osvaldo, I think you are going to need it.

Also leaving this season would be chairman Nicola Cortese, who resigned from his position just a few days after this match against West Brom. Rumours of a strained relationship between Cortese and club owner Kathrina Liebherr surfaced, although no one outside of the club can say with any certainty why Cortese left.

His replacement would be a bit of a surprise, as it turned out to be Ralph Krueger, a man whose background was as an ice hockey player and coach. This appointment smacked of the similarly left-field appointment of Clive Woodward by Rupert Lowe about ten years previously. Could a man who has no experience of football really be the right man to lead the club forward? At the time of writing, I have to say that he has done a good job, and the club has steadily improved both on and off the pitch during his tenure.

On the field, and by the time this match came about, Saints had won only one match out of nine, which had caused us to drop to ninth after having been as high as third at the beginning of November.

I attended this match with my mate Damien, and he kept up his lucky unbeaten run going thanks to a solitary Adam Lallana goal that lit up an otherwise dire match.

That poor run, which encompassed most of November and all of December, would ultimately prevent us from qualifying for the Europa League, but an eighth-place finish was still reward for a solid season.

The only downside to finishing so high in the table was the fact that Pochettino was beginning to garner interest from other clubs, most notably Tottenham.

The rumours had in fact started before the end of the season, and the speculation increased each time Pochettino dodged questions about his future at the club whenever probed about it by the press.

Just weeks after the end of the season, pictures emerged online of a man sporting an uncanny likeness to Pochettino arriving at the Tottenham training ground. Despite the lack of news from the club, it was obvious to most Saints fans that Pochettino had taken control of his last match for Southampton. When the news broke a few days later that Pochettino was indeed the new Tottenham manager, the news surprised nobody.

Pochettino's departure would just be the beginning, as the club seemed intent on selling as many players to Liverpool as possible during the close season.

The first to leave were Adam Lallana and Rickie Lambert, with Dejan Lovren following them to Merseyside a few weeks later.

Lambert's departure was a particular blow, as he had quickly gained legendary status amongst the Saints supporters, but most Saints fans agreed that as a Scouser and Liverpool fan, Rickie deserved one last chance of glory with his hometown club. On the other hand, the departures of Lallana and Lovren would leave a bitter taste in the mouths of the majority of Southampton fans.

Lallana would be the first to provoke the ire of Southampton supporters when pictures emerged of him signing a Liverpool fans shirt whilst on holiday before his transfer was finalised.

If that got the goat of Southampton supporters, it was nothing to the furore surrounding the departure of Dejan Lovren.

The club rejected an original bid from Liverpool, but all this tough stance did was to provoke Lovren to state "my head is already at Liverpool." Facing a situation where a player no longer wanted to play for the club, the Southampton board had no choice but to reluctantly agree to sell Lovren to Liverpool.

Lovren would also go on to say that he would have stayed had the club not sold Rickie Lambert, Adam Lallana, and Luke Shaw (to Manchester United), as he tried desperately to deflect the blame of his defection towards the club's board. The fans weren't buying this excuse, and the reception that Lallana and Lovren, in particular, would get when they returned to St. Marys the following season would be aggressive and hate filled, to say the least. Rickie, on the other hand, received a warm welcome, the kind only afforded to those players who have become legends in the fans eyes.

For now, though, Southampton faced the forthcoming season with no manager, a depleted first team squad, and only a limited backroom staff. With the new season fast approaching, the next managerial appointment was going to have to be a good one.

Goals, Goals, Goals

Saints 8 Sunderland 0   Premier League   18 October 2014

When the club announced that Dutchman Ronald Koeman was to take over as the first team manager, I was more than just a little bit pleased. In my opinion, he was just the high profile manager we needed to attract the kind of players who could take the club forward. Okay, so his stints at Valencia in Spain and at AZ in Holland didn't stand up to close scrutiny, but he was fantastic as a player, being one of the world's top centre-backs, as well as holding the record for the most goals by a defender in the world.

He also had a sense of humour as proved when he posted on his Twitter account a photo of an empty training ground on his first day in the job. This was a joke in relation to a number of players that had left the club during the summer. Not only had Rickie Lambert, Adam Lallana and Dejan Lovren left for Liverpool, but Luke Shaw had signed for Manchester United, Callum Chambers had signed for Arsenal, and after a season out on loan, Billy Sharp signed for Leeds United. Oh, and Dani Osvaldo had his contract terminated, and others leaving on free transfers were Lee Barnard and Guly Du Prado. Whereas, Midfielder Gaston Ramirez who had not settled at the club joined Hull on loan, with goalkeeper Arthur Boruc heading for Bournemouth on a similar deal. Thankfully, Koeman and the club wasted no time in filling those many gaps in the squad by signing a number of top quality replacements.

The new additions included goalkeeper Fraser Forster from Celtic, defenders Florin Gardos and Ryan Bertrand from Steaua Bucharest and Chelsea respectively (Bertrand initially joined on loan but the move was made permanent in the January transfer window), attacking midfielders Dusan Tadic (FC Twente) and Sadio Mane (RB Salzburg) and strikers, Shane Long (Hull) and Graziano Pelle (Feyenoord).

With such a turnover in playing staff, it worried me that the new players would take time to gel as a team, but those fears proved to be groundless as the club made a flying start to the new Premier League season.

Despite an opening day 2-1 loss to Liverpool at Anfield, which was followed by a tepid 0-0 draw at home to West Brom (have we ever played an entertaining game against West Brom?), the Saints won their next four games. It was a run of results that helped us up to the dizzy heights of second place in the embryonic Premier League table.

Also during this winning run came a League Cup third round trip to Arsenal. Saints had beaten Millwall away in the second round, but this second trip to the capital would be an altogether more difficult proposition.

The Emirates is an impressive stadium, and the padded seats are a nice touch, although to be fair, most of us in the away end decided to stand throughout the entire 90 minutes. Standing in an all-seater stadium has always been a bone of contention amongst those fans who wish to actually sit down, and those fans who miss the good old days of terracing at football grounds.

The match against Arsenal was everything I hoped it would be, and despite going a goal behind inside 15 minutes, the Saints players dug in and produced a wonderful display.

Our equalising goal came from the penalty spot when Sadio Mane's jinking run ended under a clumsy challenge in the box, and Dusan Tadic dispensed the penalty to level the scores with just twenty minutes on the clock.

Things would get even better before the break when right-back Nathanial Clyne decided to let fly from fully twenty-five yards, and his shot dipped and swerved as in flew past Ospina in the Arsenal goal to give us the lead. It was a stunning strike of unnerving accuracy and reminded me of that Barry Horne goal against Bolton at The Dell back in 1992.

Being 2-1 up at Arsenal at the break would make you think that the second half would be one-way traffic, as the Gunners would go all out to find the equaliser, but that wasn't the case. Yes, they had more possession than we did, but we actually had more shots at goal than them, and we managed to match their shots on target total too.

That didn't prevent the last few minutes from being a nail-biting experience though, and there were one or two close calls, but we held on for a famous victory, our first away at Arsenal since 1987.

If that result left us purring, then the visit of Sunderland three weeks later would leave every Saints fan breathless.

After spending so much money travelling to London for the Arsenal game I couldn't afford to go to the two consecutive home games we had in October. The first of these was against Sunderland, whilst a week later we would welcome Stoke City. On paper, neither of these fixtures got me excited, and in the end, I decided to buy a ticket for the Sunderland game purely because it came first.

My decision to opt for the Sunderland game opened me up for a bit of leg-pulling by a couple of my work colleagues, who took great pleasure in reminding me that we hardly ever beat Sunderland at home, and the games typically produce few goals. This much was true, as we hadn't beaten them at home in our last three fixtures, and matches between the two teams very rarely produced more than three goals.

This match would be so different in many ways, and we had the added bonus of greeting our old nemesis Gus Poyet, who since his dismissal from Brighton, now had the unenviable task of trying to keep Sunderland in the Premier League.

The opening goal was comedy at its finest, and one of the most incredible own goals I have ever had the pleasure to witness. The 18-yard volley into the corner of the net by Sunderland defender Santiago Vergini will forever be one of those strikes that appear in football blunders DVDs for years to come.

Once everyone had stopped laughing (even some Sunderland fans I expect) we witnessed a master class in attacking football, helped by some of the most inept defending I have ever seen by a professional football team. Graziano Pelle doubled our advantage on 18 minutes

304

before Jack Cork made it 3-0 a few minutes later thanks to some chocolate-wristed goalkeeping from Sunderland keeper Vito Mannone.

Even though we happened to be three goals up at the break, and in total control of the match, there was still no sign of the rout that was about to take place as Sunderland shipped another five goals in the final 27 minutes of the second half.

Our fourth was another own-goal as the Sunderland keeper saved a shot from Pelle on the goal line, but the rebound hit Liam Bridcut and his touch was enough to nudge the ball over the line.

Pelle's second would come six minutes later when he ran onto Tadic's defence-splitting pass before scoring from a tight angle. Tadic himself would get in on the goal scoring action when he made it 6-0 thanks to another blunder by the Sunderland goalkeeper.

This time Mannone's weak clearance from a back pass whilst under pressure from Pelle found Tadic twenty-five yards out to the right of the goal, and his first-time shot flew past the desperate dive of the red-faced keeper.

For the Saints players, this was like shooting fish in a barrel, and everyone wanted to get on the scoresheet. Next up was defensive midfielder Victor Wanyama who fired home a fierce 12-yard drive from Tadic's deft low cross.

The rout was completed when Tadic again got in behind the Sunderland defence and his low fizzing cross was sidefooted home by Sadio Mane, although the goal would later be taken away from him and classed as a Van Aanholt own goal. It was a strange decision as Van Aanholt's touch was minimal and most pundits agreed that the ball was going in any way.

Either way, 8-0 was a phenomenal scoreline and just reinforces why so many people go to football, it's because you never know what is going to happen. This match could have been a dour lifeless 0-0, but

305

instead, it turned out to be our biggest winning margin since the formation of the Premier League. It was also the first time we had scored eight goals in a league match since an 8-2 win over Coventry City at The Dell back in 1984, but this squad hadn't finished yet.

The Push for Europe

Saints 6 Aston Villa 1   Premier League   16 May 2015

After that thrashing of Sunderland, the Saints carried on their unbeaten run with another three wins and a draw in their next four matches, which kept us in second place, albeit 6-points behind unbeaten Chelsea. It seemed as though an unlikely title challenge was forming but any hopes of battling for the title took a body blow when our form hit the skids in November and December.

We lost three out of four games in November, although to be fair there was no shame in losing at home to both Manchester Clubs and away at Arsenal, the only real disappointment came in a 1-0 loss at Burnley, a result that dropped us to fifth.

The team recovered, and recovered well, winning five out of their next six matches and drawing the other, as we climbed back up to third, although we were now 10 points adrift of leaders Chelsea.

Our topsy-turvy form continued though, as we had to endure a run of 3 home games without a victory, or indeed a solitary goal, and as the goals dried up, the worry amongst the fans was that we would miss out on European qualification altogether.

Tight home wins against Crystal Palace (revenge for an awful 3-2 home defeat in the FA Cup third round in January), Burnley and Hull steadied the ship, although now it was our away form that was suffering. Defeats at Everton, Stoke, Sunderland, and Leicester were proving to be quite damaging as we desperately tried to hang on to a Europa League qualification spot.

The defeats to relegation-threatened duo Sunderland and Leicester were particularly annoying, and now we found ourselves in seventh place, four points behind fifth-placed Liverpool.

As it turned out, Aston Villa were going to have a big say when it came down to us qualifying for Europe. Firstly, they would be the visitors for the final home game of the season, and secondly, despite fighting a relegation battle, they had somehow found themselves in the FA Cup Final, where their opponents would be Arsenal.

With Chelsea having already won the League Cup and the Premier League, it meant that the Europa League qualification spot for winning the League Cup would now go to the sixth-placed Premier League team. And with Arsenal already assured of a Champions League place, if they were to beat Villa in the FA Cup Final, then the Europa League spot would go to the seventh place side, whereas, a win for Villa and they would get to play in European competition the following season.

The match was a 12:45 kick-off due to live television coverage, and what a game they chose to broadcast to the nation. Not only did we run out comfortable 6-1 winners, but also, anyone who watched this game live was able to witness a record-breaking hat-trick.

The previous record for the fastest hat trick in a Premier League match was set by Liverpool's Robbie Fowler back in 1994, an impressive 4 minutes and 33 seconds. Not too shabby. However, Sadio Mane blew that time right out of the water when he scored three goals in a mere 2 minutes 55 seconds, a record that is going to take some beating.

Such was our utter dominance of this match that we were leading 5-1 at half time, and I dreamed of another victory on the scale of the Sunderland mauling back in October. As it was, the second 45 minutes yielded a solitary goal to complete a rout that gave us the chance we needed to finish high enough in the table to qualify for Europe.

A win in our final game at Manchester City could have propelled us up to sixth and certain qualification. However, a 2-0 defeat meant that we had to be content with finishing a respectable seventh, but now we had to sweat on the FA Cup Final result, and every Southampton fan was suddenly a Gunner for the day.

In the end, we had nothing to worry about as Arsenal blew Villa away with a resounding 4-0 victory at Wembley, a result that meant that we would enter the Europa League at the Third qualifying stage the following season. Not ideal, as that meant that our season would now begin in July rather than August, but I didn't care, as it meant that the usually barren Thursday night would now mean more football, lovely!

The Europa League

Saints 1 FC Midtjylland 1   UEFA Europa League Playoff Rnd 1st leg
20 August 2015

Our first foray back into European competition since 2003 saw us given what looked to be a tricky two-legged third qualifying round clash against Dutch side Vitesse Arnhem. With the first leg at St. Marys, it was imperative that we built up a solid lead that would enable us the see the tie through in the second leg in Holland.

As I have mentioned before, an opposition that looks good on paper doesn't necessarily look good on grass, and that is exactly what happened here, as not only did we win the home leg 3-0, but we travelled to Arnhem and won 2-0, giving us a resounding 5-0 aggregate victory.

Next up was Danish champions FC Midtjylland, who had lost in the Champions League qualifiers and had parachuted into the Europe League qualifiers instead.

After dismissing Vitesse so easily in the previous round, expectation amongst the Saints fans of securing a place in the group stages of the competition, (where there was the potential to draw some of Europe's bigger clubs) was high.

You can count Southampton's moderately successful European campaigns on the fingers of one hand, and even if that hand has three digits missing, you could still manage it.

Our first foray into European competition came when the club qualified for the Inter-Cities Fairs Cup (the forerunner to the UEFA Cup (now the Europa League)) in 1969. We made it through to the third round where we were unlucky enough to draw against English opposition in the form of Newcastle United. A 1-1 score at The Dell followed a 0-0 draw in the first-leg, and Saints got their first taste of going out of a competition on the away goals rule.

If you exclude the short-lived Texaco Cup (a completion that was basically a cup competition that involved English and Scottish clubs that had not qualified for one of the UEFA competitions), which we were runners-up in during the 1974-75 season, our only other half decent Euro campaign came in the Cup Winners Cup in 1976-77.

Pathetic, would be the word I would use to describe Southampton's forays into European competition with first round exits happening on four occasions, which included a humiliating away goals rule loss to Norwegian unknowns Norrkoping in 1982.

Other pathetic performances include a star-studded Southampton side containing Kevin Keegan, Mick Channon, Alan Ball, and David Armstrong losing 4-2 at home to Sporting Lisbon at The Dell in 1981. Some shocking Southampton defending would help the Portuguese side through to the next round, and if you're a Saints fan who is in a particularly masochistic mood, you can watch the Sportsnight highlights of the game on YouTube.

The first leg of our Europa League Playoff round tie was probably on par with many of our past poor European performances, as we went behind to a sloppy goal, only to huff and puff our way towards an equaliser.

We were hopeless on the night and had to rely on a Jay Rodriguez penalty to prevent us from going into the away leg a goal behind. Any thoughts that our route into the group stages would be easy were quickly quashed by the performance the team put in during this game. As it was, there was still the second-leg to come in Denmark, and surely, we couldn't be that bad again?

As it turned out they could, as they produced an even more inept performance in the away leg, and as I listened to our 1-0 defeat on the radio, I couldn't help but feel that the players had somehow underestimated the opposition, something that seemed to be happening a lot in cup competitions under Koeman.

With our European dream halted before it had taken on any kind of significance, it was back to the League, where we also made a poor start.

Despite an encouraging 2-2 draw at Newcastle on the opening day, Saints would only win one out of their opening six matches, in total contrast to the start they had made the previous season.

For the first time since he took over, Ronald Koeman's ability as a manager was coming into question by certain sections of the support. Had he reached a point where he couldn't get any more out of the players? That was just one of the questions that appeared on social media in the days following the feeble exit from Europe.

Things did improve, which included a 3-1 win at a below-par Chelsea side, a draw at Liverpool and a 2-0 home win against newly promoted Bournemouth.

Then in November and December, we hit the skids once more and a run of one win (ironically a 4-0 spanking of Arsenal at St. Marys) in eight sent us crashing down the table to a lowly thirteenth position.

Those rumblings of discontent amongst the fan base were becoming louder and more widespread, with rumours that unless he could turn our form around quick, Koeman's job was under threat.

It didn't help that we lost at home to Crystal Palace in the third round of the FA Cup, the second season in a row that Palace had come to St. Marys and triumphed in the competition. It was a depressing time to be a Saints fan, as a season that promised so much seemed to be fizzling out into nothing other than a battle to stay in mid-table mediocrity.

The only highlight of the season so far was the fact that we had reached the quarter-finals of the League Cup for the second season in a row.

Stuffed

Saints 1 Liverpool 6   League Cup 5th Round   2 December 2015

As a reward for taking part in the Europa League, Saints earned a bye into the third round of the League Cup, a privilege that all teams taking part in continental competition would receive.

Our League Cup campaign got off to a six-goal start when we dispatched MK Dons 6-0 at Stadium MK in the third round.

A comfortable 2-1 home win against Aston Villa followed in round four, and that set up this tie with Liverpool, and a chance to put deserters Adam Lallana and Dejan Lovren in their place.

As I mentioned earlier, this was the second season in a row where we had qualified for the quarter-finals of this particular competition. The

311

previous season we had to face League One side Sheffield United at Bramall Lane, in a match that, with no disrespect to them, we should have won and won without too much trouble. They beat us 1-0, as the team Koeman selected put in an abject performance in a match that should have seen us through to our first League Cup semi-final since the late 80s.

This time we had home advantage, but there was no doubt that Liverpool would prove to be a sterner test than a third tier team from the steel city.

I wasn't too hopeful of a win, mostly due to the fact that this match took place slap bang in the middle of that horrendous run of league performances. What we needed was to get off to a quick start, and I could not have hoped for a better start when Sadio Mane put us in front after just 39 seconds. Unfortunately, I wasn't inside the ground to see it, as I was still queuing to get in.

Heavy traffic meant that I was late getting to St. Marys, and although I still had 15 minutes or so to enter the ground the queues were unbelievably long, and it seemed as though I wasn't the only one who had had their journey to St. Marys delayed by the pre-Christmas traffic.

I still had about twenty people ahead of me in the queue when I heard the cheers from inside the stadium that signalled Mane's opener. A strange mix of emotions enveloped me as I waited to get through the turnstiles, euphoria mixed with regret and frustration at having missed the goal.

I made it into my seat about five minutes after Sadio Mane had given us the lead, and I was pleased to see that we were still taking the game to Liverpool, and in fact, we wasted a few chances to extend our lead.

Then midway through the first half, a lightning quick Liverpool break led by the tricky but often inconsistent Daniel Sturridge ended with the ball in the back of our net and teams on level terms. After that equaliser, I'm afraid to say that it was all one-way traffic, and it seemed as though Liverpool were going to score with every attack.

They had seven shots on target during the 90 minutes, and they scored with six of them, as Sturridge bagged two, and striker Divock Origi grabbed himself a hat-trick, with Nathan Ibe's goal completing the rout.

It doesn't take a genius to work out that our defending was beyond abysmal that night, but the two worst performances came from the two loanees that Ronald Koeman had signed during the summer. Defender Steven Caulker and goalkeeper Martin Stekelenburg had arrived on season long loans from QPR and Fulham respectively.

With Fraser Forster out indefinitely through injury, a new goalkeeper was needed, but I don't think that Martin Stekelenburg was the answer, and he had too many games where he just didn't look confident enough, despite having a solid back-four in front of him.

As for Steven Caulker, he looked so far out of his depth playing in the Premier League that I was surprised that he didn't take to the field wearing water-wings. Yet, this didn't stop him from ending his loan stay in January and moving on loan to Liverpool. An amazing switch that left most Saints fans flabbergasted, to say the least, although he would go on to play as many games for them (3) as he did for us, before returning to his parent club QPR, where he currently resides at the time of writing. He is a classic case of an average footballer who must have a very good agent.

This humiliating defeat to Liverpool came during that run of poor league form, and it did look like we were only heading in one direction and that was down the table. Thankfully, as we were now out of all three of the cup competitions, we could concentrate on the league, and qualifying for European competition once more.

We stopped the rot with a 2-0 win over Watford at St. Marys, and this was the catalyst of a six-match unbeaten run where we didn't

313

concede a single goal, which also coincided with the return of Fraser Forster in goal.

That mini revival ended with a 2-1 home defeat to Chelsea, and a 2-0 loss at Bournemouth followed a few days later. An awful 1-1 draw at home to Sunderland, where a Van Dijk equaliser three minutes into stoppage time salvaged a point against a team battling relegation, completed a miserable week.

European qualification was now firmly in the balance, and we had fallen eight points behind fifth place West Ham with nine games to play. Those nine games included home games against Liverpool, Newcastle, and Manchester City, whilst away from home, we had to face Everton, Tottenham, and surprise league leaders Leicester City. Was I optimistic that we would qualify for a second successive Europa League Campaign? No, I wasn't, and neither were the majority of the Saints fans on the internet forums either.

From somewhere though, the players seemed to up things a gear, and we won seven of our remaining nine games (a loss at Leicester and a draw at Everton the only blips) as we stormed up the table to finish in sixth place. It was our highest finish since the formation of the Premier League, and our best finish in the top division since 1984 when we finished as runners-up.

It also meant that we had once again qualified for Europe, as Manchester City's qualification for the Champions League meant that the Europe League place they would have earned for winning the League Cup went to the sixth place finishers.

Last year we had to watch the FA Cup Final in the hope of getting into Europe, now we had to watch it see if we would enter the Europa League at the third qualifying stage or go straight into the group stages.

The scenario was simple. Manchester United had finished fifth, so they already had a Europa League spot. However, if they won the FA

Cup Final against Crystal Palace that would mean that the seventh place team (West Ham) would go into the third qualifying round of the Europa League, and we'd be bumped into the group stages. A win for Palace would see them go into the group stages, us into the third qualifying round, with West Ham missing out.

When former Saint Jason Puncheon opened the scoring for Palace in the 78th minute, it looked as though we would have to go through the qualifying stages for the second season in a row. However, Juan Mata equalised for United three minutes later to send the game into extra-time, where a solitary Jesse Lingard goal was enough to secure the cup for United and a Europa League group stage entry for us.

I remember the unusual feeling of actually wanting Manchester United to win a match, something I only usually reserved for when they played Portsmouth, and as soon as the final whistle went, I was relieved that not only had we got a group stage place, but that I could go back to detesting United once more. It was a sentiment shared by many of my fellow Southampton fans if the comments on social media were anything to go by.

It had been a rollercoaster ride of a season, with a poor start, a winning run, a long losing streak, and it ended with two unbeaten runs that had propelled us to the lofty heights of sixth place.

Now there were rumours circulating about manager Ronald Koeman's future, with serious interest coming from Everton. Koeman quickly allayed any fears the fans had of his departure for pastures new by stating that too many managers leave clubs for more money and that they should do the honourable thing and see out their contracts. It would be a statement that would come back to haunt him.

The Lying Dutchman

Saints 1 Watford 1   Premier League   13 August 2016

If Pochettino's departure two years previously had felt like a kick in the teeth, then that was nothing when compared to the feelings amongst the Southampton fans when the announcement finally came that Koeman was leaving to take over at Everton.

At least Pochettino hadn't led fans up the garden path by making statements that he was staying. Questions regarding his future were swiftly dealt with by changing the subject, and as annoying, as it was to lose an up and coming manager, he never said he wasn't going.

Koeman, on the other hand, had not only made a statement suggesting that managers should be more loyal to their clubs, it also turned out that he had all but agreed a new deal with the club. This included a new contract for himself, one that would have made him the highest paid manager in the clubs history, but also a new five-year plan for the club, with player transfer budgets set in stone for the duration of his contract.

Koeman could have taken us to the next level, but instead, he decided to follow the money and move to Everton, where he stated that the reason for his departure was a lack of ambition from the Southampton board, something that one or two players mentioned when they had left us the previous two summers. Something wasn't right, and someone wasn't telling the truth. Were the clubs owners and directors lying to the fans, or were the players and managers who left just trying to deflect the blame away from their own greed?

With Koeman gone, the search for our fourth manager since our return to the Premier League began in earnest, whilst the fans sat back and waited to see which players would leave during the now traditional summer exodus.

We didn't have long to wait, as Liverpool came in for striker Sadio Mane, and Pochettino swooped to sign Victor Wanyama as soon as the transfer window opened on 1 July, with the combined transfer fees were rumoured to be over £30 million pounds. Also leaving us was Graziano Pelle, who left for a stint in the Chinese Premier League, a relatively new league where money seemed to be no object, and the lure of overwhelming sums of money was starting to turn many players' heads.

Also saying goodbye was Kelvin Davis who retired from football to become the club's Football Development Executive, a position that would help to provide support to players in the first team.

We also finally saw the back of midfielder Gaston Ramirez. The club released him from his contract, and he quickly signed for Premier League newcomers Middlesbrough, where once again he has only shown glimpses of the quality he undoubtedly possesses.

For now, though, we needed a new manager, and a few names appeared in the press over the following days after Koeman's departure from the club was finalised. The most well-known of these names was Manuel Pellegrini, who had recently left the managerial post at Manchester City, and he was seen by the fans as an ideal replacement for Koeman.

However, Pellegrini didn't get the job, nor did the other front runner Unai Emery, a man who had taken Spanish side Seville to three consecutive Europa League wins. Another Dutchman, Frank De Boer would also find his name linked with the vacant manager's post at St. Marys, but in the end, the club opted for a relatively unknown Frenchman who was managing French first division side Nice.

Claude Puel's name had been mentioned concerning the Saints manager's job, but bookmakers, the press and fans alike had seen him as a bit of an outsider, and his appointment wasn't met with much enthusiasm amongst the fans. My feelings were similar, and I wasn't sure if this man was the right guy to take us forward. Had the club done their homework, or had their first choice turned them down and they were making do with second best? This was either going to be a shrewd appointment or a bit of a gamble. I guess only time and results would tell.

With a new manager at the helm, it was now just a case of sitting back and waiting to see which players would come in to replace those that had left.

The wait wasn't a long one, with the club announcing the signings of winger Nathan Redmond from Norwich and midfielder Pierre-Emile Højbjerg from Bayern Munich, just a day after the appointment of Puel as boss. The speed of these signings suggested that the club had already identified them and that these were not Puel signings.

Jérémy Pied and Sofiane Boufal (our new record signing at £16 million) definitely looked like Puel signings, with Pied coming from Puel's former club Nice, and Boufal was also known to Puel through his connections at Lille FC where had also managed in the past.

The new season kicked off at home to Watford and Damien and I went along to cast our eyes over the new players, and to see how the new manager would have the team set up.

As I've said before, the opening game often sets the precedent for the rest of the season, and unfortunately, that is what happened in the home opener against Watford. The match was slow tempo, with lots of sideways and backwards passing. Watford were content to sit back and hit us on the counter-attack, whilst our attacks were slow enough to let Watford's defence regroup and thwart our advances.

It was no great surprise when Watford took the lead on 9 minutes, and they then proceeded to sit back, whilst our players lacked the imagination to break down their resistance. When the equaliser did come, it was from a corner-kick, when Tadic's corner found

Redmond unmarked just inside the penalty area, and he skilfully volleyed home through the crowded six-yard box.

The lack of cutting edge was clear for all to see, as was the wasteful finishing, with twenty-four shots at goal, but only six on target. But hey, it was early days and the players needed time to get used to a different formation as well as the new signings. Things would surely improve.

They didn't really, and we even struggled to get a draw in our next home game against perennial relegation candidates Sunderland, a result which sandwiched losses at Arsenal and Manchester United.

This wasn't the kind of form we needed to take into our forthcoming fixtures in the Europa League, and now it was starting to look like our squad wasn't deep enough or strong enough to play so many extra fixtures.

Hollow Victory

Saints 2 Internazionale 1 UEFA Europa League Group K Matchday 4
3 November 2016

The Europa League was what I was really looking forward to this season, as the draw for the group stages not only included Sparta Prague but also Internazionale, the Italian giants from Milan. This was particularly exciting for me as for many years I have had a soft spot for Inter's city rivals, AC Milan.

This goes back to when Channel 4 used to show live games from the Italian Serie A on Sunday afternoons back in the early 90s, which coincided with a lack of live English top-flight football on terrestrial television. As soon as Sky TV acquired the rights to the Premier League, free football on television was severely limited, and Channel 4's coverage filled a gap. It also helped that at the time Serie A was arguably the best league in the world, with players such as Roberto Baggio, Gabriel Batistuta, Gianfranco Zola, Gianlucca Vialli, and Englishman David Platt.

For me though, it was the AC Milan side that I fell for and what a team they had back then. World-class international players such as the Dutch trio of Ruud Gullit, Marco Van Basten and Frank Rijkaard gave the team an attacking flair that had rarely been seen in Italian football. The three Dutchman complemented the existing Italian players at the club, and the likes of Paolo Maldini, Franco Baresi, Alessandro Costacurta and Roberto Donadoni soon became household names not only in Italy but in the UK too. That Milan side won three consecutive Serie A titles, as well as appearing in three consecutive Champions League Finals (their one win being a 4-0 thrashing of Barcelona in 1994), and I have followed their fortunes ever since.

As a Southampton and AC Milan fan, the next best thing to seeing my two loves squaring off against each other (and in case you are wondering, I would want Saints to win) was the chance to see Saints beat AC Milan's arch rivals.

Firstly, we had to negotiate a home game against Sparta Prague and an away game at a virtually unknown Israeli team called Hapoel Be'er Sheva, a side that had narrowly lost 5-4 on aggregate to Celtic in the Champions League qualifiers.

The match against Sparta Prague was actually a straightforward 3-0 win, thanks to a penalty in just the fifth minute when one of the assistant referees spotted a handball in the area.

Charlie Austin duly converted the spot-kick, but only after a confrontation with teammate Dusan Tadic. Austin grabbed the ball from Tadic who had been our regular penalty taker, and some pushing and shoving occurred between the two before captain Virgil Van Dijk calmed the situation down.

Austin scored his second on 27 minutes, and with Sparta not offering much in attack, the three points was ours for the taking, and a Jay Rodriguez goal two minutes into second-half stoppage time put the seal on a fine win.

A fortnight later, and the Saints travelled to Israel for the first of two consecutive away games (Inter would follow three weeks later), and they came away with a point from a goalless draw against Be'er Sheva.

In a game we should have won, we somehow contrived to miss a number of clear-cut scoring chances, something that would be the leitmotif of our season.

Away at Inter was another example of what happens when you don't convert chances into goals, as again we should and could have come away with more than just a 1-0 defeat. Inter were not exactly taking the competition seriously at this point, and they had lost both their opening matches after fielding under strength teams.

The return match against Inter at St. Marys was now only two weeks away, and it was now a must win game if we wanted to finish in the top two in the group and thus qualify for the next round.

The first half-an-hour of the match passed by without incident, but that all changed when Inter captain Mauro Icardi put the visitors ahead with their first real attack on goal just past the half-hour mark.

From then on, the match became a tense niggly affair, with both sets of players displaying short fuses, and this increased when the ref awarded Saints a penalty for handball by Ivan Perisic just before half time.

As some of the Inter players surrounded the referee in protest, Saints player Sam McQueen seemed to be clouted in an off the ball incident by Antonio Candreva, a clash that was spotted by the officials. Despite being an obvious red card offence, for some reason, the ref only deemed it suitable for a yellow card, much to the annoyance of the Saints players and fans.

321

To make matters worse, Dusan Tadic missed the penalty-kick (starting a trend amongst Saints players for the season), and as the half-time whistle blew, more confrontations between both sets of players continued as they left the pitch.

The second-half started well for Southampton as they increased the pressure on the visitor's goal, although the strikers were not having much luck converting their chances, and it took a goal from a centre-back to restore parity.

Captain Virgil van Dijk scored the equalising goal on 65 minutes when the Inter defence failed to clear a corner, Romeu's shot cannoned back off the crossbar and found van Dijk unmarked at the far post, and his fierce volley flew past the keeper.

The winning goal came five minutes later, when Tadic's fizzing cross looked to be an easy one for the Inter defence to clear, but for some reason, two Inter defenders left the ball, and it cannoned off the unfortunate Yuto Nagatomo and into the net to give us a deserved lead.

We held on quite comfortably for the win, and those three points cemented our place of second in the table, with two games to play, away to Sparta Prague, and at home to Hapoel Be'er Sheva.

One win out of those two games would be enough to see us through to the knockout stages of the competition.

So We Meet Again

Saints 1 Liverpool 0 League Cup Semi-Final 1st Leg 11 January 2017

As it turned out, two points would have been enough to see us through to the knockout stages of the Europa League, but somehow, we would contrive to get a solitary point from those two remaining games and crash out of the competition.

322

The return game in Prague was one of the most disappointing matches I have ever seen by a Saints side in recent times. Watching from the comfort of home, I really felt for those fans who had invested the time and money to go to the Czech Republic to watch such an abject performance.

Sparta had somehow recovered from their opening round 3-0 drubbing at St. Marys to lead the group, thanks to three consecutive wins (two against Hapoel and one against Inter), and now they would get their revenge against us.

The 1-0 loss in Prague coupled with Hapoel's 3-2 home win against Inter meant that it was winner takes all going into the final match against the Israeli club at St. Marys.

We were hanging on to second place by goal difference from Hapoel Be'er Sheva, and the equation was simple. A win or a goalless draw would be enough to see us through, but because head-to-head results involving teams on the same number of points would count before goal difference, a score draw would be enough for Be'er Sheva to finish second thanks to our goalless draw in Israel. It was going to be another tense nervy night at St. Marys.

For some inexplicable reason, Saints manager Claude Puel seemed to set the team up to defend in the hope of securing the 0-0 draw that would see us through. Maybe he thought that Be'er Sheva wouldn't score if we sat back and didn't leave ourselves open to the counter-attack.

It was a risky strategy, and it did nothing to ease the overwhelming feeling of tension that was evident inside St. Marys. The atmosphere was obviously filtering down from the stands to the players, as the team struggled to find any kind of cohesion in their play.

The longer the game went on, and the more we wasted the goal scoring opportunities that came our way, the more I knew that the inevitable Be'er Sheva goal was coming and it came twelve minutes from the end.

A Be'er Sheva attack down the left looked contained by the sheer number of defenders we had back, but a misplaced pass on the edge of the penalty area by Oriel Romeu presented the ball to the opposition, and the ball found its way to Maor Buzaglo who scored with a low shot from the edge of the area.

A devastating blow if ever there was one, and it now meant we needed to score twice to progress from the group stages on a night when never looked like scoring one.

Faced with our first home defeat in European competition since that 4-2 home humbling to Sporting Lisbon back in 1982, the Saints players poured forward in a desperate attempt to salvage their Europa League campaign.

In the final minute, Virgil van Dijk scored to level the scores and set up a tense period of stoppage-time, where his central defensive partner Maya Yoshida almost won the match at the death, but he put his far post header the wrong side of the post.

It was a disappointing way to go out of the competition, and this was the match where the fans opinions regarding the manager Claude Puel and his tactics began to change, as, after that good start against Prague, we failed to score in three of our remaining five fixtures. Now, more fans than ever started to question Claude's defensive and slow tempo football, especially at home where we had been banging in the goals in the past few seasons.

Despite crashing out of the Europa League, things were going a lot better in the League Cup, as we had progressed to the semi-final stage.

Wins over recent cup bogey sides Crystal Palace and Sunderland in rounds 3 and 4, set us up for another away trip to Arsenal in the quarter-finals.

Even though most Saints fans knew that Arsenal manager Arsene Wenger would field an under strength team, it was not going to be an easy match as even a weakened Arsenal team would still be full of quality players.

Unlike the previous season, however, we didn't need to fight back from a goal behind, as a lacklustre Arsenal side failed to create too many goalscoring chances, and we took full advantage.

The first goal in our 2-0 win came from Dutch midfielder Jordy Clasie who hit a lovely shot from outside the penalty area, and the second was another long-range effort, this time from left-back Ryan Bertrand.

That victory put us through to the League Cup semi-finals for the first time since 1987, and now we had to face Liverpool over two legs, with the home leg first.

I went to the match with the memory of Liverpool's 6-1 win at St. Marys the previous season still fresh in my mind, and to be honest, although I was expecting a tighter match, I didn't fancy our chances of getting to the final.

Yet, for all Liverpool's early possession, it was the Saints who broke the deadlock, when Nathan Redmond beat the Liverpool offside trap thanks to a perfectly weighted through ball from Jay Rodriguez.

One goal up with 20 minutes on the clock, and by half-time we were unfortunate not to be even further in front as Redmond saw two goalbound shots saved well by the Liverpool goalkeeper Loris Karius.

The second-half followed the same pattern, with Liverpool having a lot of possession but not managing to do much with it, and again we wasted two chances to increase our lead. First to miss was right-back Cedric Soares, who shot wide when it looked easier to score, and later on Redmond hit the crossbar with a chipped shot.

A narrow one-goal lead was all we had to take with us to Anfield, a ground we hardly ever do well at, and I really did think that those

325

missed opportunities to increase our first leg lead would come back to haunt us.

I was so nervous going into the second leg that I couldn't even watch the match on television. Instead, I busied myself watching other TV channels but not really concentrating on what was happening on screen. Occasionally, I would open the Twitter app on my phone just to see what was going on and whether we had conceded a goal yet.

As the game wore on and with reports that Liverpool was totally dominating the match but couldn't score, I had the feeling that maybe, just maybe we could hold out for the 0-0 draw that would take us to Wembley.

With nerves jangling, the match entered stoppage-time, and with curiosity getting the better of me I switched on Sky Sports just in time to see the goal that sealed our passage to our first League Cup final since 1979.

As Liverpool players poured forward in a desperate bid to find the equaliser that would send the match into extra-time, the ball fell to substitute Josh Sims, and he set off on a speedy run through the middle. As Liverpool's defenders tried to get back into position, Sims spotted the supporting run of Shane Long, and his perfect through ball put the Irishman in on goal, and he made no mistake, slotting the ball home past the keeper to cue delirium in the away end at Anfield, and in my living room.

My jumping up and down and screaming "yesses, get the f**k in!' was all the more satisfying as I know that the people who live in the flat downstairs are Liverpool fans.

Once I got my breath back, it was time to make plans for a trip to Wembley and the final against Manchester United, and as a fully paid-up member, I was hopeful that my membership card would give me an edge over those who had been to games but who weren't members.

Apparently, spending £25 on a membership card before the start of the season was of little benefit. No sooner were ticket details for the final released, then it soon became clear that the club was still selling memberships to anyone who wanted one, which allowed people to jump the queue for cup final tickets.

I had been to six home matches during the season. The opening day game against Watford, all three home Europa League games, a terrible home loss to West Brom over the New Year period, and I was also one of the hardy souls who happened to be in a crowd of little over 13,500 for an FA Cup replay against Norwich, a match played on a bitterly cold January night. A night so cold and a match so bereft of entertainment, that as the game entered the 90th minute I was hoping for anyone to score, even Norwich, just so I didn't have to suffer another 30 minutes in the freezing cold.

Now I faced the prospect of someone who hadn't purchased a membership card at the start of the season, but who had been to seven matches, buying a membership and jumping the queue. Silly me for shelling out the money up front during the summer, I'll just wait to we get to a cup final next time and buy a membership then.

In my opinion, the club just kept selling memberships to make more money, as they knew that the clamour for cup final tickets would be immense. Memberships need selling in the same way as season tickets, in that there should be a limited time to buy them before the season starts. If we get to a cup final and you have bought neither a season ticket nor membership, and you want a ticket, then tough, pay some money up front before the season starts otherwise wait your turn. Rant over.

Oh Gabbiadini

Saints 2 Manchester Utd 3   League Cup Final   26 February 2017

After much fretting and sweating, I managed to secure a ticket to the final, although I was right up in the nosebleeds, midway up the top tier in one corner of Wembley Stadium. I didn't care though, I had a ticket, and anyway, even from the top tier, the view isn't so bad.

Now I had to think about the best way to get there. With the match being played on a Sunday, it didn't help that train spaces which would be limited anyway, would be even more scarce on the Sabbath. Even though South West Trains promised to run a couple of extra trains there and back, I didn't fancy the lottery of trying to get a seat for the 90-minute journey to the capital.

That left the coach, but I didn't fancy going on one of the official travel club coaches, which would go from St. Marys to Wembley and back again. I wanted to see a bit of London, make a day of it, and so I decided to book a seat with National Express, that way I could get to London earlier than the travel club coaches, and make my way to Wembley on the Tube at my leisure.

A few pre-match pints, some lunch and a mooch around the Tower of London later, I made my way to Wembley on a Metropolitan line train, a train that was sparsely populated until the train pulled into Paddington station.

Being on a tube train surrounded by hundreds of fans from the opposing team was not the way I would have chosen to spend the next 20 minutes or so of my journey to Wembley, but here I was doing just that.

Manchester United fans are just arrogant by nature, and sneering at every other team they face must be in their DNA, as they began mocking the Saints line-up.

328

A couple of United morons (one sat opposite me, the other next to me) began discussing the team selections for the final. After dispensing some wisdom about their own lineup, the guy next to me who was checking the starting lineups on his phone began reading out the names of the Southampton players.

"Are these even Premier League players?" he snorted as he finished reading out the team. I could feel my anger rising, but I told myself that saying something in this situation would be a bad idea. I just thought to myself, "you'll find out mate when we stick a few goals past you," and I left it at that.

Even though this would be my second visit to Wembley Stadium, getting a first glimpse of the arch and the towering stands never ceases to get the pulse going just a little bit quicker. It's not just a stadium, it's a national icon, and it also means that your club has done something special to be here for a match.

From my vantage point, I watched Saints take the game to United from the kick-off, and we deservedly took the lead just a few minutes into the game when Manolo Gabbiadini prodded home from close range. At least we should have taken the lead, had the linesman not flagged for an offside. Even from where I was sat at the other end of the stadium it looked like a wrong decision, and this was confirmed a couple of minutes later when I checked Twitter to see the posts from Saints fans watching the game on television remark about it being a ridiculous decision.

So, no goal, and now Manchester United were starting to get a foothold in the game, and their attacks carried more threat with each passing minute.

It was from one of their attacks that they were awarded a free-kick about 25-yards from goal. It looked to be too far out even for United's Swedish striker Zlatan Ibrahimovic, but he stepped up and hit a perfect shot that flew in beyond the reach of Saints stopper Fraser Forster.

Worse was to come, as although we were dominating possession and playing the better football, we just couldn't carve out a decent goal scoring opportunity, something that had been a problem all season.

As the match swung from end to end, I remember thinking that if we didn't equalise soon, then it was almost inevitable that United would score the second goal, and that prophecy came true seven minutes before the break.

Some slack defending allowed United's Marcus Rojo all the time in the world to dribble the ball from the right side into the centre of our defence, and as our defenders stood still he picked out Jesse Lindgard who took his chance from the edge of the penalty-area, to extend United's lead.

It was a horrible goal to concede, as it seemed as though no one in our defence was prepared to take the initiative and close down either Rojo or Lindgard, it was the kind of goal you would expect to see scored on a local park on a Sunday afternoon, not in a cup final at Wembley.

I remember thinking that this could be a long afternoon, and with defending like that, this could easily be a four or five goal defeat. Had I come all this way and spent all that money to watch us be humiliated on the biggest stage of all, or could we somehow yet pull this game out of the fire?

What we really needed was to score before half-time but that looked unlikely until in injury-time when Gabbiadini finally got the goal he deserved. Nathan Redmond started the move when he played a neat ball into space on the right, and James Ward-Prowse got to the byline before whipping in a low cross to the near post. Making one of his customary late runs into the box, Gabbiadini lost his marker and nipped in to slot the ball home from close range.

It was just what we needed, and was no more than we deserved for our attacking efforts, and now United's boss Jose Mourinho would have to tear up his half-time team talk.

The second-half was just three minutes old when Gabbiadini scored *the* goal of the final to level the scores.

Saints had narrowly failed to score the equaliser just a few seconds before, and we had to settle for a corner. The United defence now rocking failed to clear the resulting corner-kick, and after a bit of head tennis, the ball fell to the feet of Gabbiadini almost on the penalty-spot and he swivelled and shot in all one movement and the ball flew past a stunned De Gea in the United goal.

That goal sparked wild celebratory scenes in the Saints half of the stadium, and witnessing thousands of Saints fans twirling their scarves above their heads (the club gave every fan a free scarf) whilst chanting "ooh Gabbiadini" over and over and jumping up and down in unison for the next ten minutes will stay with me for a long time.

The United players didn't know what had hit them, from being two goals up and looking comfortable, they had lost their lead in under four minutes of play either side of half-time. Now it was all Saints, and we were unlucky not to take the lead when Oriel Romeu was left unmarked on the edge of the United 6-yard box, but he put his free header against the post.

As the game wore on and the more we squandered chance after chance, the more I knew that the inevitable United winner was waiting to ruin my day, and it duly happened three minutes from the end of normal time.

It was another piece of slack Saints defending that led to the United winner as Ibrahimovic was left completely unmarked on the edge of the 6-yard box, and unlike Romeu's effort, he didn't miss, and the game was up.

331

As the game entered stoppage-time I started to make my way down to concourse. I really wanted to stay and applaud our players for a fantastic effort, and a great fight back, but equally, I didn't fancy getting the tube back surrounded by dozens of jubilant United fans.

Anyone who has been to Wembley will know how long it can take to get the tube train, and with tens of thousands of people trying to get into the station, the queues can stretch back two-thirds of the way up Wembley Way.

I hung around in the concourse, just in case we scored the equaliser that would mean another thirty minutes of football, but it was not to be our day, and I quickly made my way out of the stadium and back towards the tube station.

What surprised me most was that although there appeared to be thousands of people who had obviously made their way out of the stadium even before the final whistle, a large number of them were wearing United colours.

I was astonished; it was obvious that these people had left the ground long before the players climbed the steps to receive their medals and lift the trophy. Why anyone would travel all that way to watch a match, watch their team win a trophy and not stay behind for the presentation is beyond me.

The tube journey was a solemn one, and in total contrast to going to the stadium, as this time I spent the journey surrounded by my fellow Saints fans. The general mood was one of pride in the performance our players had put in, whilst there was still plenty of anger towards the assistant referee for disallowing Gabbiadini's opening goal.

I made it back to the coach station but with over an hour to kill before the coach was due to leave I made for a nearby pub. It was in this pub that I saw Gabbiadini's disallowed goal in close-up for the first time, and the Sky Sports report confirmed what I felt at the time, that it was a travesty of a decision. Gabbi was onside when he put the ball past De Gea, but Ryan Bertrand was in an offside position as the ball crossed the line, but he never touched the ball, and under the current rules, he wasn't interfering with play.

The 2017 EFL Cup Final will always be remembered for the hat-trick that never was. How often does a player score a hat-trick in a major cup final? Gabbi deserved to take the match ball home with him, and we deserved to take the trophy back to St. Mary's, but a confused and inadequate official undid us.

I have always been against the use of video technology in football, but after this incident, I have changed my stance somewhat, and with FIFA now trialling the use of a video officials, it seems inevitable that incidents such as our disallowed goal will become a thing of the past, but typically, it's all too late for us.

Thank You and Goodbye

Saints 3 Crystal Palace 1   Premier League   5 April 2017

Despite reaching the EFL Cup final, there were still plenty of question marks over the future of manager Claude Puel, both in the press and amongst the supporters. He came in for particular criticism for constantly rotating his starting line-up, whilst dropping players who were in form, yet those who were struggling to find any consistency seemed to be immune from losing their starting place.

When Damien and I attended this match against Crystal Palace in early April, Saints still had another five home games to play. As we celebrated the third goal in a convincing win over a team fighting against relegation (one that had recently beaten both Chelsea and Liverpool away), little did we realise that we were watching the last goals we would score at home this season.

The Saturday prior to this game we had played out a tepid 0-0 draw at home to Bournemouth, who were unlucky not to win when they missed a penalty late on, so with that blank, it meant that we failed to score in six of our last seven games on home soil. Any way you look at it, it wasn't good enough.

Southampton fans have always demanded entertaining attacking football, especially at home, yet under Puel's leadership, the play had seemed to become pedestrian and the number of sideways and backwards passes seemed to rise with every game. The irony is that we could attack when we wanted to, with the cup final against Manchester United a prime example.

Our home scoring tally was second lowest in the Premier League with only relegated Sunderland scoring fewer goals than we did on home turf, and that is not good enough for a team in the top half of the table.

People will look back on this season and say that we finished eighth in the Premier League and reached a major cup final, so why should the manager's position be in any jeopardy?

To those people, I would point out the fact that they obviously haven't watched us many times this season, and if you take a closer look at the final Premier League table you will see that the gap in points between us and Everton in seventh is bigger than between us and the last relegation place.

In what was a poor Premier League season all round, our eighth placed finish meant that we were just best of the dross in this league, and if you take away a couple of wins, we would have been right in the mix for relegation.

The speculation regarding the manager's future carried on into the close season, and it typical Southampton fashion, the decision on whether to give Puel another season or replace him dragged on through May and on into June.

In mid-June, the club announced that Puel had been relieved of his duties, and I couldn't help but think that even his sacking was laboured and boring, but I did feel a sense of relief as I'm sure a majority of Saints fans did. There were a few dissenters of course, those fans who thought he deserved another season on the strength of getting us a top-half league finish, and a cup final, but these were in the minority.

Did he deserve another season? On paper possibly, but on overall team performance, no. In my opinion, the transfer window has a lot of influence when it comes to a club retaining or firing a manager. If Puel were to stay, he'd have money to strengthen the squad, but if early season results were poor, the pressure on him would be immense, and once that transfer window slams shut, it makes it difficult for a club to make any changes to their staff until it opens again in January. As we know from experience, getting out of the relegation zone when you are in it in January is difficult, even with a new manager, so why leave it to chance.

It is better to replace him in the summer, get the new guy in and let him spend the money in transfer window on the players he feels we need, and this is exactly the way the club felt too, as only a week or so after announcing Puel's departure, the club announced the appointment of a new boss.

Mauricio Pellegrino is the new man at the helm of Southampton Football Club going into the 2017/18 season, and his mandate is to provide entertaining football with an emphasis on a high-tempo pressing game, similar to that which we enjoyed under Pocchetino and Koeman.

As a football fan, I hate summers, especially those years with no World Cup or European Championship to fill the void, but as a Southampton fan, I've grown to hate the close season even more.

Every year since our return to the Premier League we have had other teams (typically Liverpool), come in for our players and managers, and every close season has seen the departure of two or more of our star players. So far, we have managed to overcome these raids on our prized assets, but just how long can we go on before our luck runs out?

The club has recently sold an eighty percent stake to Chinese business tycoon Jisheng Gao for £210 million, and Gao now becomes the clubs majority stakeholder with Katharina Liebherr retaining a twenty percent stake in the club.

Chinese ownership of English clubs has been less than successful so far, so we'll have to wait and see if this particular takeover will take the club forward, or leave us high and dry. The lower leagues of English football are littered with clubs whose takeovers have gone awry, and I don't really want to see us back in the third tier anytime soon.

Whatever happens, the soap opera that is Southampton Football Club will continue to throw up some surprises, both good and bad in the years ahead, but that's what keeps us all coming back week in week out, and I for one wouldn't have it any other way.

Printed in Great Britain
by Amazon